Technology-Enhanced Learning in Higher Education

Technology-Enhanced Learning in Higher Education

John Branch
Paul Bartholomew
Claus Nygaard

THE LEARNING IN HIGHER EDUCATION SERIES

LIBRI
PUBLISHING

First published in 2015 by Libri Publishing

Copyright © Libri Publishing

Authors retain copyright of individual chapters.

The right of John Branch, Paul Bartholomew and Claus Nygaard to be identified as the editors of this work has been asserted in accordance with the Copyright, Designs and Patents Act, 1988.

ISBN 978-1-909818-61-3

A CIP catalogue record for this book is available from The British Library

Cover design by Helen Taylor

Design by Carnegie Publishing

Printed by TJ International Limited

Libri Publishing
Brunel House
Volunteer Way
Faringdon
Oxfordshire
SN7 7YR

Tel: +44 (0)845 873 3837

www.libripublishing.co.uk

Contents

Foreword

Past and future perspectives on online education

I have worked with online education since I taught my first online courses and wrote the article *In Search of a Virtual School* in 1987. Now, nearly 30 years later, I'm heading *Campus NooA* [www.campus.noaa.info]– the Nordic open online Academy. It is an entrepreneurial initiative building on my Virtual School experiences and my Theory of Cooperative Freedom and Transparency in Online Education, Based on these experiences, I venture to reflect on some long-term and current trends in online education.

Looking back at some long-time trends

Online education has gradually become more available, global, mobile, and multimedial. The ICT systems have continuously become faster and more powerful. The most important breakthrough for online education came with the web in the middle of the nineties. The second most important development was the proliferation of the learning management systems. Later, open educational resources and social media became increasingly more important for online learning. It is also significant to point out that the technology gradually has become more mobile and wireless. However, the most significant difference is that very few people were online in 1987. Now, almost everybody is online – all the time – with a variety of gadgets that have huge potentials for learning.

There is a lot of focus on technology and digital learning resources, but I will speak up for people who succeed in utilizing the systems well. Learning platforms and online learning resources are important, but I will argue that it is more important how we implement and use the systems and resources. Well-organized models, effective student- and teacher support, quality content and teachers who really care about their students – are crucial for high quality online education.

Maybe this is why online pedagogy has not changes so much as I expected 25 years ago. The classroom metaphors and mind-sets are still too strong. Email and online discussion forums are still central elements in online courses and the teacher workload remains high. The students get too little flexibility, especially regarding individual start and progression. At the same time, they want swift and insightful feedback from teachers and support personnel. As far as I can see, we have not improved much in these areas during the last 25 years. I therefore urge online educators to focus on how we can organize online education better, for the benefit of all the excellent and hardworking online students and teachers.

Currents trends in online education

In a longer perspective, the following current developments are promising, but immature. One important challenge is how learning providers could develop sustainable business models to maintain these services as an important part of the future learning environment.

Open educational resources (OERs)

Freely accessible documents and media resources that are useful for teaching, learning, education, assessment and research purposes. These resources are growing in numbers, usefulness and popularity along with international, national and institutional support. UNESCO has for example named several prominent open education institutions as Chairs of OER. Another example is the European POERUP project (www. poerup.info) that provides national surveys of available OERs.

Social networks and Web2.0 services

Online learners are facing a growing number of social networks and web2.0 services that can be used for flexible and informal learning. The social networks provide access to experts and peers that can be very helpful for advice and learning. The Web2.0 services allow people to share a vast diversity of multimedial learning resources. Some of these opportunities are for example discussed in the article *Transparency in Cooperative Online Education*, which I wrote together with Christian Dalsgaard in 2006.

Personal learning environments (PLEs)

All the open educational resources, social networks and web2.0 services allow people to set up their personal learning environments (PLEs) according to their interests, learning styles and ambitions. This is both an opportunity and a challenge for the individual learner, as well as a challenge for the traditional educational institutions and providers that are used to be in control of the curriculum.

Open Badges

One challenge related to all the available OER and informal learning in the social networks is how this informal learning could be acknowledged and certified. As a result of this, the open badge movement (See for example http://openbadges.org and http://badgestack.com) challenges the traditional education institutions "monopoly" in issuing certificates and diplomas.

MOOCs

Massive Open Online Courses, and there is a growing number of such courses that could be of interest for adult learners. The design of and participation in a MOOC may be similar to college or university courses, but MOOCs typically do not offer credits awarded to paying students at schools. The open badge initiatives could therefore be of special interest for MOOCs. More information on MOOCs is available on http://mooc. ca and http://en.wikipedia.org/wiki/Massive_open_online_course

To conclude, I have spent nearly thirty years of my life to study, develop, teach, innovate, research and promote online education. It has given me the fascinating opportunity to take part in numerous discussions between people, cultures, institutions, and subject areas. Technology-enhanced learning and online education functions like a huge meeting place for educators were researchers and practitioners can work together to develop the field. So, I'm pleased to see that this book discusses technology-enhanced learning from various theoretical and practical perspectives. The chapters are inspiring to read and help us further reflect on our use of technology in higher education.

February 2015
Professor Morten Flate Paulsen

Bibliography

Dalsgaard, C. & Paulsen, M. F. (2009). Transparency in Cooperative Online Education. *The International Review of Research in Open and Distance Learning*, Vol. 10, No. 3., np.

Paulsen, M. F. (1987). In Search of a Virtual School. *T.H.E. Journal*, December/January 1987/1988, pp. 71-76.

Chapter One
Introducing technology-enhanced learning

John Branch, Paul Bartholomew & Claus Nygaard

Teacher as gardener

There is no shortage of analogies for the practice of education. Consider
the orchestra analogy, for example. In this analogy, the teacher takes on
the role of conductor. Students are members of the orchestra, the classroom serves as a concert hall, and the administrator is the artistic critic.
Education, therefore, is a kind of process in which the teacher directs
– instructs, cajoles, encourages, nudges – students to perform, despite
different students' abilities.

There is also the tourism analogy, in which the teacher is guide and
students are tourists. Curriculum is a travel book, and the tour considered more of a process than a destination. Of course, each student will
take different lessons from the tour, drawing on different experiences and
extant knowledge. Other analogies for the practice of education include
teacher as lighthouse, coach, performer, water, muse, even bowl of soup.

Taking forward perhaps the best-known analogy for the practice of
education – teacher as gardener; we might consider a learning opportunity as a seedling, and the role of the teacher as someone who nurtures
all seedlings (of different varietals) in the classroom garden. The teacher
as gardener plans the growth of each seedling, provides nourishment, and
controls for weeds and pests. And of course the hope is that, at the end of
the 'growing season', each seedling has blossomed and thus each learning

opportunity grown leads to real and tangible learning for our students.

This gardener analogy can be taken further; with each new season, for example, gardeners are offered a dizzying array of new clothing and gadgets – the purpose of which, of course, is to enhance gardening – to improve the activity of gardening and, more importantly, its outcomes. Teachers are likewise offered new technologies – directly from educational vendors and from life in general – with the potential to improve the practice of teaching and, more importantly, to enhance student learning.

Let us consider the introduction of technologies into the teaching 'garden' – it may help us to think first of all of the garden as 'learning environment' with the introduction of technology (as a holistic entity) as being analogous to gaining more space within which to grow learning opportunities (our seedlings). This raises some interesting questions:

- Do we even need more space?
- What do we want to grow?
- What tools do we need to ensure the garden blossoms?
- Do we have the time and the skills to tend the garden?

Do we even need more space?

The first consideration we should make when considering the deployment of learning technologies into higher education is whether there is a need for it in our specific context at all. What aspect of learning are we trying to enhance, and will the 'extra space' afforded by the utilisation of learning technologies help us address that need?

What do we want to grow?

If our seedlings are learning opportunities, then specifically – in terms of actual learning outcomes – what are we trying grow? What activities will benefit our students and how are we able to make informed judgements that the seedlings we choose will blossom into the learning opportunities we need to make available to our students?

What tools do we need to ensure the garden blossoms?

In many ways the term 'technology-enhanced learning' is unhelpful; it infers a singular entity – i.e. that 'technology' is a readily identified homogenous tool that we can deploy in the service of learning enhancement. Instead, technology is of course an overarching term for a myriad of specific tools – each of which is designed to support a specific type of learner behaviour. So, just as we have the trowel, the fork, the hoe, the spade and the secateurs to shape our garden, we have the forum, the wiki, the online quiz, the blog and the repository of online resources to shape our online environment, and from such environments the seedlings of learning opportunities may grow.

Do we have the time and the skills to tend the garden?

In answering the last question we said: "...*from such environments the seedlings of learning opportunity may grow*". As indicated by the emphasis, the 'may' is important – success is conditional upon us tending to the garden regularly and knowing how to use our tools. This speaks to the human agency that is required to be an effective gardener and also to being an effective designer of technology-enhanced learning opportunities. Both require vision and a clear sense of design; both require us to act at certain times of the year, to make interventions based on what we see is happening and to respond to things that may not be growing as well as we would like. Knowledge, patience and a caring attitude are a requirement.

In reflecting on our answer to question above, we are mindful that those traits of knowledge, patience and having a caring attitude are often found in effective University teachers as they practise their craft in university classrooms all around the world. We all understand that learning is a social process and that our humanity is extraordinarily important in making it happen. This remains true for technology-enhanced learning contexts too; the technology-based proxies we construct in our stead to, for example, facilitate peer discourse, to offer instruction or to manage assessment practices need to retain and reflect the agency of the teacher. The technologies we choose to use need to reflect our vision and intent; like the gardener, we need to be careful what we plant, to have knowledge of how our seedlings are likely to grow and have a realistic and pragmatic understanding of whether we have the skills and time to tend to what we plant.

Like gardening, technology-enhanced learning is a process that benefits from design, planning and dynamic human agency and it is within this realisation that we present this anthology.

LiHE

This anthology is the product of a symposium hosted by the Institute for Learning in Higher Education (LiHE), an academic association which, as intimated by its name, focuses entirely on learning at the post-secondary level. The focus of the Association reflects the shift from a transmission-based philosophy to a student-centred, learning-based approach. And its scope is limited to colleges, universities, and others institutions of higher education.

The main activity of the Association is a symposium. About 10 years ago, Claus noted that professors often attend conferences at which they present their scientific research in a 10-20 minute session, receive a few comments, then 'head to the bar for a drink'. He proposed an alternative, therefore, which returns to that ancient Greek format— the symposium— at which co-creation is key.

So, about 12 months prior to a symposium, a call for chapter proposals which has a relatively tightly-focused theme is announced on the Association's website and on various electronic mailing lists. The October 2013 symposium, for example, had the theme *Learning Spaces in Higher Education*; previous themes have revolved around case-based learning, games and simulations, classroom innovations, and creativity (in higher education).

Authors submit chapter proposals accordingly, which are then double-blind reviewed. If a proposal is accepted, its author is given 4 months to complete it. The whole chapter is then double-blind reviewed, and if it is accepted, the author is invited to attend the symposium. There, all authors revise their own chapters, work together to revise each other's chapters, and collaborate to assemble an anthology which, a few months later, is sent off to the publisher.

The symposium

Higher education is currently experiencing rapid transformation, with the introduction of a broad range of technologies which have the potential to enhance student learning. The purpose of the symposium, therefore, was to draw upon the experiences of those practitioners who were pioneering new applications of technology, thereby highlighting not only the technologies themselves but also the impact which they were having on student learning in higher education.

For the symposium, therefore, we (the editors) sought chapters which explored technology-enhanced learning within the domain of higher education, as per the focus of LiHE. The definition of technology was relatively broad, and included e-learning platforms, learning management systems, Facebook, blogging, and websites, plus newer technologies such as robotics, augmented reality, Google glasses, Geographic Information Systems, GPS, and mobile Apps. We hoped to advance our understanding of the nature, function, and impact of technology in higher education. We welcomed chapters from all scientific disciplines and which followed any methodological tradition.

The call for chapter proposals resulted in more than 20 submissions from around the world which explored a variety of different aspects of technology-enhanced learning in higher education. The subsequent review and re-submission process, however, whittled these down to the 9 chapters which follow in this anthology. The LiHE symposium at which the chapters were revised and the anthology was assembled was held in June 2014 on the Greek Island of Aegina, about 50 km off the coast of Athens. In addition to the academic symposium activities, authors explored the ruins of the 5th century B.C.E. Temple of Aphaea, visited the monastery of Saint Nektarios, climbed the islands highest point Mt. Oros, and, naturally, sampled the culinary delights of the Mediterranean.

The editors and technology-enhanced learning

As editors, of course, we bring our own perspectives to the role, which are based on our own experiences with technology. We have our own disciplinary backgrounds, which come with their own specific approaches to technology. And we have our own philosophical assumptions about human nature which, in turn, influence our views about technology.

Paul

Writing a reflective piece on one's experience of and engagement with technology-enhanced learning is interesting; one begins to draw links between early experiences and one's current teaching identity and practice. For my part, I remember being at school in 1980 and joining my school's nascent computer club. To begin, we didn't have a computer... it was on pre-order. And it was highly anticipated, with all of us in the club counting the days to its arrival. In the interim period, we programmed. We programmed human activities with the English language as our code. The first programming task was to boil a kettle:

- Unplug kettle
- Pick up kettle
- Move kettle to be under the water tap
- Turn tap on
- When kettle is full, turn off water
- ... [You get the picture]

I still remember the glee which the teacher had in letting us know that our routine was a failure as we had not included an instruction to remove the lid of the kettle! It was a formative lesson though – that a well-considered sequence was fundamentally important for any form of instruction. Later in my career, I would find myself designing learning sequences for students within a virtual learning environment (VLE) and similar care – to think through the sequence – was required.

Fast-forward 21 years and I was applying for my first substantive post in higher education, and as part of the interview process I was asked to offer a presentation on my vision for 'the future of clinical placement education in diagnostic radiography and radiotherapy'. Here, I advocated for the use of technology to connect students to their peers and to their tutors for the purposes of supporting reflection on clinical practice experiences and the fusion of theory and practice.

These two potential uses of technology, to support the sequencing of learning opportunities and to facilitate connections between people, became central pillars of my teaching practice and indeed my underpinning philosophy in learning design. My first foray in using technology to support learning was in the use of an online asynchronous conferencing tool called *WebBoard*. I supported postgraduate students to work collaboratively to solve weekly problems – specifically to agree on a diagnosis of a radiological image. The task was regular and fairly highly structured – the task was defined, duration for completion was set, and a model for the structure of the peer discourse was offered. Curious as to the degree to which the level of structure of the learning opportunity influenced student engagement, I set up other *WebBoard* spaces for two other groups of students. These were characterised by having less structure than my original model. One of the others (the semi-structured model) was a task-based space for the sharing of relevant references so that peers could pool links to useful literature. The other (the unstructured model) was a completely open space for peers to discuss aspects of their learning as they saw fit.

There was no engagement at all with the unstructured model, very limited engagement with the semi-structured model and excellent engagement with the (original) structured model. This was an unsurprising finding. As I moved forwards with my practice, new technologies became available; I moved my lectures out of the 'classroom' and onto a CD ROM as a set of video lectures, expecting students to view a lecture prior to coming to class (a model of delivery now known as 'flipped teaching'). This effectively liberated the classroom, allowing me to reclaim the space for social learning whereby (mostly) passive receipt of information was replaced by collaborative and active solving of relevant problems.

When my institution adopted a VLE, I was able to add greater resolution to the learning sequences I was offering: 'video lecture – problem solving classroom session – [repeat]' became 'video lecture – emergent questions posted on VLE – discuss questions in class and solve problems – consolidate learning with VLE-based quizzes – [repeat]'. This was a highly successful method of teaching that led to very high levels of engagement and enhanced learning outcomes as measured by performance at the point of assessment. Critical to success of the approach was having a clear understanding about what sorts of learning were best deployed where – i.e. what is *best* done in the classroom, what is *best* done within the VLE, what is *best* done when students study alone, what is *best* done when students study together. If we can put sequences of learning together that make best use of all of the resources we have available to us, then we give ourselves an excellent chance to optimise the learning opportunities we offer the students we teach.

It has been this sense of using technology as a means to enhance learning – even where that has meant, somewhat paradoxically, using it to find ways to do more technology-free face-to-face learning – that has been fundamental to my use of technology to support my own teaching. Of course, as I have progressed in my career and I have become responsible for the successful delivery of a wide range of programmes, I have shifted my aspirations. Now, I see technology not only as a way to enhance what we do in the classroom, but as a way to grow markets and to widen participation in higher education; and although some trans-national modes of higher education don't allow for significant amounts of face-to-face contact, a thorough and well developed understanding of what can be achieved through the use of technology helps greatly in the design of effective wholly-online provision.

John

To be honest, I have been for many years a bit of a luddite when it comes to technology in higher education. I suppose that it is not just in higher education, but also to some degree in life more generally. You see, I have no mobile telephone – I have never had one – and at home, my family only enjoys a few television channels because I refuse to pay for cable or satellite service. In higher education, my logic was simple— a great teacher does not need technology… nope, just a white board and a good story. Yes, of course, I have been using learning management systems, in fact since the early 2000s. But I have only really employed the posting function, never really exploiting the more advanced features such as discussion forums, testing, or wikis.

My view on technology in higher education changed dramatically in 2012 during the annual conference of the Society for Marketing Advances, a disciplinary association of which I am currently President (it is somewhat ironic, because about a decade earlier at the same conference, I won a set of clickers in a lucky draw, which I immediately donated to my colleague, pooh-poohing the entire notion of electronic question-and-answer devices.). At the conference, I was fortunate to attend a session by Fred Miller from Murray State University, who presented a number of teaching modules which he had created for teaching segmentation and other marketing concepts. The modules exploited a geographic information system (GIS), allowing students to harness in real-time the mass of information in a national database. They could explore voting patterns from state to state, itemise purchases at the county level, and even zoom down to the household to see family make-up. I was transfixed. I had been teaching segmentation for years; using mini-cases which I was convinced were effective. But I could see oh so clearly the value-add of this technology. And so began my foray into technology-enhanced learning in higher education... although I still do not have a mobile telephone.

Two projects are worth mentioning here. Recently, in my role as Academic Director of Part-Time MBA programmes, I was approached by a large pharmaceutical company which is interested in developing a customised MBA for its employees. The company wants some traditional face-to-face teaching, but because of the geographic dispersion of the potential students, also mandates alternative delivery methods. Consequently, I have been exploring the variety of synchronous and asynchronous technology platforms which could be used as the foundation for such a programme of study. I am not limiting my exploration; however, to traditional e-learning platforms or learning management systems, instead trying to be completely open to other new and creative solutions.

Last year, I was also approached by the Dean to develop a protocol for the flipped classroom. The motivation was the 'wasted classroom time' which has traditionally been allocated to lecturing on canonical material... material which could just as easily be learned by students on their own time. So, why not flip this lecture out onto the web, therefore, and use the value classroom time for application-oriented activities?

Contemporary usage of the term "flipped course", however, often means just that – a flipping, in which the classroom lecture is simply replaced with an online video version. This relatively unsophisticated flipping limits the full potential of the flipped classroom to transform education through a blend of student-centred learning and instructor-led application. That is to say, by equating the flipped course to an online lecture plus classroom activity, instructors have failed to exploit the variety of instructional tools which can be employed to facilitate student learning both in and out of the classroom. Stated in more general terms, a flipped course ought to be aimed at enhancing student learning by employing the instructional tools which meet learning objectives most efficiently and effectively.

Designing a flipped course, therefore, suggests that instructors need some kind of procedure to aid in the choice of which instructional tools are indeed most effective and efficient at meeting learning objectives. And so for the past few months, I have been working on a syllabus-making tool which will help professors design their courses, from learning objectives, to instructional tools, to assessment… and with a view to adopting new technologies which not only improve teaching but, more importantly, enhance student learning.

Claus

In the mid 1980s I started programming in Comal80, Basic, GWbasic and Dbase languages. My interest in learning led me to program software for the training of primary school children in Danish, Geography, History, and Politics. At that time, computers were all new to education, and in Denmark I was pioneering learning software together with my good friend Jens-Erik Kjeldsen, a passionate school teacher. We had the idea of using mainframes to store the test results of school children on a national scale, to enable benchmarking across school environments. At that time our ideas were too progressive and thought of as the introduction of a 'Big Brother Society', where government could misuse the knowledge of the learning of its individuals. Today it is a common feature of learning software to aggregate learning results and use big data to drive education. The feedback we got from school teachers taught me that learning software is highly engaging – if the difficulty level progressively balances the competencies of learners, if the gameplay is easy to understand, and if there is constant feedback about the progress.

At the time I moved into university, I had stopped grounded-programming, and was acting more as a passionate super-user of learning software. In the mid 1990s when the Internet became available, I started doing HTML-programming, and was now designing online cases for students, linking academic content with empirical material. My passion for case-based learning had me design a suite of learning software (Case-Maker), which was programmed as a beta-version at Copenhagen Business School in 2006. Following on from this, we won an EU-research grant to develop CaseMaker into a full functioning learning software, and at the time of writing, Libri Publishing Ltd is about to publish a book world-wide with the learning results from the CaseMaker-project. It is edited by Nigel Courtney and colleagues. The feedback we got from students and teachers working with the beta-version of CaseMaker taught me that collaborative features in the software enhance student engagement and learning – if the collaborative features enable dialogue, analysis, and synthesis. The sharing of information in a folder open for multiple users, doesn't lead to engagement and learning. In other words, there is a big difference between content management systems for information storing and sharing, and collaborative learning software.

Currently I am engaged in executive education at universities and through my company cph:learning. I rarely design curricula without an online component which holds a discussion forum and a learning log. For this purpose I use Wordpress, which I find easy to use. The multiple plugins enable me to tailor the online learning environment to the specific curriculum. I use the online component as a supplement to the physical learning environment (blended learning). The feedback I received from students using the online component in my executive courses taught me that students in general are willing to engage in online activities – if there is a direct link to the activities taking place in the physical learning environment, if the online activities are seen as a natural progression to their learning.

The latest technology-enhanced learning component with which I am working is app development within the domain of augmented reality. It is my hope that we shall succeed in developing an app, which enable students and practitioners to document their learning progress by linking data to 3D-representations of the world around them. It may sound far out, but with the technology's ability to recognise 3D-objects, it becomes possible to add data to them and also draw big data from recognised objects. Say a student points a phone to a map of Europe, data about economy, policy, health, education, etc can appear on the fly as a digital overlay on the phone. This will enable empirical data to be represented in a new way in learning situations. For me, who started in the mid 1980s, this journey from Comal80 to Augmented Reality has been a fascinating one. I have learned that technology may enhance learning if – and only if – it is designed with the learning-process of students at its core. To me the use of technology in education is more linked to pedagogy than it is to bits and bytes.

Policy and practice

A significant challenge when editing an anthology is developing a framework for structuring its chapters, even when they all share a common theme. During the symposium, therefore, together with the authors we settled on a very simple framework: policy and practice. Each of the 9 chapters of the anthology, therefore, explores technology-enhanced learning in higher education in terms of either policy and practice. The anthology is divided into 2 sections, each with a section overview which introduces the purview of either policy or practice of technology-enhanced learning in higher education.

The anthology, chapter by chapter

Chapter 2 by Claus Nygaard presents a rudimentary strategy for technology-enhanced learning in higher education by explicitly integrating technology, learning, and curriculum. It begins by reviewing cognitive and social learning theories. It then conceptualises technology-enhanced learning from both teacher-driven or student-driven perspectives, with a focus on either distribution, dialogue, or construction. Chapter 2 continues with a presentation of the promised rudiments of a strategy for technology-enhanced learning in higher education. Finally, it formulates some recommendations which may hopefully be useful for university staff engaged in the development of curricula for technology-enhanced learning. The key lessons from Chapter 2 are: 1. learning and technology are both equally important components in a strategy for technology-enhanced university learning, 2. without a strategy for learning it is not viable to formulate a strategy for technology-enhanced learning, 3. it plays an important role for student learning whether technology-enhanced activities are teacher-driven or student-driven, and whether these are planned with focus on either distribution, dialogue or construction, and 4. every planning of technology-enhanced activities should rest on a formulated strategy that takes into account both learning and technology.

Chapter 3 by Deborah Newton proposes a new performative approach for the use of technology-enhanced learning in higher education which may be described as a 'real world' approach which is ethically justifiable and respectful of the importance of the 'student voice'. It begins by radically re-defining technology-enhanced learning within a performance studies context through the use of critical theory. It then explores the theoretical foundations of technology-enhanced learning from a social constructionist perspective. Finally, Chapter 3 illustrates an innovative and creative application of technology-enhanced learning in performance studies. The key lesson from Chapter 3 is that technology in and of itself does not enhance learning, but instead through its intelligent use in carefully designed curricula which challenge and collapse cultural binaries and shift the perspective of learning to a teacher-learner relationship accepting of shared responsibility and empowerment for learning outcomes.

Chapter 4 by Eva Dobozy, Jim Mullaney, and David Gibson critiques the uses of new and emerging technologies in higher education. It begins by developing a theoretical framework for the the critique by examining the growing gap between technology-enhanced learning theory and practice. It then presents examples of 'revolutionary' and 'evolutionary' educational change. Chapter 4 continues by raising the the 'digitisation of pedagogy' dilemma, thereby pointing to the need for clear focus of technology in higher education. Finally, it draws some conclusions, outlines implications, and offers recommendations for practice. The key lesson from Chapter 4 is that new and emerging technologies must not be adopted blindly, but instead integrated mindfully in pedagogical practice.

Chapter 5 by Paul Bartholomew and Sarah Hayes challenges the assumption that through the introduction of technology (within a given context) learning will be enhanced. It begins by critiquing the very term 'Technology-Enhanced Learning' and the associated implication that the use of technology will enhance learning as an 'exchange value' transaction. It then takes a critical discourse analysis approach to substantiate this specific critique. Chapter 5 continues by placing this critique within a wider socio-political context which considers the reality of UK Higher Education in 2014. Finally, it advocates for the reconnection of human endeavour with the claimed (economic) gains which are attributed technology in higher education. The key lesson from Chapter 5 is that the academic community would benefit from having ongoing constructive debate which is characterised by a language of critique and possibility, not by a transactional account aligned to 'exchange value'.

Chapter 6 by Nicola Bartholomew and Graham Kelly explores potential strategies for implementing *iPad* technology to support student self-assessment. It begins by exploring the overarching drivers for implementing technology-enhanced learning and the potential pitfalls to be considered when investing in tablet technologies at an institutional level. It then critiques the application of tablet computers such as iPads, as personal learning tools for study management, and considers alternative uses to promote self-assessment, self-regulation and active learning. Chapter 6 continues by examining the multimodal nature of *Apple's iBook* technology, within a blended learning context, as a means to accommodate diverse learning styles. Finally, it reviews the authors' own practice which explores the use of an interactive formative eBook built using *iBooks Author*; made available on *iPads* within a higher education classroom environment. The key lesson from Chapter 6 is that tutor ownership of the pedagogic design principles which underpin the deployment of learning technologies is a primary factor for ensuring successful learner engagement.

Chapter 7 by Sarah King and Emma Flint examines the use of ePortfolios to enhance learning in higher education. It begins by exploring the philosophy and theory underpinning ePortfolio use and developing reflective and experiential learners. It then presents two contrasting case studies from Birmingham City University in which ePortfolios are embedded within the undergraduate Law programme to support personal and skills development in students. Finally, Chapter 7 examines critical incidents which can impact upon the use and value of ePortfolios in higher education. The key lesson from Chapter 7 is that the lived experience of technology use demands flexibility and responsiveness in design and subsequent implementation to enhance learning in higher education.

Chapter 8 by Steve Drew and Wayne Pullan describes an innovative, Web-based managed learning system (JPL) which was devised to scaffold novice Java language computer programmers. It begins by introducing the underlying learning challenges which these students experience when learning to program in Java. It then leads the reader through the learner-driven, evidence-based design and development of the JPL system components. Finally, Chapter 8 presents evidence of the effectiveness of the system by discerning the student learning experiences and outcomes. The key lesson from Chapter 8 is that technology can increase the flexibility of access to the learning environment, and the teacher's access to student progress for timely intervention, thereby enhancing learning in higher education.

Chapter 9 by Diane D. DePew, Frances H. Cornelius, and Carol Patton demonstrates the use of the ApprenNet technology for assessing students' application of critical thinking to guide appropriate responses in challenging nursing situations. It begins by examining the theoretical foundation of cognitive apprenticeship and experiential learning. It then introduces the ApprenNet technological process. Chapter 9 continues with an in depth review of the application of this technology to support learning in a specific nursing programme. Finally, it discusses the value, limitations, and broader applications of the ApprenNet technology. The key lesson from Chapter 9 is that technology can be utilised to link classroom to practice via structured learning activities which permit faculty members to assess student performance.

Chapter 10 by Leon Cygman examines the use of mobile telephone technology for assessing the performance of student pilots. It begins by describing the general problems which are faced by instructors who are unable to assess students as a result of the limited interaction which is inherent in field education. It then illustrates a technology solution which was implemented in flight education. Finally, Chapter 10 discusses how the implementation of this technology supported meaningful dialogue, strengthened the learning outcomes, and enhanced student engagement. The key lesson from Chapter 10 is that technology can enhance learning in situations in which student-instructor interaction is limited.

In summary

The global gardening industry was estimated to be nearly 190 billion USD in 2011, with an annual growth rate of some 3.5%. Contributing to this growth is the constant barrage of new chemicals, clothing, and gadgets – new tools, hybrids, and mulching's – all of which promise to make gardening more efficient and effective. In other words, an integral component of the gardening industry are the technologies which not only improve gardening, but also enhance its outcomes.

With this anthology, the editors aspired to showcase some of the latest pedagogical technologies and their most creative, state-of-the-art applications to learning in higher education from around the world. As such, it might be considered a kind of gardener's catalogue, offering up the latest seedlings, planters, and trellises which you might adopt in order to enhance the student-learning in your higher education garden. Happy gardening!

About the authors

Professor Dr. Paul Bartholomew is Director of Learning Innovation and Professional Practice at Aston University in Birmingham, England. He can be contacted at this email: p.bartholomew@aston.ac.uk

Professor Dr. John Branch is Academic Director of the part-time MBA programmes and Lecturer of Marketing at the Stephen M. Ross School of Business, and Faculty Associate at the Center for Russian, East European, & European Studies, both of the University of Michigan in Ann Arbor, U.S.A. He can be contacted at this email: jdbranch@umich.edu

Professor Dr. Claus Nygaard is founder and executive director of the Institute for Learning in Higher Education and owner and CEO of cph:learning. He can be contacted at this email: info@lihe.info

An introduction to technology-enhanced learning policy

Paul Bartholomew and Sarah Hayes

Introduction

This short piece seeks to introduce the concept of policy as it relates to technology-enhanced learning (TEL) as explored within this anthology. By so doing, the chapter outlines the role policy plays in shaping practice through the potential it has to define and even create practice contexts. Policy is often linked to a notion of 'a problem' and the strategies needed to solve it (Harman, 1984). Whilst problem solving is important, such an approach can tend towards a declarative model where a document provides a guide for all principles, actions and routines conveying a belief that, when strictly followed, will bring about desired change (Trowler, 1998). With these ideas in mind, we define a policy as *a set of principles that communicates expected actions within a stated context*. Accordingly, a policy seeks to reflect a context and to define responses to that context. For technology-enhanced learning, the context includes the challenges of our time, where a global economic downturn has contributed to the reshaping of many institutional priorities. Institutional aspirations to grow student numbers and the emergence of a students-as-consumers rhetoric have contributed to a teaching context that foregrounds efficiency, scalability and responsiveness to consumers' (students') perceived interests.

It is within this context that the deployment of technologies to support learning is discussed and the risks associated with what we would contend as narrow policy approaches are explored. But first we offer a small note as to author intent; throughout this piece, and indeed in our substantive chapter (in this volume), we are critical of policy and what we see as the dehumanisation of the technology-enhanced learning agenda. This should not be construed as an indication that we consider the institutional aspirations outlined above to be in anyway illegitimate – we appreciate and understand that universities must respond to economic and societal realities and that they must remain dynamic in relation to their mission and strategy. We simply critique a demonstrable (Hayes & Bartholomew, in this volume) conception of technology as an anthropomorphised agent of influence cast in the role of an autonomous and automatic 'solution' to current higher education challenges. We argue that expressing principles that foreground technology in this way through policy discourse is counterproductive, as it simply limits human involvement to be able to socially construct environments where technology plays a part in transformative learning.

Indeed, in relation to our empathy for current university priorities, we contend that our argument actually gives service to the furtherance of such university aspirations, for without the realisation that technology-based solutions to emergent challenges require human agency to be actioned, investments in technology-enhanced learning systems may not yield hoped-for solutions. We therefore see our critique as enabling solutions to economic realities rather than being in opposition to university aspirations to address them.

Defining policy as it relates to TEL

As outlined above, we contend that *policy defines a set of principles that communicates expected actions within a stated context* and below we discuss our understanding of how policy responds to economic challenges within a wider political context; but first we discuss policy as it relates to TEL in an institutional context. In higher education, policy has agency and can be seen as a 'proxy' of institutional authority. By 'proxy' we mean a functional representation of the views and intentions of another or others – in this case a representation of the authority of the policy writers. Policy, we contend, exists within the hierarchy of an institution and can play an important mediation role between the empowered agents who hold (actual) authority (senior management for example) and other agents within the institution. Figure 1 shows where we place policy, as it relates to the setting of the context for an institution's approach to designing and implementing TEL 'solutions', within an institutional hierarchy. If the policy's focus is on technology-enhanced systems, design and implementation is focused on TEL as a commissioned product; this leads to the development of institutional technical capacity without (necessarily) the recognition of, or support for, human labour. The systems-focused limb of the lower part of Figure 1 represents such a focus.

Alternatively, if the policy's focus is on people then the design and implementation is focussed on TEL as a social process. This focus has human engagement with technology 'built-in' to its precepts and, we contend, a truly (technology-) enhanced learning context emerges as a consequence.

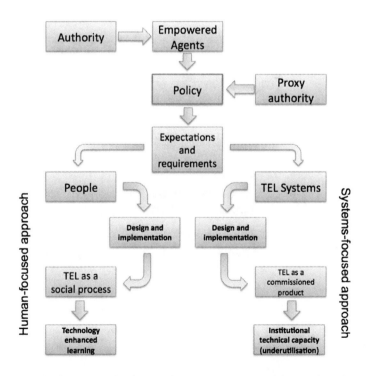

Figure 1: The location of policy within an institutional hierarchy of technology-enhanced learning design and implementation.

Hayes & Bartholomew (in this volume) demonstrate how policy documents are very often written in a way that leads to a prevalence of thinking that aligns with the systems-focused side of Figure 1. As a consequence acknowledgement of human labour, as the vital ingredient to drive and steer learning with technology, is absent from the discourse and potentially from the resource models that must underpin successful use of technology as a way to enhance learning. Such an approach, made manifest through such language use within policy documents, can lead ultimately to an underutilisation of commissioned systems as an institutional outcome.

Nygaard (in this volume) reminds us that well-established principles to support an effective learning context must be a feature of technology-enhanced learning environments too, that they must be facilitative of the human cognitive processes that lead to learning and be responsive to the dynamic needs of learners. Achieving this requires human design agency and any university that seeks to write policy for the design and implementation of TEL should do so with a clear focus on what university staff should actually be doing in order to successfully enhance learning (Nygaard, this volume). This places the author's argument in full support of the human-focussed side of Figure 1.

If we focus not just on the design and implementation of technologies as a means to support learning, but also on the lived experience of actually using the technology as a learner, Newton (in this volume) argues that learning is owned by the learner and is enacted performatively within a wider socially-constructed context. For Newton, for meaningful student-centred learning to occur, engagement with technology itself must be a social process. She contends that for TEL to be truly effective, control of learning must be returned to students with the planned support of teachers. Once again, the human-focused side of the diagram is advocated and the responsibility for universities, through policy, to reflect human labour as a necessary ingredient to achieve success is underlined. Dobozy et al (in this volume) offer some cautionary commentary on the seductive nature of TEL and the futility of focussing on systems as a route to enhancing learning opportunities. The authors remind us that trusting in a socially-based 'learning before technology' paradigm in relation to the design and implementation of TEL is much more effective route to success.

As a consequence, and as a preface to our substantive chapter (in this volume), we argue that the way policy is written (the way sentences are constructed and the way in which policy documents can inadvertently or deliberately 'write-out' human agency as an explicit and necessary resource) can lead to problematic institutional contexts where investment in technologies alone is seen as being sufficient to address the challenges identified earlier in this chapter. Such a policy position can lead to great expenditure without much in the way of impact or the delivery of solutions. By highlighting the important place policy has in defining institutional contexts for the design and implementation of TEL, we hope to persuade the reader of the crucial role policy plays in shaping these institutional contexts. Below, we outline how policy (and its writing) may play a part in responding effectively to the challenges discussed earlier in this chapter and how a particular approach to actively 'writing-in' human agency into policy can lead to a technology-rich institutional context that is facilitative of the enhancement of learning opportunities as laid out in the human-focused side of Figure 1.

The policy response to challenges

Policy responses to global economic challenges often seem to take a rather 'crude' and 'quantifiable route' (Strathern, 1997). The principles that are then communicated become 'one-dimensional' (Marcuse, 1964, 1991), suggesting that improved performance is simply guaranteed by the use of technology. We contend that TEL is often implicitly, but inextricably, ascribed an anthropomorphic role for improving learning opportunities in institutional contexts as demonstrated by the systems-focused side of Figure 1. In the wider context of society, the organising principles of economic and social provision that have impacted on education policy are those of neoliberalism. Drawing on arguments from Jessop (1994), we contend that the economic crisis has forced a move from more hierarchical forms of industrial management to neoliberalism. This has completely re-shaped social policy, which is now subordinated to the demands of market innovation. Policy now promotes business enhancement and reinforcement of the norms of structural competitiveness (Jessop, 1994:8). Ball (1997:263) describes these changes as "*a move from one state of affairs with a set of dominant characteristics, to a new state of affairs with different dominant characteristics*". Interestingly despite these changes, a fundamental view in policy that foregrounds technology deployment as a route to the inevitable enhancement of learning and modernisation of higher education has remained, and has even been strengthened, across different decades and governments.

These policy responses to economic challenges have led to a framework around policy for TEL that implies students are the focus – whose needs are being addressed through the mere deployment of technology. Unfortunately, at the same time, this takes control from them (along with their tutors), as they rarely appear as individuals in the discourse. Paradoxically, this is despite this replacement of humans with nonhuman technology being undertaken as an activity that is intended to yield greater 'control' (Ritzer, 1998). Policy documents may advocate the capturing of examples of 'best practice', but in reality a 'best practice' cannot be known, or proved to exist, when technologies are experienced by individuals as "*a complex and often problematic constellation of social, technological and educational change*" (Bayne, 2014) – i.e. the prominent availability of TEL without properly organised human design agency inevitably leads to under-designed solutions that are unlikely to be a good 'fit' for the great diversity of learner need.

With regard to new technologies, there have been "*important changes in the contemporary world that now allow us to practically intervene and shape the social conditions that circumscribe our everyday experience*" (Kellner, 1999). Of course, such potential does exist and humans might be empowered through the possibilities this presents – or, 'static models' may confine them, where a document defines a set of principles intended to bring about desired change without reflecting the myriad of social prerequisites that need to be put in place to achieve success.

We may then ask, who actually writes policy for the design and implementation of TEL? To use the UK as an example, government strategy documents have titles, but not many of these texts have author names. In university policies too, it may not be at all clear to teaching staff how policy documents actually come into being and who is charged with writing the communication media which directs that which people should do in relation to their practice. Short-term and casual staff and those on fixed contracts may find understanding these processes even harder. With these concerns in mind, many staff may simply react to policy, rather than actively seeking routes where they might input into it or actively manage its iteration. If this is a state of play recognised by readers of this anthology then perhaps we might ask what problems these arrangements present? For example, if policy does not bear the accounts of practitioners then what elements of practice *are* present to inform it? If policy directs us on a restricted route for TEL, effectively writing out our human presence, then what responses might revitalise links between practice and policy? Understanding how policy and practice either feed or restrict each other, and how the role of power and control within this nexus plays out, is we suggest, central to developing a broad, critical and creative understanding of TEL and its place in policy and wider socially constructed contexts.

A political economic focus in TEL policy language

If practitioners treat policy for TEL as something that simply 'emerges' and do not critically question how the discourse about TEL is constituted in relation to their own position, they lose the power to effect change resulting in the system-focused side of Figure 1 being the dominant model in higher education. So far, we have defined policy as it relates to TEL and also discussed the broader socio-economic context in which it resides. We now examine how commonly constructed policy language is a reflection of the wider political and socio-economic context, and how it drives a propensity for the system-focused side of Figure 1 to be dominant by default. We then proceed to consider what the taking of a more emancipatory approach might entail and how it allows us to change the 'default setting' for policy documents that seek to codify required TEL responses to socio-economic challenges and new institutional contexts.

If we believe policy responds as *a set of principles* to economic and social challenges, then these are also 'political' challenges (Hay, 2002:3). We suggest that to understand better what constitutes policy for TEL, it is necessary to examine the powerful political economic base that structures a global discourse of TEL. Language provides a vehicle for political economic agendas to make simplified claims in the name of technology to meet economic challenges, but these may also distort the values of human learning communities in higher education causing the human-focused side of Figure 1 to become relatively, if not completely, unacknowledged. By drawing attention to a normalising of capitalist social relations (and neoliberal values) within the discourse of TEL in UK higher education policy, through later chapters, we reveal what becomes prioritised (see Hayes & Bartholomew, this volume). Economic ideals can drive approaches where policy emphasises what *technology* can do to improve practice (as an exchange value), but it does not firstly question which theory-informed practices of human labour actually help people to learn with technology (see Nygaard, this volume). For example, if we understand as Newton (this volume) suggests, that TEL is enacted in student learning contexts as a 'performance' then a co-construction of the individual learning conditions of students needs to takes place.

The elements of *technology*, *language* and *learning* that are embodied within the terminology of TEL are enacted through human labour as a social practice, yet in policy texts, human labour as a tacit encounter with technology, may be overlooked. In TEL policy we are often urged to improve 'the student experience' (singular) – but we would stress that such 'reified' (Lukacs, 1971) language reduces our tangible human presence in these texts, erroneously classifying the diverse practices of many individual students as a single entity (Hayes & Bartholomew, this volume).

Naïve expectations of TEL coincide with agendas for economic growth

Rapid changes worldwide in the university system in recent decades have politically repositioned universities as engines of economic growth (Finlayson and Haywood, 2010:1). Traditional academic values of research, teaching, learning and free inquiry have been eroded, as emphasis has been placed on getting value for money and improving efficiency. 'Technology-enhanced learning' as a compound term, links 'use of technology' with the claim that learning is inevitably 'enhanced'. However the assumption that new technologies can (in themselves) enhance the effectiveness of education has always been in doubt, even as these new systems emerged: *"The history of educational technology shows that every new technology (television, computers, hypertexts, multimedia, Internet, virtual reality...) raise a wave of naive expectations regarding to the intrinsic effects of these technologies*" (Dillenbourg, Schneider, and Synteta, 2002:11).

It is not difficult to see how policies focused on global economic enhancement and reinforcing norms of structural competitiveness (Jessop, 1994) might then colonise people's 'naive expectations' of technology. A rhetoric of flexible and performance-driven goals for higher education benefits from a vision of TEL as simply a vehicle to support this. Dobozy *et al.* (this volume) argue that one effect from policy that seeks to modernise pedagogical practices in higher education through technology, is that some educators experience fascination with new and emerging technologies and bring these rapidly into the context of teaching, without a clear pedagogical understanding of what might be achieved for student learning. They describe a 'glitter effect', which leads to more and more technology being introduced into education, but without pause to question for what pedagogic purpose it is being introduced (Dobozy *et al.*, this volume). Critical theorists would argue that this approach is dictated by a 'mass culture' in capitalism where technology restructures people's work and leisure, influencing their lives from the organisation of their labour to their very modes of thought (Marcuse, 1964, 1991). In other words, what may sound beneficial in terms of suggested global 'enhancement' could actually threaten human criticality – an important pedagogical value (Freire, 1972).

Later in this anthology, to demonstrate how policy for TEL can reinforce assumptions we would wish to challenge, Hayes & Bartholomew (in this volume) take a Critical Discourse Analysis (CDA) approach (Fairclough, 2007) to draw on political economic theory from Marx (1867). By doing so, they reveal how simplified claims in the name of technology are made, suggesting there are strong assumptions of 'exchange value' from the implementation of TEL. Yet this is a focus that can inhibit questions even being raised about more diverse ways students experience technology, in their learning, and indeed throughout life.

Conclusion

While the focus on TEL remains on the technology, as opposed to powerful social and political forces that surround them (including language), important academic questions are simply not being asked.

Questions, for example, which address the neo-liberal (and in capitalism more generally) trend for ever-more technologies to intervene between people, or to replace them (Matthewman, 2011) within (in our case) the higher education context. Additionally, questions about why policy is written with such a focus, rather than constructed based on decades of critical theory about the politics of technology and also theory about how people learn (see Nygaard, this volume), remain under-examined.

Although the issue we raise is widespread and somewhat pervasive, there are simple steps we can take to manage how policy is created and maintained within an institution and although the reader could be excused for assuming that we regard the *production* of policy to be absent of human engagement, we do not. We contend that although policy, as a *product*, can be absent of an acknowledgement of human engagement, the production process of a policy *does* engage people and is itself a product of human engagement and potentially rich discourse. This engagement of people in the production of policy *should* enable us to develop it in a way that represents a human-focused approach, but as Hayes & Bartholomew (this volume) demonstrate through their Critical Discourse Analysis work, this tends not to be the case. We would like to conclude this chapter with a speculation as to why that is the case, and what can be done.

When policy is first developed and 'launched' within an institution, it is done through a process that is socially supported; for example, it emerges through the workings of a committee and is shared with members for cascading throughout the institution. As such, the policy is shared with colleagues with accompanying social processes that communicate context and implied caveats. The policy can be argued to be a hybrid agent – a co-agent comprising document and authors. Clarifications can be given, questions can be answered and the policy is manoeuvred into place with the use of social and (institutional) political influence. Accompanying human management of the process of 'launching' the policy offsets the paucity of explicit acknowledgement of the crucial nature of human labour within content of the document.

However, what of those people who encounter the policy without the policy-author co-agent being present – say months after introduction or after key authors have left? What of unwritten contexts and caveats then? Instead, all that is left is the document and the language and consequent reader interpretation of documented policy instruction. This is why we must be careful with policy language; after the author-co-agents of policy have distanced themselves in time or institutional topography from the document component of the policy, how will the original intent of policy documents be accurately discerned and interpreted by those who have to use it?

We conclude this chapter with two recommendations. Firstly, for all policy documents to include within its authors those practitioners who will be subject to the policy and who are the everyday designers and implementers of TEL practice (Figure 2):

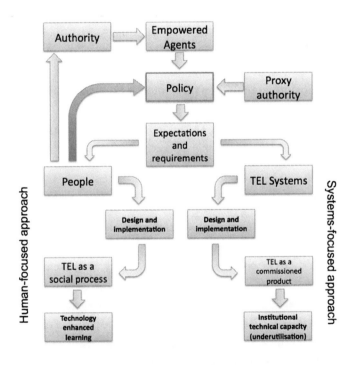

Figure 2: 'People' who design and implement TEL have the authority for, and responsibility to, write applicable policy.

Secondly, for all policy to be made dynamic; to be insulated against the risk of author co-agents drifting away, in conceptual or organisational distance, from the policies they have written. Accordingly, we suggest that each and every policy have, as its concluding paragraph, the names of the authors, the date of last authoring and crucially the mechanism through which the policy can be challenged or modified. Additionally we would like to recommend the inclusion, as the final paragraph of any policy that seeks to define the parameters for practice with TEL, a statement similar to the following:

> "This policy has been written to support the work of people to use technology to support the learning of students. It is meant to be useful, relevant and used. If you find there are aspects of this policy that aren't fit for purpose or are inhibiting you from designing and implementing learning technologies in a way that successfully enhances learning, then we want to know. Please use the mechanism above to let us know how you think the policy needs to change. We want, and need, to hear from you."

By implementing an ongoing practitioner-led approach to dynamic policy authoring and maintenance, we hope a systems-focused approach to policy writing will eventually be eradicated, and in the meantime be effectively mitigated through the strengthening of the human component of the document-human hybrid policy agency.

About the authors

Professor Dr. Paul Bartholomew is Director of the Centre for Learning Innovation and Professional Practice at Aston University, Birmingham, England. He can be contacted at this email: p.bartholomew@aston.ac.uk

Dr. Sarah Hayes is a Lecturer in Technology-Enhanced and Flexible Learning in the Centre for Learning Innovation and Professional Practice at Aston University, Birmingham, England. She can be contacted at this email: s.hayes@aston.ac.uk

Bibliography

Ball, S. J. (1997). Policy sociology and critical social research: A personal review of recent education policy and policy research. *British educational research journal*, Vol. 23, No. 3, pp. 257-274.

Bayne, S. (2014). What's the matter with 'technology-enhanced learning'? *Learning, Media and Technology*. Vol. 40, No. 1, pp. 1-16.

Dillenbourg, P.; Schneider, D. & P. Synteta (2002). Virtual Learning Environments. In *Proceedings of the 3rd Hellenic Conference 'Information & Communication Technologies in Education'*, pp. 3-18.

Fairclough, N. (2007). Global Capitalism and Change in Higher Education: Dialectics of Language and Practice, Technology, Ideology. In *BAAL conference: Edinburgh*.

Finlayson, G. & D. Hayward (2010). Education towards heteronomy: A critical analysis of the reform of UK universities since 1978. Online Resource: http://bit.ly/aJOJB1 [Accessed October 14, 2014].

Freire, P. (1972). *Pedagogy of the Oppressed*. Middlesex: Penguin Education

Jessop, B. (1994). The Transition to post-Fordism and the Schumpeterian Workfare State. In R. Burrows & B. Loader (Eds). *Towards a post-Fordist Welfare State?* London: Routledge.

Harman, G. (1984). Conceptual and theoretical issues. In J. R. Hough (Ed.) *Educational Policy: An International Survey*. London: Croom Helm.

Hay, C. (2002). *Political analysis: a critical introduction*. Basingstoke: Palgrave Macmillan.

Kellner, D. (1999). Theorizing/resisting McDonaldization: A multiperspectivist approach. In B. Smart (Ed.) *Resisting McDonaldization*, London: SAGE Publications Ltd, pp. 186-207.

Lukács G. (1971). *History and Class Consciousness*. London: Merlin.

Marcuse, H. (1991). *One-Dimensional Man: Studies in the Ideology of Advanced Industrial Society* [1964]. London: Routledge.

Marx, K. (1867). Capitalism and the modern labour process. Capital, volume 1. In R. C. Scharff & V. Dusek (Eds). (2003). *Philosophy of technology: The technological condition: An anthology*. Oxford, UK: Blackwell.

Matthewman, S (2011). *Technology and Social Theory*. New York, NY: Palgrave.

Ritzer, G. (1998). The Weberian Theory of Rationalization and the McDonaldization of Contemporary Society. In P. Kivisto (Ed.) *Illuminating Social Life: Classical and Contemporary Theory Revisited*, Thousand Oaks, CA: Pine Forge Press, pp. 37-61.

Strathern, M. (1997). From improvement to enhancement: an anthropological comment on the audit culture. *Cambridge Anthropology*, Vol. 19, pp. 1-21.

Trowler, P. (1998). *Education Policy: A Policy Sociology Approach*. Eastbourne, East Sussex: The Gildridge Press Limited.

Chapter Two

Rudiments of a strategy for technology-enhanced university learning

Claus Nygaard

Introduction

This chapter forms the basis for a discussion of what constitutes a strategy for technology-enhanced university learning. The chapter explicitly integrates technology, learning and curriculum. My aim is not to formulate a complete strategy but to inspire a motivated discussion of what a strategy for technology-enhanced university learning may contain. The chapter has four sections. In the first section, I conceptualise learning. In the second section, I conceptualise technology-enhanced learning. Following this, the third section presents the rudiments of a strategy for technology-enhanced university learning. In the fourth section, I formulate some recommendations that may be useful for university staff engaged in the development of curricula for technology-enhanced learning. Consequently, this chapter will:

1. show you how learning and technology are equally important components in a strategy for technology-enhanced university learning;
2. invite you to work with eight statements about learning drawn from an integration of cognitive- and social-learning theories;
3. outline the possible roles and value of both teacher-driven and student-driven technology-enhanced activities.

Conceptualisation of learning

While learning itself is a human process, 'technology-enhanced' represents a certain range of activities we can access to achieve learning. I contend that, in order to understand the design and effect of technology-enhanced higher education, we need to have a clear understanding of learning as a human process. The use of technology itself is not learning – the development of human capacity is. I shall come back to that in more detail below but will begin by conceptualising learning. Within the modern learning discourse, we can see two important learning theoretical orientations, each with its own understanding of how people learn. One is cognitive learning theory (Bloom *et al.*, 1956; Piaget, 1970; Bruner, 1996; Freeman, 1999). The other is social learning theory (Bandura, 1975; Vygotsky, 1987; Kolb, 1984; Lave & Wenger, 1991; Wenger, 1998). Understanding the differences between these two main discourses within learning theory will help us address the design and effect of technology-enhanced university education more clearly.

Cognitive learning theory

Cognitive learning theory was developed mainly by cognitive psychologists and focuses on the role of cognitive processes in learning. Cognitive processes are sometimes referred to as mental processes and we will see discussions of how students observe, categorise and form generalisations to make sense of the information provided. The focus is on learning as a result of internal mental activity and not from externally imposed stimuli. It is argued that the learner (student) holds knowledge, skills and experiences which have an effect on learning. In the cognitivist view, learning is individual as the learner receives information through the senses and processes that information in the brain. Terms like short-term memory and long-term memory are used as indicators of how learning is stored by the individual. Cognitive learning theory sets the individual (the learning subject) in a learning environment (among objects). The main focus is on the capacity of the individual to learn, and learning is largely seen as an individual matter. Subscribing to cognitive learning theory, the role of the teacher is to make available to the student the right information within the theoretical domain studied and see to it that the learning environment enables to student to perform (learn). Leaving the responsibility for learning to the student, as long as the information and the learning environment are perceived to be suitable, curriculum design becomes a matter of designing specific ways in which information can be distributed to students (i.e. through lectures, books, or technology-enhanced techniques). Since learning is a cognitive process, and because what is learned is stored in either short-term or long-term memory, it becomes possible to assess students based on their learning (often measured as well-defined learning outcomes). Students can then be divided into groups of excellent students, good students or poor students. As I shall show later when I present a possible typology for technology-enhanced university learning, the focus on teacher-driven distribution of information to individual students engaged in cognitive learning processes seems to be dominant in universities.

Social learning theory

Social learning theory was mainly developed by sociologists and socio-psychologists. It also focuses on the individual but studies how the social relationships (also called social embeddedness) and language (also called discourse) of the individual contribute to the individual's understanding of the world. The argument is that learning occurs in social situations (also called situational learning) so learning is a social issue, not an individual matter. When social learning theory explains that individuals learn by developing practice in communities with other individuals and argues that learning is situated, a distinction appears between the individual and the environment which is also found in the cognitive learning theory – but there are some clear differences. Where cognitive learning theory sets the individual (as the learning subject) in a learning environment (among objects), social learning theory situates learning (an embedded process) in a context (embedded in ongoing social relations). McDermott (1999:15) writes that: "...context is not so much something into which someone is put, but an order of behavior of which one is a part". Seeing context as an order of behaviour, rather than as an architecture or structure of objects, enables a focus on relational processes between individuals and context. Although it is the individual who learns, learning is seen as a socially embedded process influenced by the individuals' position in "ongoing systems of social *relations"* (Granovetter, 1992). The argument of embeddedness is defined as: *"...the argument that the behaviour and institutions to be analyzed are so constrained by ongoing social relations that to construe them as independent is a grievous misunderstanding... Actors do not behave or decide as atoms outside a social context, nor do they adhere slavishly to a script written for them by the particular intersection of social categories that they happen to occupy. Their attempts at purposive action are instead embedded in concrete, ongoing systems of social relations."* (Granovetter, 1992:53-58).

With Granovetter's concept of embeddedness, it can be argued that learning (and knowledge production) cannot be taken for granted, even with curriculum structured a certain way. Learning is socially situated (tied to a particular order of behaviour) and unfolds anew in any learning situation as the student engages in the learning process and interacts through ongoing social relations. In university settings, these relations can be between students and students, students and teachers, students and administrators, students and technology, students and physical learning facilities, and students and the social and cultural environment of the wider institution. Indeed, many more relations are possible – these are only some of them. From the point of view of social learning theory, ongoing social relations are multiple and endless. The order of behaviour may well be regulated by curriculum, institutional structures, ICT-systems, physical learning facilities, etc., but there is no one best way of interacting and learning in such situations. The argument that systems of social relationships are 'ongoing', and that context is an order of behaviour, tells us that the relation between the student and the learning environment is never stable but constantly unfolds in new formations over time. Thus, any learning environment, no matter how it is designed, cannot be perceived as an identical setting for learning for all students, and thus the distribution of information or the design of technology-enhanced learning environments cannot in itself lead to a particular level of learning.

Subscribing to social learning theory, the role of the teacher is to make available to the student the right conditions for taking part in ongoing systems of social relations which, through an academic discourse, enables the student to see the world in a new way (thereby arguably having learned). The responsibility for learning is not left to the student alone but is shared between student and the actors and artefacts that constitute the order of behaviour. Curriculum design becomes a matter of designing the ways in which students can make effective use of their social embeddedness (through lectures or technology-enhanced techniques). As learning is a social process, it may not be suitable to assess students based on their individual learning and divide students into groups of excellent students, good students or poor students. If universities really wish to develop a strategy for learning, they need to address issues much wider than how students perform as individuals within a well-defined curriculum. As I shall show later when I present the possible typology for technology-enhanced university learning, a focus on student-driven dialogue and construction may be a way forward.

Eight statements about learning

Following this synopsis of cognitive and social learning theories, I find it useful to broaden the concept of learning from focusing on *what* students have to learn to *how* students learn, and subsequently how students can further develop their capacities for learning. I find useful insights from both positions and I believe it is possible to bridge the two and use them in the formulation of a strategy for technology-enhanced university learning. Consequently, I end this section with eight personal statements which, for me, conceptualise learning:

1. Learning is the construction and continual articulation of meaning.
2. Learning is based on experiences which make it different for each individual.
3. Learning involves acquiring new personal knowledge, skills and competencies that can be used to resolve forthcoming challenges in life.
4. Learning is the ability to doubt and to question one's own assumptions.
5. Learning is both an individual and a social process.
6. Learning is a contextual process tied to an order of behaviour that changes over time.
7. Learning is a process affected by (and a process that affects) the identity of the learner.

8. Learning is a process affected by (and a process that affects) the social position of the learner, and the learners' embeddedness in ongoing social relations.

The immediate reason for articulating eight statements about learning is that they enable us in universities to make a more qualified discussion and evaluation of our strategies for learning – including those for technology-enhanced learning.

Conceptualisation of technology-enhanced learning

Having looked at learning in more detail, how do we link the knowledge of learning to technology? In the research on technology in higher education, it is difficult to find a coherent focus on the use and role of technology. Success seems to have many fathers. Some link technology with online learning (Carliner, 2004; Hiltz & Turoff, 2005; Rhode, 2009) and distinguish the classroom or lecture hall (the traditional settings for learning) from the 'newer type' of electronic environments for online mediated learning. Others name similar situations 'e-learning' (Nichols, 2003). Others again talk about 'distance learning' or 'distance education' (Keegan, 1996; King et al., 2001) to distinguish between on-site learning at universities and off-site learning in a geographical setting away from the university (typically containing an online component). This is also called 'distributed learning' (Stupans, 2014). Still others talk about situations where traditional on-site settings are mixed with online off-site settings and label those 'blended learning' (Garrison & Kanuka, 2004; Helms, 2012). In the debate on technology-enhanced learning, the notions of synchronous and asynchronous learning (Pilkington & Walker, 2003; Hrastinski, 2008) pinpoint the differences in time between learning activities – either students learn at the same time (synchronous) or at different times (asynchronous). Although technology-enhanced learning differs in mode from traditional learning (what may be called analogue learning) in its technology, pedagogy and curriculum, learning itself does not differ in its ontological or epistemological sense. Regardless of technology, pedagogy and curriculum, the ways in which a human being learns do not change. It therefore makes no sense to talk about technology-enhanced learning (or e-learning, online learning, distributed learning, blended learning, etc.) without bringing in our knowledge of learning. So, what could result from this fusion of technology and learning?

A possible typology of technology-enhanced learning activities

There are multiple typologies of technology-enhanced learning activities. Based on the university context, where learning can be argued to be the key element and the true purpose of curriculum development, I define three types of technology-enhanced learning activities: 1) distribution; 2) dialogue; and 3) construction (Figure 1). It is my argument that there are fundamentally different learning outcomes for students in these scenarios. These three technology-enhanced learning activities should be viewed as educational activities that would normally indicate the way study methods (including education) are performed. 'Distribution' describes the situation where a sender sends a message to a recipient. 'Dialogue' describes the situation where two parties actively communicate with each other about a topic. 'Construction' describes the situation where one or more parties construct knowledge together (which may be based on previously completed distribution or dialogue). By definition, these three technology-enhanced learning activities are not epistemologically different but the typology points out educational differences between them. The technology-enhanced learning activities contained in the distribution column tend to be teacher-driven and focus on students' learning outcomes (much like with cognitive learning theory). Distribution usually creates assimilative learning within existing cognitive structures. The technology-enhanced learning activities contained in the dialogue column tend to be student-driven and focus on the relational process between students, which are argued to lead to learning (much like with social learning theory). The same is the case for technology-enhanced learning activities in the construction column, which has the built-in requirement that students construct knowledge with other students, or make use of interactive methods that enable them to construct knowledge on their own. The technology-enhanced learning activities in the dialogue and construction columns usually create accommodative learning where students actively rearrange existing cognitive structures through the challenge of their own presuppositions and the creation of new knowledge.

Overall, it can be argued that technology-enhanced learning activities, to be their best, should aim toward dialogue and construction and away from distribution. Student-directed learning is important because learning takes place through the active behaviour of the student. It is what the student does that leads to learning, not what the teacher does.

I also distinguish between whether the technology-enhanced learning activities are governed by a student-driven or teacher-driven paradigm. Here, it is my argument that the teacher-driven paradigm, in which information is distributed equally to all students, or activities planned based on the teacher's horizons, tends to create assimilative learning. The student-driven teaching paradigm, where students themselves are responsible for creating the information base or knowledge, tends to create accommodative learning. Overall, one can say that it is important that technology-enhanced learning activities are directed away from a strong teacher-centred expression and toward a student-centred expression. Figure 1 outlines possible teaching paradigms and combinations of technology-enhanced university learning.

Teaching paradigms	Technology-enhanced learning activities		
	Distribution	Dialogue	Construction
Teacher-driven (subject and format decided by teacher)	podcast video broadcast online test	blogging session chat online conference	online review online assignments online case challenge online collaborative role play games
Student-driven (subject and/or format decided by student)	online presentation	blogging session chat online conference	online discussion forum wiki e-book / iBook ePortfolio academic blog online research tools academic Facebook pages online review / opponent web 2.0 design creation of academic database online collaborative role play games

Figure 1: A possible typology of technology-enhanced learning activities.

The examples in Figure 1 are not exhaustive but show some of the typical technology-enhanced learning activities in use at universities. It is not suitable for universities to have teachers apply teacher-driven technology-enhanced activities without any reflection on the learning processes of students. It is my observation, from 20 years in the university sector and having followed the technological developments in higher education, that the majority of university curricula see technology as a vehicle for teachers to distribute information to students. Even the recent MOOC (Massive Open Online Course) hype is built on experts distributing information to students via video broadcasts and podcasts. After participating in four MOOC's myself, it is my experience that as an educational model it is very tiresome and as a vehicle for learning it is somewhat limited. In my view, universities must try to use technology-enhanced learning activities that create accommodative learning among students, which requires at least dialogue and, at best, construction. Technology-enhanced learning activities should be integrated with a comprehensive strategy for curriculum development that explicitly links technology to student learning. I am not implying that this isn't already being done at some universities. Recent case studies show prime examples of technology being used for student-driven construction. Hager (2013) shows how ePortfolio is used at the University of Oregon, USA, to engage students in learning for the 21st century. Rowley (2012) shows how ePortfolios for music education at the University of Sydney, Australia, are an innovation in the transmission of learning for both students and staff. Lenstrup (2013) shows how the application of Web 2.0, in which students construct case-based social-media learning environments, improves students' second-language learning at Copenhagen Business School, Denmark. Raiker (2013) shows how computer-supported collaborative learning enables the professional development of schoolteachers in a university led programme at Bedfordshire University, England. Hardy & Totman (2012) show how university student engagement in online role play exercises at Deakin University, Australia, improves their level of understanding of the political dimensions of the Middle East. Other inspiring case studies are presented in this anthology. Following these discussions of learning and technology, I now present the rudiments of a strategy for technology-enhanced university learning.

Rudiments of a strategy for technology-enhanced university learning

How can we use our knowledge of learning theory and the examples of technology-enhanced activities we have seen to formulate a strategy for technology-enhanced university learning? What would it look like? It is my judgement that such a strategy should take its cue from our knowledge of learning. I would also argue that it should be designed and implemented to increase students' learning outcomes while reducing the barriers for both students and staff to engage in technology-enhanced activities. Figure 2 reiterates the eight statements about learning and reflects on their implications for technology-enhanced activities.

Statements about learning	Implications for technology-enhanced activities
1. Learning is the construction and maintenance of meaning.	Technology should be used in such a way that students are inspired to construct and maintain meaning. This can be a result of teacher-driven distribution where students are inspired from a podcast. It can be achieved through a dialogue between two students in a student-driven blogging session. It can also be reached through the creation of a student-driven wiki on a subject chosen by the teacher. My hypothesis is that by moving from distribution (which calls for assimilation) to dialogue and construction (which call for accommodation) there is a higher possibility that students construct and maintain meaning that leads to improved learning outcomes.

Statements about learning	Implications for technology-enhanced activities
2. Learning is based on experiences which make it different for each individual.	Technology should be used in such a way that students explicitly draw on their past experiences, because when doing so it becomes apparent to them how they can link new knowledge to their existing knowledge. At the same time, technology, with its asynchronous abilities, enables students to reflect on their own learning in relation to the learning of other students. This can be achieved through both teacher-driven and student-driven technology-enhanced activities. It could be by a student-driven online presentation in which experiences and learning outcomes are distributed online. It could be by a teacher-driven dialogue in a chat-forum in which students are asked to contextualise their own experiences in relation to the subject studied. Or, it could be achieved in a teacher-driven case assignment in which students are asked to construct arguments for use of the studied subject in practice.
3. Learning involves acquiring new personal knowledge, skills and competencies that can be used to resolve forthcoming challenges in life.	Technology should be used in such a way that it enables students to become aware of their new knowledge, skills and competencies which arise from using technology-enhanced activities. It should not be used only for the sake of technology or the distribution of information alone. A teacher-driven distribution of information through a podcast or a video broadcast does not allow insight into what students are learning. Teacher-driven or student-driven dialogues, like blogging sessions, in which students reflect on their new knowledge, skills and competencies, provide a deeper insight into learning outcomes. The same is the case for technology-enhanced activities that lead to construction, such as students writing e-portfolios about their own learning outcomes.
4. Learning is the ability to doubt and to question one's own assumptions.	Technology should be used in such a way that it enables students to doubt and question their own assumptions and invites them to further reflect on the use of their knowledge, skills and competencies. Teacher-driven online tests may enable such reflection. Student-driven dialogues in an online conference can do the same. Student-driven construction of an academic blog about using their knowledge, or applying online research tools that make students question the scope and utility of what they have already learned (or think they have learned), can also encourage critical thinking.

Statements about learning	Implications for technology-enhanced activities
5. Learning is both an individual and a social process.	Technology should be used in such a way that students are required to interact with other students, with cases, and with practice. This moves the use of technology away from teacher-driven distribution to technology-enhanced activities designed for dialogue and construction. These can be teacher-driven dialogues in online conferences or student-driven construction of academic Facebook pages, web 2.0 design, or similar activities where students use technology to interact with other students and reflect on the use of their learning and their learning outcomes.
6. Learning is a contextual process tied to an order of behaviour that changes over time.	Technology should be used in such a way that it opens up for both engagement and flexibility over time, student learning is an ongoing process. Students do not all learn in the same way or continue learning in the same way as individuals. This also moves the use of technology away from teacher-driven distribution to technology-enhanced activities designed for dialogue and construction. The technology-enhanced curriculum should be developed so students engage in changing dialogues, which may be achieved through blogging sessions, chat sessions and online conferences, either teacher-driven and student-driven. Dialogue may also be achieved by students taking part in activities for construction, such as a wiki, an academic blog, academic Facebook pages, etc. We know that learning changes over time, and we can use technology-enhanced activities to support this development.

Statements about learning	Implications for technology-enhanced activities
7. Learning is a process affected by (and a process that affects) the identity of the learner.	Technology should be used in such a way that students get immediate feedback on their learning outcomes and their progress as learners. This can be achieved by teacher-driven online tests. Technology-enhanced activities based on dialogue and construction, in which students interact with other students and with members of faculty, allow students to reflect on their own performance in relation to the performance of other students, thereby helping them understand their own role and identity as students. Finding oneself as a student and understanding the requirements of that role may be difficult if one is listening mainly to podcasts or video broadcasts from teachers. Using technology to invite students to take part in dialogues (online conferences, chat sessions, blogging sessions) or construction (reviewing other students' work, taking part in the creation of an academic database, writing an e-book on a particular subject) helps students understand their own role and identity as students.
8. Learning is a process affected by (and a process that affects) the social position of the learner and the learner's embeddedness in ongoing social relations.	Technology should be used in such a way that it enables and/or requires students to interact with a large variety of other students. Technology-enhanced activities impact how students are seen by other students and thus change their social position in the student network, both online and offline. Technology should be used to broaden the social relations of students and invitations for dialogue and construction should be facilitated through a wider group of students. This may be done through teacher-driven activities for dialogue and construction, in which the teacher decides which students are going to work together. It may also be done through student-driven activities for dialogue and construction, in which students decide on the subject but invite a larger group of participants to their online conference, academic Facebook page, etc. It is important to be aware that using technology-enhanced activities does affect the social position of students, and a wider mix of facilitated dialogue and construction will enable students to become part of a broader network of students. It is my hypothesis that this will benefit both student identity and student learning.

Figure 2: Eight statements about learning and their implications for technology-enhanced activities.

From my own experience, it seems that often technology is introduced as a mere add-on to analogue teaching and not used for its abilities to enhance student learning. Investing vast amounts of money in the introduction of online content management systems to distribute lecture notes, lecture slides, and allow students to upload assignments electronically doesn't seem to me to be a strategic move. If universities wish to make intelligent use of technology for enhancing student learning, they have to formulate an explicit strategy for doing so.

The following eight statements about the use of technology form the rudiments of a strategy for technology-enhanced university learning.

1. Technology should be used in such a way that students are inspired to construct and maintain meaning.
2. Technology should be used in such a way that students explicitly draw on their past experiences because doing so makes it apparent how they can link new knowledge to their existing knowledge.
3. Technology should be used in such a way that it enables students to become aware of the new knowledge, skills and competencies that arise from using technology-enhanced activities.
4. Technology should be used in such a way that it enables students to doubt and question their own assumptions and invite them to reflect further on the use of their knowledge, skills and competencies.
5. Technology should be used in such a way that students are required to interact with other students, with cases, and with practice.
6. Technology should be used in such a way that it opens up both engagement and flexibility over time, as student learning is an ongoing process.
7. Technology should be used in such a way that students get immediate feedback on their learning outcomes and their progress as learners.
8. Technology should be used in such a way that it enables and/or requires students to interact with a large variety of other students.

Figure 3: Rudiments of a strategy for technology-enhanced university learning.

It is my advice that universities, when investing in technology, formulate a strategy for technology-enhanced university learning. Doing so will put normative requirements on university staff because they have to live up to the strategy. In the final section of this chapter, I formulate some normative recommendations for implementing such a strategy.

Normative recommendations for implementing a strategy for technology-enhanced university learning

At Copenhagen Business School, I was involved in a university-wide study of the barriers that kept study administrators, teachers and students from engaging in technology-enhanced learning activities (CBS Learning Lab, 2004). The findings are summarised in figure 4. It is my argument that, in order to implement a strategy for technology-enhanced university learning, universities have to work to eliminate such barriers.

Barriers identified among study administrators	Barriers identified among teachers	Barriers identified among students
Lack of academic and pedagogical knowledge about the use of technology-enhanced learning activities.	Lack of a vision for technology-enhanced learning activities at the university-level.	Expert-biased (they think that the best learning comes from listening to the teacher).
Lack of time to engage in technology-enhanced learning activities.	Lack of overall goals for technology-enhanced learning activities at the university-level.	Wish to have more lectures.
Lack of economic resources to develop interactive technology-enhanced learning activities.	Lack of knowledge about multiple uses of technology-enhanced learning activities.	Act like pupils (waiting to be told what to read, which assignments to hand in, etc.).
Technical issues.	Lack of skills and competencies to design and develop interactive technology-enhanced learning activities.	
	Lack of time to engage in technology-enhanced learning activities.	
	Lack of economic resources to develop interactive technology-enhanced learning activities.	
	Lack of motivation.	
	Scepticism about the benefits of the use of technology-enhanced learning activities.	
	Unclear as to where to get technical and pedagogical support.	
	Technical issues.	
	Copyright issues.	

Figure 4: Barriers that possibly keep study administrators, teachers and students from engaging in technology-enhanced learning activities.

Eliminating such barriers doesn't happen by management directive. It requires systematic work with student culture, curriculum development and administrative practices. And it will take time. One way to start is to take a normative approach and formulate a strategy for technology-enhanced learning based on a conceptualised learning strategy. At the same time, it is important to bear in mind that words on paper alone don't change practice (see Hayes & Bartholomew in this volume). A natural second step is to formulate a normative curriculum development guide which requires study administrators and teachers to reflect on their use of technology. Such a guide could come in the form of questions for reflection that each educational programme should answer when developing curriculum. This could be in the form of a template for curriculum design where the links between learning and technology are made explicit. The aim of this chapter is to inspire closer links between learning and technology, not to discuss aspects of organisational practices or implementation of new practices among study administrators or teachers. The following five questions for reflection are meant to inspire your normative implementation of a strategy for technology-enhanced university learning at your institution.

Question 1: Have you formulated a learning strategy at your university?

Question 2: Is there a coherent understanding of learning as concept and process among key stakeholders at your university?

Question 3: Have you formulated a strategy for technology-enhanced learning at your university?

Question 4: Is there a coherent understanding of technology-enhanced learning as concept and process among key stakeholders at your university?

Question 5: Have you formulated a normative action plan for linking together learning and technology for the benefit of your university students' learning process and learning outcomes?

Conclusion

It is my hope that by making explicit eight statements of learning and eight statements that may form the rudiments of a strategy for technology-enhanced university learning, I can help inspire a more reflective use of technology in university education. From my own experiences, it seems that often technology is introduced as a mere add-on to analogue teaching and not for its abilities to enhance student learning. It is a shame that the power of technology is far from optimised in our university educational experiences. As the cases in this anthology show, there are many possibilities for linking technology to learning in an inspiring way. If reading my chapter and the other chapters in this volume will spark a new idea for the normative implementation of a strategy for technology-enhanced university learning, I shall be more than happy.

About the author

Professor Dr. Claus Nygaard is founder and executive director of the Institute for Learning in Higher Education and owner and CEO of cph:learning. He can be contacted at this email: info@lihe.info

Bibliography

Bandura, A. (1975). *Social Learning & Personality Development*. New Jersey: Holt, Rinehart & Winston.

Bloom, B. S.; M. D. Engelhart; E. J. Furst; W. H. Hill & D. R. Krathwohl (1956). *Taxonomy of educational objectives: The classification of educational goals. Handbook I: Cognitive domain*. New York: David McKay Company.

Bruner, J. (1996). *The Culture of Education*. Cambridge, Mass.: Harvard University Press.

Carliner, S. (2004). *An overview of online learning*. Amherst, MA: Human Resource Development Press.

CBS Learning Lab (2004). *Barrierer for implementering af e-learning*. CBS Learning Lab, Whitepaper, Copenhagen Business School, Denmark.

Freeman, W. J. (1999). How brains make up their minds. Phoenix: Orion Books.

Garrison, D. & H. Kanuka (2004). Blended Learning: Uncovering Its Transformative Potential in Higher Education. *Internet and Higher Education*, Vol. 7, No. 2, pp. 95-105.

Granovetter, M. (1992). *The sociology of economic life*. Boulder: Westview Press.

Hager, L. L. (2013). ePortfolios and the Twenty-first Century: Learning in Higher Education. In C. Nygaard; J. Branch & C. Holtham (Eds.). *Learning in Higher Education – contemporary standpoints*. Oxfordshire: Libri Publishing Ltd., pp. 151-166.

Hardy, M. & S. Totman (2012). From Dictatorship to Democracy: Simulating the Politics of the Middle East. In C. Nygaard; N. Courtney & E. Leigh (Eds.). *Simulations, Games and Role Play in University Education*. Oxfordshire: Libri Publishing Ltd., pp. 189-206.

Helms, S. A. (2012). Blended/hybrid courses: a review of the literature and recommendations for instructional designers and educators. *Interactive Learning Environments*, pp. 1-7.

Hiltz, S. R. & M. Turoff (2005). Education goes digital: The evolution of online learning and the revolution in higher education. *Communications of the ACM*, Vol. 48, No. 10, pp. 59-64.

Hrastinski, S. (2008). Asynchronous and synchronous e-learning. *Educause Quarterly*, Vol. 4, pp. 51-55.

Keegan, D. (1996). *Foundations of distance education*. London: Routledge.

King, F.; M. F. Young; K. Drivere-Richmond & P. G. Schrader (2001). Defining distance learning and distance education. *AACE Journal*, Vol. 9, No. 1, pp. 1-14.

Kolb, D. A. (1984). *Experiential Learning*. Englewood Cliffs: Prentice Hall.

Lave, J. & E. Wenger (1991). *Situated Learning: Legitimate peripheral participation*. Cambridge: Cambridge University Press.

Lenstrup, C. (2013). Social-media Learning Environments. In C. Nygaard; J. Branch & C. Holtham (Eds.). *Learning in Higher Education – contemporary standpoints*. Oxfordshire: Libri Publishing Ltd., pp. 29-44.

McDermott, R. P. (1999). On Becoming Labelled – the Story of Adam. In P. Murphy (Ed.). *Learners, Learning & Assessment*. London: Paul Chapman Publishing, Ltd., pp. 1-21.

Nichols, M. (2003). A theory of eLearning. *Educational Technology & Society*, Vol. 6, No. 2, pp. 1-10.

Piaget, J. (1970). *Main trends in psychology*. London: George Allen & Unwin.

Pilkington, R. M. & S. A. Walker (2003). Facilitating debate in networked learning: Reflecting on online synchronous discussion in higher education, *Instructional Science*, Vol. 31, pp. 41-63.

Raiker (2013). Using Computer Supported Collaborative Learning to Enhance the Quality of Schoolteacher Professional Development. In C. Nygaard; N. Courtney & P. Bartholomew (Eds.). *Quality Enhancement of University Teaching and Learning.* Oxfordshire: Libri Publishing Ltd., pp. 103-122.

Rhode, J. F. (2009). Interaction equivalency in self-paced online learning environments: an exploration of learner preferences. *The International Review of Research in Open and Distance Learning,* Vol. 10, No. 1.

Rowley, J. (2012). Innovation and Student Learning: ePortfolios for Music Education. In C. Nygaard; N. Courtney & C. Holtham (Eds.). *Beyond Transmission – Innovations in University Teaching.* Oxfordshire: Libri Publishing Ltd., pp. 45-62.

Stupans, I. (2014). The design of distributed learning spaces. In Scott-Webber, L.; J. Branch; P. Bartholomew & C. Nygaard, (Eds.). *Learning Space Design in Higher Education.* Oxfordshire: Libri Publishing Ltd., pp 21-36.

Vygotsky, L. S. (1987). *The collected works of L.S. Vygotsky. Volume 1: Problems of general psychology.* London: Plenum Press.

Wenger, E. (1998). *Communities of Practice. Learning, Meaning and Identity.* Cambridge: Cambridge University Press.

Chapter Three

Using technology-enhanced learning to pave the way to a new performative teaching and learning culture

Deborah Newton

"*The paradigm of performance is best understood not as a stable mono-lithic concept but as a carnival caravan; a heterogeneous ensemble of methods and ideas which are constantly on the move.*" (Dwight Conquergood, 1995:140).

Context and scene-setting definition

The intentional performative style of this chapter has been designed to enable you, the reader, to personally experience and embody the unique interactional nature of the performance context. As an exercise in performative writing, I take a postmodernist or avante-garde approach to enacting the argument I seek to propose in this chapter with the intention of creating the reading conditions for the ephemeral experience associated with performance. It is an exercise in aesthetic communication exemplified in the case study climax of the chapter.

I propose the following segmented and philosophically constructed definition of Technology-Enhanced Learning (TEL) to set the scene for a contextualised and provocative discussion of its use in the performance studies (PS) classroom, where its learning enhancement effects within this interdisciplinary environment are potentially at least as effective, if not more so, as in any other discipline. Accepting the loss of descriptive concision for precision of meaning and placing heavy emphasis on the 'how' rather than the 'what' of TEL, it is defined as:

- the intentionally structured use of a broad spectrum of contemporary information and communication technologies;
- having the specific purpose of enhancing goals-based student learning outcomes, through their innate ability to collapse terminal cultural binaries, in a poietic environment of performativity;
- encouraging co-responsibility and accountability;
- returning control of learning to students with the required planned support of teachers;
- enabling co-construction of conditions;
- maximising the enhanced learning gains;
- the development and active manifestation of a re-defined teacher-learner relationship unique to this blended learning context.

Embracing this guiding definition of TEL, attention is turned to providing a concise understanding of Performance Studies, paving the way to a discussion of the theoretical foundations of TEL prior to outlining its use in the Performance Studies context.

What is Performance Studies?

In asking the question "What is Performance Studies?", Richard Schechner (2006:1), considered by many to be the founder of the subject, maintains: *"The one overriding and underlying assumption of performance studies is that the field is open. There is no finality to performance studies, either theoretically or operationally…Anything and everything can be studied 'as' performance. But this does not mean performance studies as an academic discipline lacks specific subjects and questions that it focuses on. Theoretically, performance studies is wide open; practically, it has developed in a certain way"*. Throughout the literature there appears to be unanimity of agreement with Schechner, although the most quoted observation about performance is that of Strine *et al.,* (1990) in their survey article which describes it as *"an essentially contested concept"*.

Marvin Carlson, another of the Gurus of Performance Studies, informs us that Performance Studies is taken from W. B. Gallie (1964), who suggested that certain concepts had disagreement about their essence built into them and that Strine *et al* argue that performance has become such a concept. This is generally argued today in seeing performance previously described by MacDonald (1993:183) as *"categorising its own problematisation"*. Despite its obvious ephemerality, Performance Studies is gaining importance and acceptance (Schechner, 2006:5) with many Higher Education (HE) establishments throughout the world offering degree programmes in Performance Studies

Although difficult to pin down and considered by many to still be an emerging discipline resisting fixed definition, and respecting Schechner's (1996:22) claim that *" any call for a 'unified field' is, in my view, a misunderstanding of the very fluidity and playfulness fundamental to performance studies"*, there is general agreement throughout the literature that *"Performance will be to the 20th and 21st centuries what discipline was to the 18th and 19th, that is, an onto-historical formation of power and knowledge"*(McKenzie, 2001:18).

For purposes herein, the understanding of performance studies that has most appeal is that of Conquergood (1995:4): *"The paradigm of performance is best understood not as a stable monolithic concept but as a carnival caravan; a heterogeneous ensemble of methods and ideas which are constantly on the move"*. This view captures the multidisciplinary nature of Performance Studies which attracted much interest in the last third of the twentieth century, informed by insights from anthropology, sociology, theatre, communication studies, literary criticism, cultural studies, ethnography, philosophy and psychology. Today, performance scholars contribute to these diverse fields of study.

Finally, a heretical challenge to Schechner's view of performance and an attempt to offer an actual definition, comes from philosopher Robert P. Crease (1993:100): *"Performance is first of all an execution of an action in the world which is a presentation of a phenomenon; that action is related to a representation (for example a text, script, scenario or book), using a semiotic system (such as a language, a scheme of notation, a mathematical system); finally, a performance springs from and is presented to a suitably prepared local (historically and culturally bound) community which recognises new phenomena in it. The field develops through an interaction of all three"*.

53

Degree programmes in Performance Studies would, I believe, benefit from the application of a non-dualistic philosophy to their design and development. By incorporating the challenge this approach would encourage, with a shift in perspective which privileges the student, an interactive environment would result conducive to motivating students to be more creative and eager to explore their own individual interests. In focusing their attention on the social construction of ideas and taking responsibility for their learning, the shift in perspective to learning through their own experience, and the attending dissolution of traditional boundaries of teacher and learner roles, creates an effective communication setting of 'sharing' rather than 'transmission'. This suggests that students should confidently take a lead role in their own learning while the teacher embraces the empowering role of facilitator, promoting an atmosphere of experimentation respectful of breaking conventions but liberating the contributions of both teacher and learner.

Clarifying TEL in context

As Morgan (1997:184) states: *"From the beginning of history, technology has served as an important instrument of power, enhancing the ability of humans to manipulate, control, and impose themselves on their environment... It provides its users with an ability to achieve amazing results in productive activity, and it also provides them with an ability to manipulate this productive power and make it work effectively for their own ends".*

Morgan's quotation captures the transformational potential of technology to enhance learning in HE (HEA, 2009; Browne *et al.*, 2010; Balacheff *et al.*, 2009) which has been researched and documented so that today it has its own acronym of 'TEL' – Technology-Enhanced Learning. Before describing and explaining the innovative use of TEL in the performance studies (PS) classroom in HE, and acceding to what Alice in Wonderland said that, *"the place to start is at the beginning. Unless, we know what we are talking about, we cannot hope to make much sense"* (Carroll, 1871), it is incumbent to clarify exactly what is meant by TEL, by considering extant definitions and by referring to its theoretical foundations, in order to develop a clear terminology for its subsequent use.

National strategies for e-learning have now formally recognised the importance of technology in learning, teaching and assessment in all sectors of education in the UK. In response, many institutions have embedded the enhancement of learning and teaching through technology into their strategic missions (HEFC, 2009). What now unites the majority of teachers in HE is enhancing the quality of learning and their own teaching, and a practical curiosity about how technology can help. What unites learners in HE is the digital world in which they are growing up, where it is reasonable and realistic to have expectations of dynamic and collaborative modern technology-driven learning environments (See Drew & Pullan, this volume).

These contexts are no longer wholly reliant on conservative lecture-based classrooms involving passive, non-questioning learners, with a culturally imposed respectful dependence upon the guidance of lecturers still using outmoded one-way transmission-reception understandings of the teaching learning process. The context in which TEL is defined is important as it appears not to have a commonly accepted precise definition. It is much more than a simple acronym for any sort of educational technology, just as it is more than a synonym for e-learning.

It is equally important to see TEL as not merely learning with technology but learning through technology and, as a result, more efficiently and effectively than might otherwise be the case. Consequently, the view adopted herein, is that any reliable and valid definition of TEL must embrace an understanding of 'how' it enhances student learning in specific HE contexts, rather than a simple general description of its form and use. Only by considering its theoretical foundations is it possible to construct a clear definition of TEL, as well as a newly proposed single specific term for its applied use in the teaching and learning of Performance Studies in HE.

Theoretical foundations of TEL

There is a general consensus in the literature (Webb & Cox, 2004) that TEL is an all-embracing term broadly inclusive of all forms of educational technology in learning and teaching, covering a broad spectrum of activities from supported learning to blended learning and learning that is delivered entirely online. Whatever the technology, learning is the vital element.

The lack of any universally accepted definition of TEL in the literature is, on one hand, surprising, given the government's increased focus on TEL in recent years. Its vision is for the UK to become a world leader in higher education e-learning within the next 10 years. On the other hand, it is less surprising when the majority of definitions appear to be based on a wide range of understanding of TEL's actual use in HE. Such definitions, however, can be meaningful in that they seek to spell out how TEL actually results in enhancing student learning.

With its emphasis on the importance of active involvement by learners in constructing knowledge for themselves and building new ideas or concepts based on current knowledge and past experience, TEL is founded on theories of learning which ask why students do not learn 'deeply' (Biggs & Tang, 2011:26) by listening to a teacher or reading from a textbook. These theories suggest that to design effective enhanced learning environments, one needs a good understanding of what the learners already know when they come into the classroom (See Drew & Pullan, this volume).

The need to adopt a 'deep' concept of learning, by which I mean learning aimed at having students extract principles and underlying meanings in order to integrate them with their previously acquired knowledge, as opposed to a 'surface' approach, can be achieved by promoting and supporting opportunities for students to become reflective practitioners (Schön, 1983). This would meet the increasing acceptance that investigation, enquiry, evaluation and innovation are all part of the performance (See King & Flint, this volume).

To enhance learning, the curriculum should be designed to build on what the students already know and develop with them. TEL can manifest itself in theoretical foundations that forcefully maintain that learning is a social activity (See Nygaard, this volume). Learners construct their knowledge and understanding not just through listening to the teacher or interacting with material knowledge, but through collaboratively constructing their knowledge with their peers, (See Drew & Pullan, this volume). Played out as social constructivism (Berger & Luckmann, 1967), the claim is that TEL better enables the acquisition of learning and highlights the importance of the student's voice in its enhancement.

Seen as a postmodern approach to enhancing student learning, TEL is a contemporary current of thought that some commentators prefer to view as 'late modern' (Giddens, 1991). This theoretical approach suggests that nothing makes sense without a social context of which both teachers and learners are the products rather than the creators. It makes the point that learners are *"creative, they are not puppets dancing at the ends of the strings of social culture"* (Butt, 2004:78). Put simply, students bring with them a personal view of the world which teachers should acknowledge, especially when this view is embedded in society's dependence on using technological resources. Technology is a rapidly advancing change in society that creates opportunities for teachers and learners to use it and then reflect upon its potential learning enhancement abilities (See Hayes & Bartholomew, this volume).

This social constructionist view (Gergen, 2001), which emphasises the role of social forces in education, questions the assumptions of dualism and makes the case for the person being formed by societal structures. TEL represents a pendulum swing towards student-centred theories of learning (Tyler, 1949) and offers well-documented benefits in its ability to help learners achieve improved learning outcomes through planned collaborative activity between them. Shuell (1986:411) captures this well when he states, *"If students are to learn desired outcomes in a reasonably effective manner, then the teacher's fundamental task is to get students to engage in learning activities that are likely to result in their achieving those outcomes... It is helpful to remember that what the student does is actually more important in determining what is learned than what the teacher does".* TEL, as Tyler (1949) stresses, enables learning to take place through the active behaviour of the student: it is what the student does that he learns, not what the teacher does (See Nygaard, this volume).

From a constructivist theory and postmodernist (Steffe & Gale, 1995) perspective, TEL involves learners in reflecting and theorising rather than simply memorising and recalling. Evidence in support of this constructivist theoretical foundation to TEL is provided in 'phenomenography' (Marton, 1981), a resurrected theory that grew out of studies on approaches to learning (Marton & Booth, 1997). Sonneman's (1954) use of phenomenography in the student learning context corroborates and authenticates the idea that the learner's perspective determines what is learned, not necessarily what the teacher intends should be learned. Both constructivism and phenomenography agree that effective learning changes the way we see the world in exactly the same way that technology enables this (Morgan, 1977, 1988). The benefits of giving over control of learning to the learner, or 'visible learning' as Hattie (2009a:271) describes it, is captured in her comment that, *"When students become their own teachers they exhibit self-regulatory attributes that seem most desirable for learners"*. Many commentators (Beetham & Sharpe, 2007; Laurillard, 2002) appear to agree that this is pivotal to why and how TEL actually enhances learning (See Drew & Pullan, this volume).

Recognising that at this point in the chapter you may be feeling a little theory weary, I simply and concisely summarise the importance of the above evidence: it is apparent from a specific review of the literature on TEL (Wellburn, 1996) that it is possible to enhance and enrich students' learning journeys in HE, particularly in the arts. The evolution of TEL in these disciplines is likely to become a revolution if learners and their learning are given the precedence they deserve over teachers and teaching, whose role, methods and responsibilities will have to change accordingly. The beginning of this revolution has already begun in Performance Studies in HE, a stimulating area of development to which I direct your attention.

TEL in Performance Studies (TELiPS)

Before describing and documenting an example of a new and innovative application of TEL in HE, it is important to the performative style of the chapter to build on the above theoretical framework and contemporary body of knowledge. Also, keeping in mind the view that any contemporary reliable and valid definition of TEL must embrace a response to the question of how technology enhances learning (see Hayes & Bartholomew, this volume), I introduce a new term, TELiPS, which I expand on below. For now, I will maintain the frustration and suspense of not knowing how the chapter ends. thus nurturing feelings that align well with the chapter's performative nature before I, unleash the real-world case study upon you!

To ensure transparency of relationship between the terminologies used with TEL applications for Performance Studies in HE and to develop a sound argument for its continued use in Performance Studies, there are a number of provocative premises that need to be explained. The significance of these premises should not be underestimated since they suggest profound implications for how HE institutions design and support learning activities. Among the more important general widely held premises relevant to the Performance Studies context that need to be highlighted are the following:

+ students clearly place greater value on technologies they have 'discovered' or selected for themselves. Ownership, personalisation and appropriation of technologies is one of the overarching themes which emerge from the data (Conole *et al.*, 2006);

+ the effective use of TEL, in respect to capitalising upon its learning enhancement attributes, is wholly dependent on returning control of, and responsibility for, learning back to the learner, requiring a re-definition of the teacher-learner relationship (Maor, 2008);

+ emphasis on the learner's voice is pivotal in capitalising on the practical application of learning technologies for improving learning outcomes and the learner's personal sense of educational achievement (Towel & Howe, 2008);

+ technology by itself does not enhance learning; it is heavily dependent on the context to which it is applied and how it is used by both learners and teachers in HE (Wingkvist & Ericsson, 2010).

Shifting to a more experiential perspective of TEL, it equally important to focus on the following nuanced authorial premises, which have emerged from my own practices in the use of TEL in teaching Performance Studies in HE:

+ PS is at least as conducive, and potentially more so, in its demands for creative learning responses by its learners, to the individual and collaborative use of TEL activities as any other HE subject area;

+ the future of TEL in Performance Studies is not some unknown, mysterious place in which its learners and teachers are uncontrollably drifting but one where responsibility is shared;

+ just as performers and audiences become co-creators in all devised performance works (Fischer-Lichte, 2008), so do teachers and learners become co-creators in the enhanced performance of learning through the naturally occurring poietic conditions of the transformative Performance Studies-classroom;

+ the contextually defined and 'performative' teacher-learner relationship extant in Performance Studies-classrooms in HE, perhaps exclusive to the discipline, provides a unique platform for the dynamic applications of TEL. Although highly provocative, its significance lies in its fundamental integration into the proposed definition of TEL offered above.

Internalising these eight premises, which intrinsically claim their influence on how TEL enhances student learning in HE (Byrom & Bingham, 2001; Marshall, 2002), I now advance an argument for the need for a new term, 'TELiPS', capturing the specific state-of the art application of TEL to Performance Studies.

TELiPS: a new technology of the performative

TELiPS is far more than a mere acronym referring to the informed use of 'Technology-Enhanced Learning in Performance Studies'. It 'performatively' grounds TEL approaches to Performance Studies in contemporary theories of communications technology, learning and pedagogy. It moves beyond proclamatory conjecture found in some of the literature describing tenuous uses of TEL, which serves only to reinforce unfounded lingering resistance held by its sceptics, and speaks to its inevitable implementation. The evidential specifics of this claim will emerge in the case study section of this chapter, which presents the unquestionable benefits of TELiPS for both students and teachers of performance studies – another performative delight to be experienced as the reader!

This attempt to gain a more salient and insightful grasp of the meaning, definition and applications of TEL in the HE context, is facilitated by using:

+ metaphor, the benefits of which have been well documented (Ortony, 1975; Morgan, 1993), to describe and explain TEL;
+ a unique definitional understanding of TEL emerging from an emphasis placed on the importance of 'poietic' context, that is, the context of creative-making found in any performative classroom and especially in the performance studies environment;

    ◆   an exemplar study, devised and driven by the above premises, involving the use of TEL activities with Performance Studies students and a blended learning approach in which common everyday hard and soft technologies are used inside and outside the HE classroom.

The overarching proposition explicit in these premises that supports the argument for the need of the contextualised approach to a definition of TEL, is that firstly, it augments and enriches creative learning by giving prominence to the learner's voice (Sharpe *et al.*, 2005; Rudd *et al.*, 2006), actuated through the 'performative' need to return the control of learning to where it belongs. Secondly, it contributes significantly to creating the necessary poietic conditions for establishing the transformative power of TEL and developing the unique teacher-learner relationship that results in the enhancement of learner outcomes. The case study to come will show further clarification of this.

Such foundational claims to TEL's potential to enhance learning are corroborated below through clear documented examples of its application with learners aspiring to be future performance practitioners. Such claims to these benefits emerging from the informed use of TEL require not only credence in, and commitment to, a number of shifting perspectives about the teaching-learning process, but also an appreciation of context and the cultural binaries which unconsciously serve to inhibit rather than enhance student learning. These binary oppositions tend to restrict and confine students' learning potential and impede their identify formation as equal players and change-agents in the teaching-learning process enacted through the teacher-learner relationship, (See Cygman, this volume).

As a remediable response to these cultural restrictives to learning, I claim TELiPS to be the practical means by which these binaries are dissolved and their dichotomous oppositions collapsed. TELiPS liberates Performance Studies students to instigate new behaviours and relationships and paves the way to a 'performative' teaching and learning culture. Learning, within this performative educational context, accedes to cultural principles of democracy, inter-dependence, shared responsibility, active engagement, collaborative encouragement and participant empowerment, (See Drew & Pullan, this volume). I strongly argue that all of these are essential to creating the poietic conditions for the application of TELiPS to emancipate the learner from inhibitions imposed by conventional and cultural morality. By this, I simply mean students and teachers need no longer feel like hostages to the conventional norms and standards found in educational settings, which tend to privilege the teacher over the learner and the institution over the teacher, locating empowerment in the hands of others. They now have the necessary means to share in the control of learning and liberate themselves from the shackles of traditional understandings of the role of teacher and learner and, in particular, the nature of their aesthetic relationship.

A critical theory (Horkheimer, 1982) is a type of social theory oriented toward critiquing and changing society by digging beneath the surface of social life and uncovering the assumptions that keep us from fully and truly understanding how the world actually works. Viewed as a critical theorisation of learning, (See Hayes & Bartholomew, this volume), TEL is pivotal because it seeks human emancipation, *"to liberate human beings from the circumstances that enslave them"* (Horkheimer, 1982:244). Such theorising aims to explain and transform the circumstances, including cultural binaries, that inhibit human beings. For TELiPS to be proposed as a distinctive example of how technology enhances learning in the Performance Studies-classroom in HE, the constraints of the cultural binaries found in all HE classrooms which have the power to diminish the enhancing effects of TEL on students' learning, and how this power can be desensitised if not diminished, must be discussed.

For TEL to be taken seriously and adopted enthusiastically by both learners and teachers as a 'real world approach' (Robson, 2002) to learning, the case for its efficacy must be made. A penetrating way to respond directly to this important challenge is to provide an existential phenomenological (Merleau-Ponty, 1962, 1963) explanation of 'why' technology enhances learning and, in so doing, establishes the criteria for proposing the unique definition of TEL proffered at the outset.

Combining the use of the power of metaphor with explanation of how the performative nature of the Performance Studies-classroom in HE enables the desensitising of binary oppositions and their eventual collapse, I contend that a strong case is presented that Performance Studies students are at least as likely, if not more so, to have their learning enhanced as students in any other discipline.

Learning as performance: collapsing binaries and shifting perspectives

In 1985, Newton and Mathews published a prophetic article in which they contended that the process of learning could be democratised and enhanced by taking a metaphorical perspective to its analysis and consequent understanding. This contention stemmed from their research in HE classrooms showing that, more often than not, 'control of learning', deemed to be the essence for its enhancement, lay not in the hands of learners but teachers. You may recall that the importance of this assertion, inherent in the appealing potential of TEL to return this aspect of control to the learner, was captured earlier in this chapter in a quoted description of teaching-learning practice by Tyler (1949:np) ending with the advice: *"It is helpful to remember that what the student does is actually more important in determining what is learned than what the teacher does"*. Adopting a Wittgensteinian (1997) position that 'all seeing is seeing as', the authors claimed that the best way to enhance learning was to hand control back to learners by seeing the *"learner 'as' teacher"* and *"teacher 'as' learner"* (Newton & Mathews, 1985:29), *"to share in the process of teaching and learning... to become partners in education"*. This metaphorical process culminated in the conclusion that seeing both learner and teacher 'as' researchers, engaging *"in essentially the same type of activity"* (Newton & Mathews, 1985:30) is the required perceptual framework for any initiatives making claim to enhancing learning in the HE sector.

While their work makes a significant theoretical contribution to an understanding of how learners and teachers should go about implementing technological attempts to enhance learning, Newton and Mathews stopped short of any guidance on how such enhancement could be effected in practical terms in HE. Accepting the significance of this perceptual context as an important cognitive framework for considering practical means of enhancing learning, it is suggested that the utilisation of TELiPS is very efficient, economic, effective and practical (See Nygaard, this volume). Furthermore, this process of enhancement can be intensified by identifying and diminishing those possible constraints and restrictions on learners, using technologies to optimise their capabilities to enhance learning. This is important because it describes not only 'how'

TELiPS can best be implemented but 'why' learning is demonstratively enhanced.

Acknowledging the potential metaphorical value of Newton and Mathews (1985) research findings, the challenge of proving the efficacy of TELiPS is taken up by conceptualising 'learning as performative'. Furthermore, in the same way the relationship between performer and audience is pivotal to the construct of performance (Freshwater, 2009; Fischer-Lichte, 2008), so too is the binary relationship between learner and teacher fundamental to the social construct of learning. In critical theory, a binary opposition is a pair of related terms or concepts that are opposite in meaning, strictly defined and set off against one another. It is the contrast between two mutually exclusive terms. In Western thought, one of the two opposites, generally the first term, is always privileged over the other and assumes a role of dominance, as manifested in the binary 'teacher-learner'. The immense significance of this is spelled out in the work of a number of theorists (Barthes, 1977; Goody, 1977) and very clearly by Jacques Derrida (1974), who maintains that all meaning in Western civilisation is defined in terms of binary oppositions. The implications of Derrida's work suggest that most perceived binary oppositions have perpetuated and legitimised approaches to HE with the teacher's role dominant over the learner's with respect to communication responsibilities and direction; a clearly unequal dichotomous opposition in favour of the teacher.

The major claim being made here is that TEL has the potential and capacity to bring about deconstruction (Derrida, 1978) of this particular binary opposition of teacher-learner which, in the majority of cases, culturally inhibits opportunities for students' learning to be enhanced. TEL, in deconstructing these binary oppositions, creates new notions or concepts, not to synthesise the opposing terms but to mark their difference and eventually bring about their collapse. Theorists such as Barthes and Derrida have, it appears, rarely been used in the debate about technology and its ability to enhance learning; yet, by understanding and appreciating how collapsing cultural binaries like teacher-learner removes the culturally perceptual barriers to the enhancement of student learning, it is possible to see just how TEL comes into its own in HE.

Within the context of Performance Studies in HE, a clear and compelling case can now be made for TEL and how it actually results in enhanced student learning outcomes. Through metaphorical analysis in which we see 'teacher as learner' and 'learner as teacher' as in the research of Newton and Mathews, and through Derridian deconstruction of the cultural binary of 'teacher-learner' by reversing the privilege from the first term 'teacher' to the second term 'learner', we remove what is possibly the most pervasive block to using technology to enhance student learning – our cultural perceptions of the process itself. Discussing the work of the post-structuralist period of Roland Barthes (1977) may help you, the reader, to more easily see the links with the non-dualistic philosophical standpoint I adopt in this chapter, and which theoretically underpins my conceptualisation of learning and position as a teacher of performance studies.

Just as Barthes (1977), in his essay 'The Death of the Author', privileges the reader over the writer and expands the concept of author to argue that the reader is also an author resulting in the subject and object becoming one, Fischer-Lichte (2008) confirms his thesis, by showing how in theatrical performance the performer-audience binary is collapsed, creating the conditions for role reversal in which subject and object become one.

This dissolving of the binary opposition 'performer-audience' comes about through deconstruction of roles, and through a rigorous analysis of the performer-audience 'relationship' which extends beyond traditional theories, Fischer-Lichte extends the explanation of how these dichotomous oppositions fuse into each other, enabling the subject to become the object. She does so by applying systems thinking (Senge, 1990) to the theatrical performance event through use of the term 'autopoiesis', defined in cognitive biology by Humberto Maturana and Francisco Varrela (1992), as the way in which living beings are seen as systems that produce themselves in a ceaseless way. It can be said that an autopoietic system is simultaneously the producer and the product. It could also be said they are circular systems, that is, they work in terms of productive circularity.

Fischer-Lichte uses the original term 'autopoietic feedback loop' to mean, in short, whatever the actors (teachers) do elicits a reaction from the audience (learners) which impacts on the entire performance (learning). Both the audience as well as the performers perceive, and subsequently respond to, these reactions. Their encountered relationship is physically, intellectually, emotionally and socially interactive, thereby remaining unpredictable and spontaneous to a certain degree. Fischer-Lichte (2008:39) claims that, as a result, *"A shift in focus occurs from potentially controlling the system to inducing the specific modes of autopoiesis"*, or, in TEL terms, the learner's voice coalesces with the teacher's in a circular process of responsibility for achieving planned learning outcomes that stimulate the conditions for their enhancement. She goes on to assert that, given this shift, it needs to be investigated how actors and audiences influence each other in performance, what the underlying conditions of this interaction might be, and what factors determine the feedback loop's course and outcome. Applying these questions to the HE classroom might well provide the stimulus for further research into how TEL can best be used by teachers, with the specific goal of creating the conditions in which their students' learning will continue to be enhanced.

While a comprehensive and detailed analysis of the autopoietic feedback loop concept in the teaching-learning event is beyond the scope of this chapter, it is reasonable to assume from Fischer-Lichte's research that, in answer to her questions, TEL has the capacity to show how teachers and learners can influence each other, how learning technologies can create the essential conditions for this unique interaction in the Performance Studies-classroom, and how TEL is a major factor in the autopoietic feedback loop's course and outcomes. Outcomes of student 'enhanced' learning result directly from the use of technology, by both teachers and learners, through their planned encounters in a performative environment. This need not be clearly defined and distinguished but allowed to blossom in an environment of equal responsibility for learning outcomes, through a unique teacher-learner relationship and the personally creative use of a wide range of technologies confidently and competently utilised in their everyday lives.

TELiPS in action – an exemplar

Researching Contemporary Theatre is traditionally a lecture-based module that focuses on journeys in performance. The first five weeks of this six-week module are based around the work of an internationally renowned theatre company called 'Forced Entertainment', who, *"through questioning and collaboration, continue to inspire audiences by making and re-making theatre about the times we live in"* (Forced Entertainment, 2013). They explore what theatre and performance can mean in contemporary life and have been acclaimed in the national press as *"Britain's most brilliant experimental theatre company"* (Gardner, 2009).

The module is described as being transformative and experiential in its explicit requirements for students to work both individually and collaboratively, inside and outside the HE classroom. Using the technology deployed ignites the beginnings of the student's research journey and acts as a provocation about 'liveness' in performance. The aim of the carefully devised tasks is to present the students with a challenge to interact with the technology and the city (within which they study), in an experiential and transformative journey, both in reality and the cyber world.

The tasks focus on students' individual experience and mostly use two different claimed learning technologies which play an important part in their everyday lives – the online social networking service 'Facebook' and a mobile phone (smart phone) with more advanced computing capability and connectivity than basic feature phones. It is apparent that most, but not all, students are conversant and competent in their use. Incorporating this knowledge, the module is designed to stimulate a modern take on performance interaction while challenging the complex and ephemeral concept of the 'performer-audience relationship'. The culmination of the six-week module is an individual creative presentation about journeys in performance enabled through each session's planned tasks, providing the students with a different and challenging learning experience and creation of original material.

To begin the intentional process of enhancing their learning, students are required, without teacher intervention, to create a new Facebook page, which presents its own difficulties of resolution to those not previously registered with Facebook. This preliminary but essential task initiates this learning enhancement process for those students familiar with the operation and use of the social network as they help those who are not, who additionally benefit from the newly acquired knowledge as well as the collaborative learning process (See Drew & Pullan, this volume). Even at the very outset of this exercise, a clearly defined enhancement of student learning is evidenced for all students as they meet the learning objective requiring them to adhere to all data protection rules and regulations; to which even the most conversant users confess to previously paying little attention.

To avoid potential difficulties of establishing so-called 'friendship' relations between students and teacher, the students create an anonymous profile using the initials of the course title to establish a profile without personal sensitive information. Once satisfactorily completed, the new profile can be used by the teacher to send 'friend' requests to all students. On acceptance of the friend request, an arbitrary selected student is asked to create a private group using as its name the title of the module. It is important to acknowledge, however, that beyond the confines of this chapter, it would be proper and wise when undertaking further research along these lines to give due attention and more ongoing consideration to ethical implications.

All participants' profiles are then added to this group with the administration function allocated to the staff involved in respect of responsibility and place for relaying all information. Following what is described in the HE student learning research literature (Biggs & Tang, 2011:31) as a 'deep approach' to learning, involving 'constructive alignment' with intended outcomes, this particular approach to TEL has been shown to be a teacher-focused response to the differing levels of ability within the group: "Good teaching is getting most students to use the level of cognitive processes needed to achieve the intended outcomes that the more academic students use spontaneously" (Biggs & Tang, 2011:7).

In reiterating the important point that enhancement of learning does not happen as a consequence of any facet of the TEL itself but rather through its considered use, we reveal why technology can enhance learning – it impacts on teachers' practice such that they focus more on learning outcomes than on teaching content restricted to a narrowly devised curriculum. This suggests that teachers committed to using technology, with the specific purpose of enhancing their students' learning rather than simply for its own use, are likely to be syllabus-free rather than syllabus-bound teachers. They also place a heavy emphasis on their students' learning progress rather than on slavish following of restrictive curricula.

Performative Studies teachers achieve their pedagogical commitment to this goal by emphasising the importance to students of continuously reflecting on their learning, and of developing creative skills through collaborative work with their colleagues and teachers, facilitated by the innovative use of readily available learning technologies, (See Drew & Pullan, this volume). In this way, learning becomes a part of their identity and everyday living, no longer restricted to the HE classroom. It is unquestionably enhanced by using the communicative power of technology to interact in ways that conservative, passive classrooms could never achieve. The results of this active, inclusive approach to using technology clearly demonstrates to students the social nature of learning and how they can use technology in different ways to enhance their learning beyond the boundaries of the HE institution. The outside world now becomes as dynamic a classroom as any traditional HE setting and provides constant opportunities for learning enhancement.

Creativity and reflection have long been held by educators as basic skill requirements for Performance Studies students aspiring to become the practitioners of the future. By developing skills in technological communication with others, they are encouraged and stimulated to use the technology not just as a potential repository of knowledge, but to become reflective practitioners (Schön, 1983, 1987). Self-reviewing their digital work records and openly sharing these with colleagues, teachers and learners to seek regular feedback is a process the technology enables, helping to develop competence and confidence in through its familiarity and effectiveness (See Drew & Pullan, this volume). Technology enhances learning by becoming an effective means of taking the fundamental step toward developing and acquiring the sense of creativity considered essential to the work of all performance practitioners. The 'why and how' of technology, in its capacity to enhance learning, now manifests itself in these practice-based examples. Its 'power of transformation' helps students grow into understanding the benefits of ongoing critical reflection and provides the opportunity to share and exchange personal and creative thought using a wide range of common information and communication technologies (ICT's), (See Hayes & Bartholomew, this volume).

In the next step, students give the teacher their mobile telephone numbers, as this and Facebook will be the only means of communication between them over the rest of the module. Students need to have access to Facebook on their mobile phones or, if not, to liaise as necessary with their colleagues. All messages providing time and location details for subsequent meeting are placed on Facebook twenty four hours before each session begins; for example, *"All students need to be stood together looking at the arrivals and departure screen at Piccadilly Train Station at 2:00 pm".* Students are requested to 'like' the message on the group Facebook page as confirmation of having read and understood the message, with the expressed expectation that they must all be at the confirmed location at the appropriate time. The lecturer, unknown to the students, will also be at the location and at the meeting time will phone one of the students and read a pre-determined message, such as: *"Dear student, this is a pre-recorded message. Please listen to your instructions very carefully. To ensure that you can hear and understand me please stand on one foot. Now get the rest of the group to shake each other's hands. This message will only continue once these actions have been completed to satisfaction. Thank you. Each member of the group must now find something within and around the station area that is lost, and that has been left behind. Once these have all been collected, you must find ten locations within the city centre and arrange the lost items together in places where they do not belong. Each location should be significantly different from each other. At each location you should take a picture and upload it to the Facebook page. You must provide comments on these pictures together with an accompanying narrative of their journey. Once completed, all students must write a 100 word artistic reflection on their personal experience today. All instructions will now be uploaded to the Facebook page should you need to return to them at any point. Good luck".*

For the duration of the phone call it is essential that the lecturer is not seen, to prevent any chance of breaking the illusion. It is important that the students are left questioning everything, constantly reflecting, questioning and debating their own existing knowledge of what performance 'is' or what they see performance 'as' (Schechner, 2006).

The above message can be altered and adapted to suit different situations and student groups. It might ask the student on the phone to repeat everything that is said, or ask the students to get a member of the public to take a photograph, using the student's phone, of them all 'standing on one leg' and immediately upload it to Facebook. This requires interactive use of the technology during the task and adds to the mystery of the teacher's location. Experience of this approach indicates that it inspires debate about whether they actually are being simultaneously observed, while also inviting the involvement of a member of the public. This adds the pivotal dynamic of audience participation essential to stimulating creative questioning about the process of performance and its claimed ability to collapse the cultural binary of 'performer-audience' and 'presence-absence' – key issues in the contemporary theory of performance. Once all pictures, commentary and reflections have been posted, the teacher uses the technology to respond, 'liking' all the data and writing a creative response to motivate and encourage the students in subsequent follow-up module tasks.

In session two, for example, the student travels to a different location where the focus of the task becomes processes of interaction and communication with the public. As previously explained, a message is posted on the private Facebook group page by the lecturer's new profile twenty four hours before the session begins, allowing time for all the students to access the Internet and check the message.

In the phone message part of the task, the students are requested to complete a number of different moves to acknowledge they understand the speaker, such as touching the ground and arranging themselves in height order. This is developed again by asking for photographic evidence to be placed on the Facebook page, followed by the message: "There are a number of questions that are being uploaded onto the Facebook page that you must each individually answer as you make your way alone around the city. Answer them literally, metaphorically and creatively. Share the questions with people in the street and use your own memories. You will also receive an individual text message which you must explore as part of your journey and think about how it could become a performance from your experience today. Your journey must be documented on the Facebook page. Do you understand?"

Asking the student to document their journey generally provokes unsolicited use and involvement of other potentially enhancing learning technologies. Some students video the public when asking questions or video their footsteps. Others utilise flip cameras, mobile phones, action cameras, video cameras, voice recorders or computer tablets. Yet others take picture with sound clips or copy their Twitter updates. There is a myriad of opportunities to enhance for student learning in this task via a plethora of technology, often owned and carried throughout this module by the students motivated to achieve creative, original and outstanding results. This aligns with and indicates the technologies' role in enhancing learning to meet all intended outcomes. Once the questions, which are of an ambiguous nature, are posted on Facebook, each student is individually texted a creative provocation to stimulate their journey. They are expected, once again, to provide a 100 word creative response to this at the end of the session.

Following sessions in the module have similar formats with changing content; for example, students are given envelopes and told not to open them until they reach their destination. Alternatively, each student is sent an individualised email or private Facebook message timed to arrive when they reach their destination. Students are asked via mobile conversation to meet in a certain location and form a circle with their backs facing inwards. They must then walk 321 steps before opening their envelopes or accessing their private media-based message and complete the task. As before, they must then produce a 100 word creative reflective statement but, on this occasion, it must be in response to each of the three individual tasks they have had to undertake.

Week five is conducted via a task which begins with a video, created and produced by the teacher and posted to the Facebook page, to explain the next tasks to the students. The task involves collecting texts obtained from a variety of sources from around the city such as litter, signs, lost items, verbatim speech, fliers or announcements. Students are encouraged to search for texts in the most unusual and enigmatic places without disclosing to anyone what they are actually doing. They are also asked to find a way of recording the words in their original location, with a camera, video, Dictaphone or other suitable technology of their choice, and then upload their favourite piece together with creative comment capturing their artistic experience of acquiring it.

The second part of the video explains the next task to the student and constructs the detail of their formative assessment explaining how their journey might come to an end. For example, "*What you have now is a text, photographs, lost items and a journey. You are now required to create a short performance for presentation to the rest of the group in our next session which combines the work, exercises, documentation and research undertaken in the past weeks. You will receive a private message detailing exactly what it is you need to do*".

Each student is then sent a confidential message with the same creative provocation that they were given but developed further with a stimulus statement such as, "*Start with explaining the lost item. Use quotes from your questionnaire as a text to complement those you found in the city. Present a journey you emotionally remember but retrace it in this space replacing certain landmarks with things from your memory. Consider how you can incorporate lists and how you can tear your city down. Finish by repeating the text from the voicemail you left yourself."* The assessment relates to all the previous tasks and, as it is requested via a creative video, it also encourages and inspires the students to be creative with their technology – what might be referred to as 'self-enhancement of learning' effected through creative use of these learning technologies.

This example of the application of TELiPS illustrates how TEL makes the learner voice count, which is seen as a fundamental requirement for students' learning to be enhanced. As a direct result of the creativity and originality of tasks that can be devised using TEL activities in the performative environment of the Performance Studies extended 'classroom', inside or outside the HE environment.

The overt attempt at deconstructing and collapsing the terminal binary 'teacher-learner' through the innovative use of technology, (See Cornelius and DePew, this Volume) and the resulting role reversal that emerges from it, together with the naturally occurring poietic conditions of performative environments found in Performance Studies 'classrooms', creates a unique relationship between Performance Studies students and teachers. That effect is perhaps unlikely to be experienced in other subject contexts, where the poiesis of the environment is less significant and there is less, if any, emphasis on pedagogical performativity. Although technology itself does not enhance learning, (See Hayes and Bartholomew, this volume) the astute and judicious use of TEL in these performative contexts enhances its potential to do so, as evidenced in this exemplar case study. It also perhaps offers further evidence and justification for the claim that Performance Studies students may benefit more from TEL applications than students from other disciplines.

In summary, the autopoietic feedback loop, as described by Fischer-Lichte (2008), initiated in, and by, performative learning contexts found in Performance Studies-classrooms in HE, makes a significant contribution to the potential power of technology to enhance student learning. Leaving the final source of evidence that technology actually does enhance student learning with the learner, here is one student's comment: *"If only I'd been able to use my love of technological contraptions in my previous schooling before coming into HE as I have on this Performance Studies course, instead of being told to leave my mobile at home for example, I'm sure I would*

*have not only enjoyed my studies much more and been much more moti-
vated, but I'm certain I would have learned far more, got better results and
'performed' better all round. Who'd have ever thought that using my mobile
and laptop would be so useful in helping me achieve my ambition of becoming
a qualified contemporary performance artist".*

In its innovative inclusion and use of technology, this module has not
only found the very satisfying outcome of genuine popularity with students
but has unquestionably resulted in a consistently improved and enriched
standard of individual performative presentations. Complementing this
important benefit and enhancing overall module satisfaction, other
gratifying observations are the improved attendance rates and increased
quantity and augmented quality of individual reflections. The module
clearly emboldens and animates students to self-explore the capacity of
technology and its use in performance and documentation, while stimulating innovative exploration of the city in a powerfully collaborative and
individually exemplary performative fashion.

About the author

Deborah Newton teaches theatre and performance at Arden School of
Theatre, part of The Manchester College. She can be contacted at this
email: debbie.newton01@gmail.com

Bibliography

Balacheff, N.; S, Ludvigsen.; A. Lazonder & S. Barnes. (Eds.) (2009).
Technology-Enhanced Learning: Principles and Products. Springer Science
and Business Media.

Barthes, R. (1977). *Image, Music, Text.* New York. Noonday Press.

Beetham, H. & R. Sharpe (2007). *Rethinking Pedagogy for a Digital Age:
Designing and Delivering e-learning.* London: Routledge.

Berger, P. & T. Luckmann (1967). *The Social Construction of Reality,*
Harmondsworth: Penguin.

Biggs, J. & T. Tang (2011). *Teaching for Quality Learning at University.* Open
University Press.

Browne, T.; R. Hewitt; M. Jenkins; J. Voce; R. Walker & H. Yip. (2010).
Survey of Technology-Enhanced Learning for Higher Education in the UK.

Universities and Colleges Information Systems Association (UCiSA). University of Oxford.

Butt, T. (2004). *Understanding People*. Palgrave: MacMillan.

Byrom, E. & M. Bingham (2001). *Factors influencing the effective use of technology for teaching and learning: Lessons learned from SEIR*TEC Intensive Site Schools*. Greensboro, NC: SERVE.

Carroll, L. (1871). *Through the Looking Glass*. Gutenberg.

Conole, G.; M. de Laat; T. Dillon & J. Darby (2006). *Student experiences of technologies*. JISC LXP. Final Report.

Conquergood, D. (1995). On Carnival and Caravans: Performance Studies in Motion, *The Drama Review*, Vol. 39, No. 4, pp. 137-141.

Craib, I. (1998). *Experiencing Identity*, London: Sage.

Crease, R. (1993). *The Play of Nature; Experimentation as Performance*, Bloomington: Indiana University Press.

Derrida. J. (1974). *Positions*. The University of Chicago Press.

Derrida, J. (1978). *Of Grammatology*. Baltimore: Johns Hopkins University Press.

Fischer-Lichte, E. (2008). *The Transformative Power of Performance: A new Aesthetics*. Routledge.

Forced Entertainment. (2013). Online Resource: www.forcedentertainment. com [Accessed 11 January 2015].

Freshwater, H. (2009). *Theatre and Audience*. Palgrave MacMillan.

Gallie, W. B. (1994). *Philosophy and the Historical Understanding*, New York: Schocken Books.

Gardner, L. (2009). We are Waging a War. *The Guardian*. 23 February 2009.

Gergen, K. (2001). *Social Constructionism in Context*. London: Sage.

Giddens, A. (1991). *Modernity and Self-Identity*. Cambridge: Polity.

Goody, J. (1977). *The Domestication of the Savage Mind*. Cambridge University Press.

Hattie, J. A. C. (2009). *Visible Learning. A Synthesis of 800+Meta-analyses on Achievement*. London: Routledge.

Irving, A. (Ed.) (1982). *Starting to teach study skills*. Edward Arnold.

HEFCE (2009). *Enhancing Learning and Teaching Through the use of Technology: A revised approach to HEFCE's strategy for e-learning*. HEFCE.

HEA (2009). *Enhanced learning and teaching*. JISC. P1-60

Horkheimer, M. (1982). *Critical Theory*. New York: Seabury Press.

Laurillard, D. (2002). *Rethinking University Teaching*. London: Routledge Falmer.

MacKenzie, J. (2001). *Perform or Else: From Discipline to Performance,* London: Routledge.

Maor, D. (2008). Changing Relationship: Who is the learner and who is the teacher in the online educational landscape? Murdoch University. *Australasian Journal of Educational Technology,* Vol. 24, No. 5, pp. 627-638.

Marshall, J. M. (2002). *Learning with technology: Evidence that technology can, and does, support learning.* San Diego, CA: Cable in the Classroom.

Marton, F. (1981). Phenomenography – describing conceptions of the world around us, *Instructional Science,* Vol. 10, pp. 177-200.

Marton, F. & A. S. Booth (1997). *Learning and Awareness.* Hillsdale, NJ: Lawrence Erlbaum.

Merleau-Ponty, M. (1962). *Phenomenology of Perception.* London: Routledge.

Merleau-Ponty, M. (1963). *The Structure of Behaviour.* Pittsburgh: Duquesne: University Press.

Morgan, G. (1988). *Riding the Waves of Change.* Jossey-Bass Inc.

Morgan, G. (1997). *Images of Organisation.* Sage Publications Inc.

Newton, R. J. & P. V. Mathews (1985). The Study Skills Paradox: "You Can Bring a Horse to Water but You Cannot Make It Drink." *Vocational Aspect of Education,* Vol. 37, No. 96, pp. 23-31.

Ortony, A. (1975). Why Metaphors Are Necessary and Not Just Nice. *Educational Theory,* Vol. 25, pp. 45–53.

Robson, C. (2002). *Real World Research.* Blackwell Publishing.

Rudd, T.; F. Colligan & R. Naik (2006). Learner voice: A handbook from futurelab.

Schechner, R. (2006). *Performance Studies: An Introduction.* Routledge.

Schön, D. A. (1983). *The Reflective Practitioner.* London: Falmer.

Schön, D. A. (1987). *Educating the Reflective Practitioner.* San Francisco: Jossey Bass.

Senge, P. (1990). *The Fifth Discipline.* New York: Currency/Doubleday.

Sharpe, R.; G. Benfield; E. Lessner & E. De Cicco (2005). Learner study – Final report.

Shuell, T. J. (1986). Cognitive Conceptions of Learning. *Review of Educational Research,* Vol. 60, No. 4, pp. 411-436.

Sonneman, U. (1954). *Existence and Therapy.* New York: Grune & Stratton.

Steffe, L. & J. Gale. (Eds.) (1995). *Constructivism in Education.* Hillsdale, NJ: Lawrence Erlbaum.

Strine, M. S.; W. B. Long & F. M. Hopkins (1990). Research in Interpretation and Performance Studies: Trends, Issues, Priorities. In G. M. Phillips & J. T. Woods, (Eds.). *Speech communication,* MacMillan, pp. 181-193.

Towle, G. & R. Howe (2008). *The learner's voice in higher education*. University of Northampton's Learning and Teaching Conference: Creating Contemporary Student Learning Environments, University of Northampton.

Tyler, R. W. (1949). *Basic Principles of Curriculum Instruction*. Chicago: University of Chicago Press.

Webb, M. & M. Cox (2004). A review of pedagogy related to information and communications technology. *Technology, Pedagogy and Education*, Vol. 13, No. 3, pp. 235-286.

Wellburn, E. (1996). *The Status of Technology in the Education System: A Literature Review*. Technology and Distance Education Branch, Ministry of Education, Skills and Training, British Columbia, Canada.

Wingkvist, A. & M. Ericsson. (2010). A Framework to Guide and Structure the Development Process of Mobile Learning Initiatives. Conference Proceedings, University of Malta.

Wittgenstein, L. (1958). *Philosophical Investigations*. Prentice Hall: New Jersey.

Chapter Four

"Look at these new gadgets!": the achilles' heel of technology-enhanced learning

Eva Dobozy, Jim Mullaney and David Gibson

Introduction

This chapter contributes to the anthology on technology-enhanced learning by critiquing uses of new and emerging technologies in higher education. Although these technologies might be perceived as enablers of educational change and the modernisation of pedagogical practices, we argue that educators must understand the 'enhancement effect' of a particular technology before integrating the technology into their teaching and learning practices.

Our motivation for writing this chapter is our fascination with new and emerging technologies and their potential to enhance teaching and learning experiences and student learning outcomes when used in educational contexts. However, we are wary about incorporating new and emerging technologies into the classroom without a clearly under-stood purpose. Our awareness comes from recent experiences in which the transfer of new and innovative technologies, from the contexts of industry and everyday use to teaching and learning situations, calls for an understanding of the value-adding nature of a chosen technology.

We write this chapter to inspire and generate debate about the real or perceived enhancement effects of new and emerging technologies, particularly in the higher education classroom. Throughout this chapter we will argue that new and emerging technologies, when used in and for education, must be evaluated for their pedagogical value and suitability. The transfer of new and emerging technologies from other contexts into the higher education landscape requires detailed and careful consideration and articulation of their teaching and/or learning enhancement. We refer to the enhancement effect of new and emerging technologies in education as 'fitness for purpose'.

Our viewpoint in this chapter is that the Achilles' heel (a metaphor for vulnerability) of technology in education is the temptation of techno-savvy educators to fall for the technology's 'coolness factor'. They may be tempted to integrate new and emerging technologies, such as augmented reality or nascent proprietary technologies such as *Google Glass*, into their teaching and learning practices without really understanding the technology's 'enhancement factor'. As Laurillard *et al.*, (2009:290) aptly noted: *"One of the strongest arguments for bringing new digital technologies into schools and other educational institutions is that, by doing so, we would trigger pedagogical innovation"*.

Although technology-enhanced learning has many benefits, the Achilles' heel is a lack of understanding by some educators of the pedagogical 'value-add' of a selected technology for teaching and/or learning, or the technology's designated role in teaching and learning. In this chapter, we will refer to this as the technology-enhanced learning theory and practice gap. The potential for an educator's personal interest in, and knowledge of, new and emerging technologies, and a desire to help tech-savvy students (see the illustrative example of 'Emily' below) use their technology skills and knowledge in the classroom, risks deploying technologies in pedagogically unsound ways. It is not a foregone conclusion that all educators with interest and knowledge in deploying new and emerging technologies in educational settings will have a comprehensive understanding of the relationship between technology, pedagogy and subject matter. A possible framework to help educators navigate this pedagogical dilemma, and help them in their development and use of technology-enhanced learning activities, is the TPACK model discussed below. We believe linking pedagogical knowledge, technological knowledge and content knowledge will help educators understand better the utility and effective incorporation of technology-enhanced learning activities into higher education.

We will develop our proposed solution to address the Achilles' heel of TEL as follows: first, the theoretical framework of our critique will be introduced by examining the growing potential for a TEL theory and practice gap. Then, examples of 'revolutionary' and 'evolutionary' educational change will be presented. A dilemma relating to the 'digitisation of pedagogy' will then point to the need for clear focus and understanding that technology should serve a pedagogical purpose in education. Finally, the narrative draws some conclusions, outlines implications and offers recommendations for practice.

The growing TEL theory and practice gap?

The focus of knowledge and skills in university educators is shifting from pure content to include more and more pedagogical and technological expertise (see The Larnaca Declaration on Learning Design [2013], for example). We refer to this concept as technology-enhanced learning and follow Laurillard *et al.*'s lead in defining it as: "*[the] role of technology [is] to enable new types of learning experiences and to enrich existing learning scenarios*" (Laurillard *et al.*, 2009).

Despite the growing popularity of technology-enhanced learning and its mushrooming literature, many researchers working in this sub-field (Conole *et al.*, 2008; Ertmer, 2005; Laurillard *et al.*, 2009; McKenney, 2013; Molebash, 2010; Plants & Rose, 2010) have pointed out that convincing empirical evidence is still scarce, fragmented and contradictory about how effective integrating technology in teaching and learning really is. Does it provide better learning experiences and more favourable learning outcomes than traditional face-to-face, low-tech teaching and learning methods and solutions? "*This leaves a problematic gap between what could be effective technology-enhanced learning (TEL) in theory, and what can be effective TEL in practice*" (McKenney, 2013:17374).

Interestingly, hybrid pedagogical strategies have been reported to outperform either no technology or all technology (Griffin & Thomson, 2008; Pelliccione & Broadley, 2010). There are also increasing studies reporting teacher and student resistance to technology-enhanced learning, their under-preparedness for technology-enhanced learning environments, and general misconceptions about the abilities and learning habits of so-called 'millennial students' (Strauss & Howe, 1991). Some even call for technological minimalism in education as a "*wide array of new tools and accessibility has led to users becoming overwhelmed by the sheer quantity and magnitude of options*" (Calvin, 2013:1). The more we research this area, the more obvious it becomes how complex the issues are that technology-enhanced learning researchers and practitioners face. Laurillard *et al.* (2009:296) note that: "*It is well recognised that teachers' practices tend to change slowly, particular if the values they hold seem to be threatened by the innovation. … TEL research provides both opportunities and threats to the teacher. The opportunities lie in the new forms of learning and teaching opened up to them. The threats lie in the disruptive nature of digital technology. This is probably the most important factor that tends to inhibit adoption of TEL. It is not a simple addition to a classroom or educational process. The opportunities it offers for more flexible, adaptive and learner-centred ways of learning require a fundamental rethink of teaching and learning. Without this, the technology can simply be an inconvenience or can even reduce learning effectiveness if it is used inappropriately*".

Most interesting is that, to emphasise the need for an enhancement effect of technology, the 'lingua franca' is technology-enhanced learning or TEL, at least in the UK and Australia, rather than e-learning (Bayne, 2014). To set the context for competing realities and truths of a technology-infused social world on one hand, and higher education realities often governed by traditional education practice on the other, we introduce Emily, a fictive first-year teacher education student.

Introducing Emily

For a more enjoyable, intuitive and perhaps safer driving experience, a newly released augmented reality heads-up display (HUD) allows Emily, a university student in Early Childhood Education, to keep her eyes on the road while accessing just-in-time virtual information in full colour, through the windscreen, just above the horizon. After parking her car and paying her parking fees via smartphone, Emily searches her handbag for her new pair of Google Glasses, sourced from a US supplier on the Internet where this 'one-of-a-kind novelty' (Swider, 2014:1) is now freely available. Emily's friends know she is an early adopter of technology gadgets. Despite her passion for and awareness of digital learning technologies, she is on her way to the new lecture hall where she will be educated using an antiquated 13th century method of teaching and learning: the lecture.

This scenario is real; it is happening right now all over Australia and elsewhere. This is where the technology-enhanced learning theory and practice gap is most evident. Why are some university educators and administrators reluctant to adopt learning models and modalities leveraged on the affordances of technology-enhanced learning (see Nicolle & Lou, 2008)? What is the role of technology-enhanced learning in Emily's university education? Should administrators and educators look to industry for inspiration to update their teaching and learning practices?

While some stakeholders yearn for a technology-mediated revolution in education, others question the logic and value of technology-enhanced teaching and learning practices in higher education (Conole, 2013; Dobozy, 2009; Laurillard *et al.*, 2009).

Through the introduction and critical evaluation of the first case narrative, *the revolutionary change case* (below), new developments in wearable computing and in human-machine interface and head-up display technology (HUD) in the car industry offer a vision of how new and emerging technologies have the potential to enter the higher education classroom and influence education provisions; not because of a perceived need and/or usefulness of the technology to enhance learning, but because of the technology's intrinsic appeal. For example, a recent research report by NESTA (2012:63-64) found that: *"Over recent decades, many efforts to realise the potential of digital technology in education have made two key errors. Collectively, they have put the technology above teaching and excitement above evidence. This means they have spent more time, effort and money looking to find the digital silver bullet that will transform learning than they have into evolving teaching practice to make the most of technology. If we are to make progress we need to clarify the nature of the goal we want to satisfy through future innovation. Much existing teaching practice may well not benefit greatly from new technologies. As we continue to develop our understanding of technology's proof, potential and promise, we have an unprecedented opportunity to improve learning experiences in the classroom and beyond"*.

NESTA's findings correspond with Laurillard and colleague's (2009) observations that the disruptive nature of new and emerging technologies affects adoption and requires practitioners to re-evaluate their understanding of the purpose of education and pedagogical practices.

The second case narrative, *the evolutionary case*, will be used to illustrate an alternative reality – the pedagogical evolution of a teaching strategy (simulation) used in a number of mainly learning-centric situations and educational contexts to one which is enriched through technology (digital simulation). We will illustrate the synergy between technology, pedagogy and content or subject matter in digital simulation pedagogy to assist and enhance teaching and learning processes.

Revolutionary change: focusing on technology

The car industry is known for high tech innovation and effective research and development. New human machine interface, especially augmented reality (AR) and head-up display technologies (HUDs) have surpassed the testing phase and are hailed as the *"next big step of personal computing"* (Starkey, 2013:1). Jet fighters have used AR HUD technology for a number of years but including it in cars is new and costly. However, test drivers note that it improves driver safety (Hibberd *et al.*, 2010). As a result, new models of luxury cars have standard fitted or after-market AR HUD displays. According to Laursen (2013), new 'clip-on' varieties allowing drivers to see vital data without looking away from the road have recently come onto the market (Figure 1), which means this advanced technology is no longer reserved for fighter pilots and luxury car drivers, improving driver effectiveness and safety so its proponents argue (Ablaßmeier *et al.*, 2007).

Similarly, *Google Glass* is a smart, real-time data processing device readily adopted by self-proclaimed technology pioneers or 'digerati'. Latest research (Kalla, 2014) notes that although *Google Glass* wearers feel disoriented at first and overwhelmed by the many new features of this new 'techno-gadget', early adopters seem to like it. One could contend that the 'glitter effect' has primacy, overshadowing arguments of the possible benefits for consumers. Consumers may benefit from *Google Glass* technology in the future and be able to explain how this technology can improve the way they connect with others and with information in real time. However, its value-adding nature is not yet entirely clear and may not even be seen as important for consumers. The fact that it 'simply IS' may be tempting enough to purchase the 'techno-gadget'. Now that the technology has been invented, tested and is ready for mass production, the time has come to create a market for *Google Glass*. To this effect,

Eisenmann and colleagues (2014) from the Harvard Business School developed a project to help formulate a marketing and distribution strategy. One may contend that the technology's user value is currently its 'glitter effect', overshadowing concerns about technological, cognitive and/or social benefits for users individually or collectively, making the revolutionary change case problematic.

These examples show that, in some cases, new and emerging technologies are created not out of a perceived social need but as an economic enterprise. The potential market value, as Susan Kalla (2014) from Forbes Magazine reports, is estimated at over 250 million units by 2019. What is the social benefit of these new and revolutionary technological gadgets? Kalla (2014) reports that wearers felt 'powerful' when they wore the wearable computer and that feeling may be more of a reason for buying than more tangible benefits.

Figure 1: After-market HUD. (Image courtesy of Garmin International).

Incorporating new and emerging technologies into higher education may disrupt current pedagogical practices, such as the 'traditional lecture,' to make teaching and learning more interactive, contextual and relevant but the entry of new and emerging technologies into our public and private lives, including our education systems, should not be viewed as unwelcome. Still, despite the impressiveness of these technological developments and their possible usefulness for education in the future, integrating technology without pedagogical consideration or understanding the subject matter to be learned, as outlined by the TPACK framework below, runs the risk of undermining the learning focus and missing its potential.

In summary, this revolutionary case points out that if we are to have the application of particular novel technologies in education (and in our view this is inevitable), using new and emerging technologies in education needs to be justifiable and have a proven enhancement effect. Research reported by Walker *et al.* (2012) suggests that novelty and convenience without clearly definable pedagogical advantages do little to convince educators and students, and that tried and tested traditional pedagogies should be discarded. Not being swayed by technology's 'glitter effect' does not mean that educators are technology-averse and that the digitisation of pedagogy is not happening (Kivunja, 2013). Educators are increasingly embracing technology-enhanced learning (see European Commission, 2014) but their technology choices seem to be pedagogically driven.

Adoption of novel learning technologies should not be based on novelty or sophistication, instead there needs to be a clear link between their implementation and improvement in learning outcomes (Laurillard, 2012). Evidence concerning alternative realities and practices is crucial to help people break free from normative cognition and associated behaviours.

Evolutionary change: focusing on TPACK integration

Over the years, many educational experts have attempted to help teachers integrate information and communication technologies (ICTs) more effectively in their teaching and to understand the potential enhancement effect of introducing novel and emerging technologies into their teaching and learning activities (Conole, 2008; Dobozy *et al.*, 2013; Laurillard, 2012). Focusing on pedagogy in general and teachers' technology-mediated pedagogical content knowledge in particular, Mishra and Koehler introduced the *TPACK framework* (Koehler & Mishra, 2005; Mishra & Koehler, 2006), which builds on Shulman's (1986, 1987) work on the inseparability of pedagogical and content knowledge. TPACK is a *"simple, yet powerful idea"* (Thompson & Mishra, 2007:38) and a way of representing what teachers know about technology. Koehler and Mishra (2005) suggest that good pedagogy is more than simply adding technology to existing teaching provisions. Rather, it is the *"representation of new concepts and requires developing a sensitivity to the dynamic, transactional relationship between all three components suggested by the TP[A]CK framework"* (Koehler & Mishra, 2005:134). The three components of the TP[A]CK model are: 'technology' (T), 'pedagogy' (P) 'and' [A] 'content' (C). Koehler and Mishra (2012) noted recently that the addition of the 'A' in TPACK was to emphasise the 'and' or *"TotalPACKage"* in relation to the concepts outlined above (Thompson & Mishra, 2007:38). In the newer literature that refers to TPACK, the 'A' is always included (Koehler *et al.*, 2013).

The framework developed by Mishra and Koehler (2006:1025) emphasises *"the connections, interactions, affordances, and constraints between and among content, pedagogy, and technology"*, indicating that these components (see Figure 2) should not be viewed in isolation. Mishra and Koehler (2006) advocate the use of pairs at the intersect points on the diagram:

+ pedagogical content knowledge (PCK);
+ technological content knowledge (TCK); and
+ technological pedagogical knowledge (TPK).

The TPACK model relies on the interplay and synergy that exists between the elements. There will be occasions where one element dominates the landscape because it is contextually appropriate. However, while the importance of each element is recognised, there are dangers in over-reliance of one at the expense of the others.

Shulman's conception was that pedagogy and content are not only inseparable, integrating them implies the need to understand that teaching specific content involves unique approaches that differ from subject to subject. Teaching mathematics requires a different set of pedagogical knowledge and skills than teaching music, chemistry or health sciences. Not only is there a general pedagogy of teaching related to how people learn but there are also highly specific pedagogies unique to each discipline. Discipline knowledge needed for teaching is not separable content; it has to be integrated with the specifics of teaching that particular discipline. For example, a mathematics teacher needs to understand that subject's common misconceptions at particular development levels and its unique metaphors, symbols and problem-solving approaches (for a more detailed exploration of this idea, see Drew & Pullan, this volume).

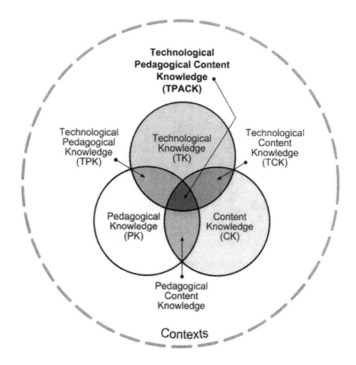

Figure 2: The TPACK model.

Mishra and Koehler (2006) extended that argument to include the unique technologies that differentiate one field of knowledge from another. For example, the technology tools needed in astronomy are different from those needed in architecture, as are the pedagogies for teaching and the content of those fields. So, TEL is similarly inseparable from the union of pedagogy and content. The paired intersections in the TPACK model (e.g. PC, PT, and TC) are helpful in thinking about the dimensions of the union of all three containing the unique content, pedagogy and technology of a particular field of knowledge.

When technology leads, the strengths include the excitement of new computational supports for acquiring, visualising, analysing and communicating information and leveraging shared expertise from around the world. However, technology alone is simply a tool; it requires a purpose and a subject (Engeström, 1999; Vygotsky, 1978) to be complete. Providing access to vast amounts of data and information can lead the learner toward knowing and understanding, but there is a facility associated with technology that can, if not monitored, gravitate towards lower-order thinking. Without the links to people and their aims, tools are as inert as content is when devoid of its community of practice.

When content leads, the strengths include the primacy of inquiry in the field of knowledge as the heart of the discipline. Acquiring content knowledge as part of a community is the 'heart before the course' that is taught by the enculturation of novices into a field along with key knowledge; the key methods, habits of mind, and professional practices of the field. Without that heart, there is a danger that content is inert and disconnected from the values and purposes of the community of practice that creates and sustains the knowledge.

When pedagogy leads, the strengths are its focus on the aims of learning and the mechanisms by which people learn. However, without tools of implementation and engagement and a community of practice for feedback and social processes, pedagogy alone is unable to accomplish its aims.

It is clear, therefore, that a harmonious relationship between the three elements can assist educators build learning experiences that are authentic, relevant and contemporary. As an example of a technology that leads to new pedagogical practice, we offer a commentary on digital simulation, which has a long history of development and is characterised by an evolutionary approach to technology-enhanced learning implementation. Digital simulations are tools for learning that have been discussed since the 1970's (Carson, 2009; Cruickshank, 1977). Recently, they have been seen to achieve dramatically higher levels of emotional power, interactivity and effectiveness for learning, compared to traditional resources such as books, lectures, videos, and student-produced artifacts like reflection papers, student research, and tests and quizzes (Aldrich, 2004; Gibson et al., 2007). Their key advantages include potential seamless integration with online resources, embedding of complex models to be discovered and acquired via mastery, and high-resolution time-based data for analysis of learning (Coulthard, 2009; Gibson & Jakl, 2013). As a result, games and simulations can effectively engage students in direct experience with the causal mechanisms and structures of systems and, through experiment and discovery, help people acquire higher order knowledge and skills (Coulthard, 2009). Airline pilots, for example, train in simulators and return to them to renew and develop further their experience base. The military uses digital games extensively to provide scalable, uniformly high quality training exercises (Prensky, 2001). Medical schools are also rapidly developing simulations for a wide variety of educational purposes (Rosen, 2008).

In education, digital simulations are used to illustrate basic principles in physics, chemistry and economics and, with the advent of simulation authoring tools such as Star LOGO, MatLab, VenSIM and STELLA, have been extensively studied. Three uses of digital simulations have been noted (Mandinach & Cline, 1993):

+ Constrained models, which are used as illustrations and examples and which allow users to conduct highly constrained experiments with a system model.
+ Parameter manipulation, which allow users to conduct open-ended experiments with a system model.
+ Epitome models, which allow users to construct new representations of systems and apply algorithms that result in an operational model.

A simulation enables researchers and practitioners to try out alternatives that are impossible to try out in real systems, and to develop intuition augmented by detailed exploration of the effects of alternative courses of action (Holland, 1995). The added value of the technology is clear: it enables people to see and interact with data in ways that are impossible without it. Implementing digital simulations is not a case of the 'glitter effect' but of seeing and taking advantage of the added value of technology enhancement in learning.

The digitisation of pedagogy dilemma

Learning in the 21st century looks very different from what it was before. *Ad lib* access to huge bodies of knowledge and new ways to communicate and collaborate have signaled the beginning of the end of the traditional Socratic model of education. But, progress is slow and inconsistent. The potential for a clear disconnect between the technological advancements experienced by our fictive first-year university student, Emily, inside the physical university classroom (lecture hall and tutorial rooms) and outside it (in her car, for example) is what we perceive to be a pedagogical dilemma. Today, there are many 'techno gizmos' that enthusiastic educators can introduce to students. Their training and professional judgement should help them make pedagogically sound decisions. Unfortunately, some educators resist the evolutionary changes and attempt to stick with the 'true and tested' pedagogies of the past. Recent evidence (Chomal & Saini, 2013) shows there are also educators who compete to see who can use 'more' or 'cooler' gizmos in their teaching, with the result that many students become overwhelmed and confused about what they need to learn or do in their assignments. Norrish (2014:2), a former history teacher and the director of technology at *United Learning*, a UK independent schools organisation, explains that: *"the temptation when you have 30 iPads at your disposal is to find ways of cramming them into every single lesson, regardless of what is being studied and how it would otherwise be taught. This is the wrong approach"*. The Achilles' heel of technology in education is, we contend, the temptation for educators to fall for the 'coolness factor' and try to integrate established (iPads) with new and emerging technologies into their teaching and learning practices without really understanding the technology's 'enhancement factor'. Although technology-enhanced learning has many benefits, the Achilles' heel is a lack of understanding by educators of the pedagogical 'value add' of a selected technology for teaching and/or learning.

Educators need to resolve the tensions that exist between the seductive nature of technology and the necessary capacity development that must underpin effective use to develop an attitude that is 'pro TEL' but balanced with sufficiently developed pedagogical skills to evaluate the usefulness of highly advanced technologies. What is needed is an understanding of learning theories and learner characteristics (see for example Nygaard, this volume) and their relevance for day-to-day pedagogical practices. This includes the selection of appropriate technology tools and with that in mind, the TPACK framework may be a good starting point to help educators deal with this challenge.

Conclusion, implications, and recommendations

A key aim of this viewpoint chapter was to alert readers to the vulnerability of technology-enhanced learning and explore some possibilities of new and emerging technologies by presenting two dichotomous case examples. Our primary aim was to explore alternative conceptions of the 'glitter effect' versus the value add TEL. The reality of higher education in Australia and many other places is a push towards more TEL. The question is not, "Should more technology be introduced to education?" but rather, "What technology and for what purpose?". This led us to contrast the desirable *Evolutionary Change* (in which development is incremental and based on the needs uncovered by pedagogy) and *Revolutionary Change* (in which step changes are driven by the desire or perceived need to incorporate novel technologies). We have argued that pedagogy should be the focus of TEL, exemplified by advancements we described in simulation technology. It is possible some techno-enthusiasts will be swayed by 'shiny new gadgets', such as the car industry's augmented reality (AR) HUD technology and transfer it into the classroom. However, we share the views of many educators who resist the introduction of new and emerging technologies into the classroom without clear evidence of its value-adding nature and clear pedagogical purpose. We advocate the need for more debate and discussion about the viability of nascent technologies, like augmented reality and heads-up displays, before we embrace them in the classroom.

Recommendations for practice

Based on our argument, we make the following recommendations for practice:

- The vulnerability of technology-enhanced learning is that some educators may be tempted to fall for the attractiveness of the technology ('coolness factor') and may attempt to integrate new and emerging technologies into their teaching without a clear understanding of how to exploit the technology's learning enhancement ability. The TPACK framework is a good starting point to self-evaluate the utility of the desired technology and to enable principled technology integration.

◆ Technology-enhanced learning is still a vague concept that needs greater clarity. There is a need for capacity building for educators and learners about the pedagogical 'value add' of new and emerging technologies. Rich case studies are needed to understand better the struggles and successes of implementing new and emerging technologies. We urge readers to contribute their ideas to the developing literature of technology-enhanced learning to increase collective understanding of informed academic innovations that translate into learning gains for all students, irrespective of their technological savvy.

About the authors

Eva Dobozy is a Senior Lecturer in the School of Education at Curtin University. She can be contacted at this email: eva.dobozy@curtin.edu.au

Jim Mullaney is academic engagement developer in the Faculty of Humanities at Curtin University. He can be contacted at this email: jim.mullaney@curtin.edu.au

David Gibson is the director of the Centre of Teaching and Learning at Curtin University. He can be contacted at this email: david.c.gibson@curtin.edu.au

Bibliography

Ablaßmeier, M.; T. Poitschke; F. Wallhoff; K. Bengler & G. Rigoll (2007). Eye gaze studies comparing head-up and head-down displays in vehicles. *IEEE International Conference on Multimedia and Expo.* IEEE, pp. 2250–2252.
Aldrich, C. (2004). *Simulations and the future of learning: an innovative (and perhaps revolutionary) approach to e-learning.* San Francisco: John Wiley & Sons.
Babbie, E. (2013). *The Practice of Social Research.* Belmont, CA: Cengage.
Bayne, S. (2014). What's the matter with 'technology-enhanced learning'? *Learning, Media and Technology.* Vol. 39, No. 1, pp. 6-36.

Calvin, T. (2013). Minimalism in Technology. Online Resource: http://www.bpsedtech.org/2013/10/28/minimalism-in-technology/ [Accessed 16 January 2015].

Carson, J. S. (2009). Introduction to modeling and simulation. *IEEE Engineering Management Review*, No. 37, np.

Chomal, S. & J. Saini, (2013). A study and analysis of paradigm shifts in education triggered by technology. *International Journal of Research in Economics & Social Sciences*, Vol. 3, No. 1., pp. 14-28.

Coulthard, G. J. (2009). *A Review of the Educational Use and Learning Effectiveness of Simulations and Games. Business.*

Conole, G. (2008). The role of mediating artefacts in learning design. In L. Lockyer; S. Bennett; S. Agostinho & B. Harper (Eds.). *Handbook of Research on Learning Design and Learning Objects: Issues, Applications and Technologies.* New York, N.Y.: Hershey, pp. 188-208.

Conole, G. (2013). *Designing for learning in an Open World.* New York, N.Y.: Springer.

Cruickshank, D. R. (1977). *A first book of games and simulations.* Belmont, Calif.: Wadsworth Pub. Co.

Damianova, M. & G. Sullivan (2011). Rereading Vygotsky's theses on types of internalisation and verbal mediation. *Review of General Psychology*, Vol. 15, No. 4, pp. 344-350.

Deloitte (2013). *Researchers' Report 2013.* European Union and Deloitte.

Dobozy, E. (2009). Learning 2.0: Teachers who choose to be left behind. Refereed Proceedings of the biannual EDUCAUSE Australasia Conference, Perth: Convention Centre.

Dobozy, E.; J. Dalziel & B. Dalziel (2013). Learning design and transdisciplinary pedagogical templates (TPTs). In C. Nygaard; J. Branch & C. Holtham (Eds.). *Learning in university education – Contemporary standpoints.* Farringdon, Oxfordshire: Libri Publishing Ltd., pp. 59-76.

Eisenmann, T; L. Barley & L. Kind (2014). Google Glass. Harvard Business School Case 814-102, *HBC Case Collection.*

Engeström, Y. (1999). Activity theory and individual and social transformation. In Y. Engestrom; R. Miettinen & R. Punamaki (Eds.). *Perspectives on Activity Theory.* Cambridge: Cambridge University Press, pp. 19–38.

European Commission (2014). *Horizon 2020.* European Commission.

Gibson, D.; C. Aldrich & M. Prensky (2007). *Games and Simulations in Online Learning: Research and Development Frameworks.* Information Science Publishing.

Gibson, D. & P. Jakl (2013). *Data challenges of leveraging a simulation to assess learning.* CA: West Lake Village.

Griffin, T. & R. Thomson (2008). *Evolution of blended learning in a large enrolment subject: What was blended and why?* Proceedings ascilite Melbourne 2008.

Hague, P.; N. Hagu & C. Morgan (2004). *Market research in practice: a guide to the basics.* London, UK: Kogan.

Hibberd, D. L.; S. L. Jamson & O. M. J. Carsten (2010). *Managing in-vehicle distractions: evidence from the psychological refractory period paradigm.* Proceedings of the 2nd International Conference on Automotive User Interfaces and Interactive Vehicular Applications.

Holland, J. (1995). *Hidden order: How adaptation builds complexity. Helix Books.* Cambridge, MA: Perseus Books.

International Academy, Research and Industry Association (2014). *The Sixth International Conference on Mobile, Hybrid, and On-line Learning.* eLmL 2014.

Kivunja, C. (2013). Embedding Digital Pedagogy in Pre-Service Higher Education To Better Prepare Teachers for the Digital Generation. *International Journal of Higher Education*, Vol. 2., No. 4., pp. 131-142.

Koehler, M. J.; P. Mishra; K. Kereluik; T. S. Shin & C. Graham (2013). The Technological Pedagogical Content Knowledge Framework. In M. Spector; M. Merrill; J. Elen & M. J. Bishop (Eds.). *Handbook of Research on Educational Communications and Technology.* New York, N.Y.: Springer, pp. 101-111.

Laurillard, D. (2012). *Teaching as a Design Science: Building Pedagogical Patterns for Learning and Technology.* New York, N.Y.: Routledge.

Laursen, L. (2013). Head Up Displays Go Down Market. *Tech Talk.*

Mandinach, E. & H. Cline (1993). Systems, science, and schools. *Systems Dynamics Review*, Vol. 9, No. 2, pp. 195–206.

McKenney, S. (2013). Designing and researching technology-enhanced learning for the zone of proximal implementation. *Research in Learning Technology.* Vol. 21, pp. 17374-17381.

NESTA (2012). *Decoding Learning: The proof, promise and potential of digital education.* London, UK.

Nicolle, P. & Y. Lou (2008). Technology adoption into teaching and learning by mainstream university faculty: A mixed methodology stud y revealing the "How, when, why and why not". *Journal of Educational Computing Research.* Vol. 39, No. 3, pp. 235-265.

Norrish, D. (2014). Classroom practice – Power up to become a tech-savvy teacher. *TEC – Connect.*

Pawson, R. (2006). Digging for nuggets: How "bad" research can yield "good" evidence. *International Journal of Social Research Methodology*, Vol. 9, No. 2, pp. 127-42.

Pelliccione, L. & T. Broadley (2010). R U there yet? Using virtual classrooms to transform teaching practice. In C. H. Steel; M. J. Keppell; P. Gerbic & S. Housego (Eds.). *Curriculum, technology & transformation for an unknown future.* Proceedings ascilite Sydney 2010, pp. 749-760.

Prensky, M. (2001). *Digital game-based learning.* New York: McGraw-Hill.

Rosen, K. R. (2008). The history of medical simulation. *Journal of critical care*, Vol. 23, pp. 157–166.

Starkey, D. (2013). New App Brings Augmented Reality HUD to Your Windshield. Blog post. Online Resource: http://www.tomshardware. com/news/augmented-reality-driving-hud-rally,24972.html [Accessed 27 November 2013].

Strauss, W. & N. Howe (1991). *Generations: The History of America's Future, 1584 to 2069.* Harper Perennial, p. 335.

Swider, M. (2014). Google Glass review: Is the Explorer Edition with the price of admission? Online resource: http://www.techradar.com/au/ reviews/gadgets/google-glass-1152283/review [Accessed 2 June 2014].

Thagard, P. (2010). *How brains make mental models.* Online resource: www. cogsci.uwaterloo.ca/Articles/Thagard.brains-models.2010.pdf [Accessed 2 June 2014].

Thompson, A. & P. Mishra (2007). Breaking news: TPCK becomes TPACK! *Journal of Computing in Teacher Education*, Vol. 24, No. 2, pp. 38-64.

Vygotsky, L. (1978). *Mind in society: The development of higher psychological processes.* Cambridge, MA: Harvard University Press.

Walker, J.; C. Dziuban & P. Moskal (2012). Transforming education with research that makes a difference. In D. Oblinger (Ed.). *Game changers: Education and information technologies.* EDUCAUSE.

Section 2

Introducing the 'practice' of technology-enhanced learning

Steve Drew & Diane D. DePew

Introduction

This section of the anthology deals with aspects of practice as experienced by educators and students engaging with technology-enhanced learning (TEL) in higher education. This chapter contributes to the anthology on technology-enhanced learning in higher education by defining and conceptualising 'practice' in that domain. Reading this chapter, you will: encounter definitions of terms and an introduction to current ways of understanding the practice of technology-enhanced learning; engage with models and theories relating to that practice; and be introduced to the contributions to practice of the following chapters in this section of the anthology. The aim of the 'practice' section is to connect from policy to design, implementation, and evaluation of technology-enhanced learning in higher education.

'Practice' in the context of technology-enhanced learning

For the purposes of this section of the anthology, the term 'practice' refers to the practical applications of technology with pedagogical and discipline knowledge to enhance learning and teaching in higher education. Practice embraces the performative aspects of design, implementation and evaluation that practitioners undertake in the pursuit and enhancement of quality education in this domain.

In contrast to policy, practice involves stakeholders at the educational 'coalface' of higher education. Practitioners, related in the chapters of this section, include students, teachers, and professionals with expertise in discipline content, educational design, and purposeful integration of relevant technology.

A key aspect of context for the practice of technology-enhanced learning is the cultures of the actors within the higher education organization. As students, many senior academics achieved their own academic success through traditional lecture, tutorial, and laboratory formats. Later employed by higher education providers based primarily on discipline research, some with only passing understanding of educational approaches based on their experiences as learners, many academics have been ill-equipped to move beyond those experiences of learning and teaching. Students approaches to learning (Marton & Säljö, 1976) and hence learning outcomes have been found to be influenced by the learning and teaching environment (Marton et al., 1984; Ramsden, 1992). Perpetuation of teacher centred approaches to learning (Biggs, 1989; Samuelowicz & Bain, 1992) and learning environment design have met with decreasing student engagement with learning activities (Kuh, 2003). As a result more organisations encourage academics to engage in relevant areas of education and technology.

Contemporary students in higher education are increasingly engaged with mobile technology to provide communication, information, and entertainment. Their arguable status as 'digital natives' (Jones et al., 2010; Margaryan et al., 2011) does imply a skill set and preference for use of these devices in everyday activities that promote expectations of their engagement with higher education beyond the classroom (Bryant, 2006). And then there are the non-traditional students (Kim, 2007; Gilardi & Guglielmetti, 2011), some of whom are not as familiar with technology-enhanced education.

Adoption and effective use of blended learning, online learning and other technology-enhanced learning strategies are business, as well as educational quality imperatives. An expansion of expertise required for creating effective learning experiences, particularly in the blended and online realms, has prompted a move towards engaging teams of professionals such as blended learning advisors, curriculum consultants, and educational designers to assist in the creation of effective learning. This addresses a key concern of many academics as teachers that are untutored in the relative strengths and limitations of the range of technologies and their affordances for enhancing learning and teaching.

Such professionalising of the higher education workforce (Whitchurch, 2008), enables interchange of requisite discipline or content knowledge, pedagogical knowledge, and technological knowledge to bear on educational design. Koehler and Mishra (2009) refer to a model encompassing these knowledge areas as Technological Pedagogical and Content Knowledge (TPACK) and are represented as a Venn diagram (see Figure 1). The three core knowledge areas create the main component sets. Each intersection set represents different specialised knowledge areas such as pedagogical content knowledge which enables design of learning activities that will best develop understanding of particular content. This is the realm of the educational designer in collaboration with the discipline expert. Technological pedagogical knowledge provides the understanding of how technology can best be used to create effective learning activities and is the realm of the blended learning advisor or learning technology consultant. Technological content knowledge provides an understanding of how the discipline content can best be represented and communicated using relevant technologies. It is usually a collaborative enterprise between the learning technology consultant and discipline expert.

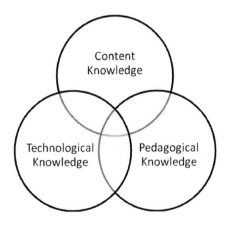

Figure 1: Practice in TEL as TPACK.

The central intersection of the three sets is arguably the 'holy grail' of combined knowledge for technology-enhanced learning and is expressed as technological, pedagogical and content knowledge or TPACK. Understandably, all the chapters in this 'practice' section of the anthology express investment and developments of knowledge from all sets and are thus positioned as cases in the intersection set in middle of this diagram.

Conceptions of 'practice' in technology-enhanced learning

Conceptions are different ways of thinking about or developing responses to an entity, concept or process. A conception might be considered a mental model (Greca & Moreira, 2000) that builds upon similarities and relationships to other known concepts and develops with deeper understanding and experience. Conceptions might also be built by considering the range of views of different actors within a system and how each view provides a lens that contributes a different perspective and perception. For example, a conception of 'technology-enhanced learning' might be built upon the reader's existing conceptions of learning (Entwistle & Peterson, 2004), learning outcomes (Marton & Säljö, 1976), pedagogy (Shulman, 1987) and educational technology (Laurillard, 2013). Further, reflection upon experiences of developing pedagogies involving educational technology to enhance students' learning outcomes will shape and refine that conception. By considering the range of conceptions shared by peers, such as will be found in the following chapters, then a shared understanding of the 'concept' of practice in technology-enhanced learning will be developed.

Via a collaborative exercise with the authors in this section of the anthology, consensus on the aspects making up the 'practice' of technology-enhanced learning generated a shared conception. As above, the performative aspects of practice are logically and temporally ordered into stages. In this case policy provides information that informs the design stage; once the design has sufficient detail including intended outcomes, methods of evaluating achievement of outcomes, and appropriate activities then it becomes the plan that informs its implementation. The implementation stage is where practice engages each of the system's actors in executing the planned activities and collects relevant data to evaluate achievement against design goals. In the evaluation stage, the analysis of data provides evidence that potentially informs each of the stages, including policy, in the next iteration of development (see Figure 2).

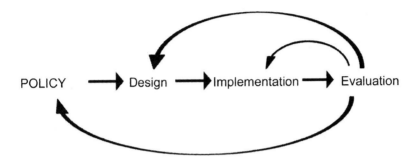

Figure 2: Conception of Practice in TEL.

Change in an organisation's operating context (see Figure 3) from influences of regulation, economics, competition, and innovation necessitates and informs changes to both policy and practice, although either one may lead the other. In an organisational sense, practice is informed by policy, but through the study of innovations and outcomes in practice so policy can in turn be informed.

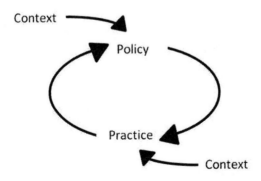

Figure 3: Organisational change cycle.

Models underpinning teaching and learning in 'practice'

Chapters in this section of the anthology each describe a fundamentally constructivist (Chen & Liu, 2006) philosophical approach; and a design for practice based on a range of models and viewpoints for learning and teaching. These models and viewpoints are 'pedagogical knowledge' and are divided between attributes being developed in learners, models for learning, and models for curriculum development.

A central theme is the focus on 'active learning' (Bonwell & Eison, 1991) that encompasses a range of activities and approaches that places the student and 'what they do' (Biggs, 2012) at the centre of the learning enterprise. In contrast to the 'passive' teacher as provider of knowledge model of classroom activity, this approach is alternatively expressed as 'student-centred learning' (O'Neill & McMahon, 2005). Experiential learning (Kolb, 1984) leads a learner through a cycle of concrete experience, reflection on what was observed, abstraction of concepts from reflection, and experimentation to test conceptual knowledge and understanding (see Figure 4). Biggs (1999) describes a more abstract but analogous cyclic model of 'action learning' that leads a learner through steps of planning, acting, observing, and reflecting as they incrementally build understanding through their actions (see Figure 5).

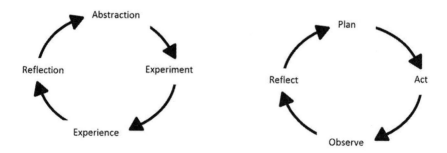

Figure 4: Experiential learning.   *Figure 5: Action learning.*

As students undertake learning activities so do teachers engage in their own 'action learning' about the nature and effectiveness of the technological pedagogical designs implemented. From a teacher's perspective this might be experienced as a quality management (van der Bank & van der Bank, 2014) or Plan, Implement, Review, and Improve (PIRI) cycle (see Figure 6). A teacher researching to improve their practice (praxis) might enter the cycle at either of two points. With evidence indicating a problem to be addressed entry is at the 'review' step. Alternatively, with knowledge derived from scholarly works about effective practice, entry is at the 'plan' step. Rather than circular as depicted, the PIRI cycle actually describes a spiral that evolves 'practice' over time.

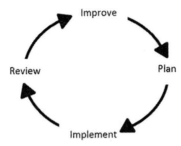

Figure 6: PIRI quality management.

Core to each of the models is an achievement goal orientation (Covington, 2000), with an element of reflection or review on what was undertaken. Reflective practice (Schön, 1987) is a process of analysis involving critical thinking (Pithers & Soden, 2000) to determine for a particular activity, what worked, what did not work, and what actions might be tried to effect improvement next time. Formalised reflection is part of a deep approach to learning (Trigwell *et al.*, 1999) that can be taught to students to enhance learning outcomes, to teachers to enhance pedagogical design, and to higher education providers to promote institutional maturity (Biggs, 2001).

For students, learner maturity is a particular issue for successful transition into higher education. Often coming from a teacher-led learning environment many students are not self-regulated learners (Zimmerman & Schunk, 2008; Nicol & MacFarlane-Dick, 2006) and lack knowledge of how best to manage their learning activity. Facilitating steps to self-regulated or self-managed learning is the essence of the cognitive apprenticeship model (Collins *et al.*, 1987; Collins, 1991). Emerging from situated learning theory (Lave & Wenger, 1991; Billett, 1996), 'apprentice learners' discover how to cognitively learn from masters such that responsibility for direction of learning starts with the master with increasing responsibility adopted by the apprentice. Cognitive apprenticeship is uses modelling, coaching, scaffolding, articulation, reflection and/or exploration for student attainment of cognitive and metacognitive strategies for manipulating knowledge to new situations and problems. At each phase, cycles of trial, reflection and discussion of what has been learned embody a formative process.

Situated learning is also a fundamental theory underpinning the engagement with learning activities and assessments that are 'authentic' to professional settings that students are likely to enter as graduates. Authentic learning environments (Herrington & Herrington, 2006) adopt real-world practices, creating professional relevance and introducing students to interdisciplinary complexity of social and organisational professional settings.

Collaborative learning (Bruffee, 1995) is a theme of the viewpoints expressed by authors in this section of the anthology. Valuing the knowledge and experience of students and encouraging sharing in learning environments provides elementary cognitive apprenticeship that leads to shared understanding. With teacher as a facilitator of learning and also 'master learner', collaboration leads to dialogue and interaction between students, teacher, and content creating a milieu that encourages contribution to the learning process.

Review of these models shows a focus on learner-centred teaching rather than on teacher-centred teaching. This bodes that the practice of which this section discusses is learner centred. Therefore, the technologies while selected and designed by the academics are actually enacted upon by the learner. It is the learner engagement with the technology that enhances education.

Introduction to chapters about practice

This section provides a roadmap to the sequence of chapters in the 'practice' section. Following the authors' conceptualisation of practice (see Figure 2), the logical flow of policy, design, implementation and evaluation, each chapter is highlighted for its contribution to the section.

This section on 'practice' begins with Chapter 6 which explores potential strategies for implementing *iPad* technology to support student self-assessment. It begins by exploring the overarching drivers for implementing technology-enhanced learning and the potential pitfalls to be considered when investing in tablet technologies at an institutional level. The chapter then critiques the application of tablet computers such as iPads, as personal learning tools for study management, and considers alternative uses to promote self-assessment, self-regulation and active learning. It continues by examining the multimodal nature of *Apple's iBook* technology, within a blended learning context, as a means to accommodate diverse learning styles. Finally, the chapter reviews the authors' own practice which explores the use of an interactive formative eBook built using *iBooks Author*; made available on *iPads* within a higher education classroom environment. The key lesson from Chapter 6 is that instructor ownership of the pedagogic design principles that underpin the deployment of learning technologies is a primary factor for ensuring successful learner engagement.

Chapter 7 examines the use of ePortfolios to enhance learning in higher education. It begins by exploring the philosophy and theory underpinning ePortfolio use and developing reflective and experiential learners. The chapter then presents two contrasting case studies from Birmingham City University in which ePortfolios are embedded within the undergraduate law programme to support personal and skills development in students. Finally the chapter examines critical incidents that can impact upon the use and value of ePortfolios in higher education. The key lesson from Chapter 7 is that the lived experience of technology use demands flexibility and responsiveness in design and subsequent implementation to enhance learning.

Next, Chapter 8 addresses 'practice' by describing an innovative, Web-based managed learning system for Java programming. It begins by introducing the underlying learning challenges driving the design of a technology-based system to enhance students' experience of learning to program in Java. The chapter then leads the reader through the learner-driven, evidence-based design and development of the Java Programming Language (JPL) system components using a participative action research approach. Finally, the chapter presents evidence that the system described is a highly effective technology-enhanced learning environment that positively impacts student learning experiences and outcomes. The key takeaway of this chapter is the design of JPL as a TEL environment has enhanced learning outcomes by providing structure to study, flexibility of access to learning environment, and teacher access to student progress for timely intervention.

Chapter 9 demonstrates the use of a technology to assess students' application of critical thinking to guide appropriate responses in challenging situations. It begins by an examination of the theoretical foundation of cognitive apprenticeship and experiential learning. The chapter then introduces the ApprenNet technological process. The chapter continues with an in depth review of the application of this technology to support learning in a nursing program. Finally, the authors offer a discussion of the value and limitations of the technology to support learning and how it may be applied to other disciplines. The key lesson from Chapter 9 is technology can be utilised to link classroom and practice via structured learning activities than permit faculty members to assess student performance.

Chapter 10 addresses the problem faced by educators who are unable to provide meaningful feedback to students due to limited interaction inherent in independent, out-of-the classroom, fieldwork environments. It then proposes a distance education solution and provides an example of how the solution was implemented in the field of aviation education. The chapter continues to discuss how the implementation of a communications medium can support meaningful dialogue, strengthen the learning outcomes and student engagement. Finally, it provides a recommendation for a technology-enhanced solution to strengthen the link between the professor and student.

About the authors

Steve Drew is Director Learning & Teaching in the Griffith Sciences Executive, Griffith University, Australia. He can be contacted at this email: s.drew@griffith.edu.au

Diane D. DePew is Assistant Clinical Professor in the College of Nursing and Health Professions, Drexel University, United States of America. She can be contacted at this email: d.depew@drexel.edu

Bibliography

Altbach, P. G. (1999). The logic of mass higher education. *Tertiary Education & Management*, Vol. 5, No. 2, pp. 107-124.

Biggs, J. B. (1989). Approaches to enhancement of tertiary teaching, *Higher Education Research and Development*, Vol. 8, No. 1, pp. 7-27.

Biggs, J. (1999). What the student does: teaching for enhanced learning. *Higher Education Research & Development*, Vol. 18 No. 1, pp. 57-75.

Biggs, J. (2001). The reflective institution: Assuring and enhancing the quality of teaching and learning. *Higher Education*, Vol. 41, No. 3, pp. 221-238.

Biggs, J. (2012). What the student does: teaching for enhanced learning. *Higher Education Research & Development*, Vol. 31, No. 1, pp. 39-55.

Biggs, J. & C. Tang (2011). *Teaching for quality learning at university*. McGraw-Hill International.

Billett, S. (1996). Situated learning: Bridging sociocultural and cognitive theorising. *Learning and instruction*, Vol. 6, No. 3, pp. 263-280.

Black, P. & D. Wiliam (2009). Developing the theory of formative assessment. *Educational Assessment, Evaluation and Accountability (formerly: Journal of Personnel Evaluation in Education)*, Vol. 21, No. 1, pp. 5-31.

Bonwell, C. C. & J. A. Eison (1991). Active Learning: Creating Excitement in the Classroom *ASHEERIC Higher Education Report* (Vol. 1). Washington, DC: George Washington University.

Bruffee, K. A. (1995). Sharing our toys: Cooperative learning versus collaborative learning. *Change: The Magazine of Higher Learning*, Vol. 27, No. 1, pp. 12-18.

Bryant, T. (2006). Social software in academia. *Educause quarterly*, Vol. 29, No. 2, pp. 61-64.

Carini, R.; G. D. Kuh & S. Klein (2006). Student Engagement and Student Learning: Testing the Linkages*. *Research in Higher Education*, Vol. 47, No. 1, pp. 1-32.

Chen, I. J. & C. C. Liu (2006). Evolution of Constructivism. *Contemporary Issues in Education Research*, Vol. 3, No. 4, pp. 63-66.

Collins, A. (1991). Cognitive Apprenticeship: Making Things Visible. *American Educator: The Professional Journal of the American Federation of Teachers*, Vol. 15, No.3, pp. 6-11.

Collins, A.; J. S. Brown & S. E. Newman. (1987). *Cognitive Apprenticeship: Teaching the Craft of Reading, Writing, and Mathematics*. Cambridge,

MA: Illinois University (Urbana: Center for the Study of Reading. Bolt, Beranek and Newman, Inc).

Covington, M. V. (2000). Goal theory, motivation, and school achievement: An integrative review. *Annual Review of Psychology*, Vol. 51, pp. 171-200.

Dede, C. (2009). Immersive interfaces for engagement and learning. *Science*, Vol. 323, No. 5910, pp. 66-69.

Dede, C.; M. Salzman; R. B. Loftin & K. Ash (2000). Advanced Designs for Technologies of Learning. In M. J. Jacobson & R. B. Kozma (Eds.). *Innovations in Science and Mathematics Education*. Mahweh, NJ,: Erlbaum. pp. 361–413.

Delfino, M. & D. Persico (2011). Unfolding the Potential of ICT for SRL Development. In R. Carneiro; P. Lefrere, K. Steffens & J. Underwood (Eds.). *Self-Regulated Learning in Technology-Enhanced Learning Environments*: Springer. pp. 53-74.

Entwistle, N. (1988). Motivational factors in students' approaches to learning. In R. Schmeck (Ed.). *Learning strategies and learning styles*: Springer, pp. 21-51.

Entwistle, N. J. & E. R. Peterson (2004). Conceptions of learning and knowledge in higher education: Relationships with study behaviour and influences of learning environments. *International Journal of Educational Research*, Vol. 41, No. 6, pp. 407-428.

Gilardi, S. & C. Guglielmetti (2011). University life of non-traditional students: Engagement styles and impact on attrition. *The Journal of Higher Education*, Vol. 82, No. 1, pp. 33-53.

Goodyear, P. & S. Retalis (2010). *Technology-enhanced learning*: Sense Publishers.

Gosling, J. (2000). *The Java language specification*: Addison-Wesley Professional.

Greca, I. M. & M. A. Moreira (2000). Mental models, conceptual models, and modelling. *International Journal of Science Education*, Vol. 22, No. 1, pp. 1-11.

Herrington, A. & J. Herrington (Eds.) (2006). *Authentic learning environments in higher education*. IGI Global.

Jones, C.; R. Ramanau; S. Cross & G. Healing (2010). Net generation or digital natives: is there a distinct new generation entering university? *Computers & Education*, Vol. 54, No. 3, pp. 722-732.

Kember, D. (2000). *Action learning and action research: improving the quality of teaching and learning*. London: Kogan Page.

Kemmis, S. (2006). Participatory action research and the public sphere. *Educational Action Research*, Vol. 14, No. 4, pp. 459-476.

Kim, K. (2007). ERIC Review: Exploring the meaning of "Nontraditional" at the community college. *Community College Review*. Vol. 30, No. 1, pp. 74-88

Kjell, B. (1997). Programmed instruction using web pages. *Journal of Computing in Small Colleges*, Vol. 12, No. 5, pp. 113-123.

Koehler, M. & P. Mishra (2009). What is technological pedagogical content knowledge (TPACK)?. *Contemporary Issues in Technology and Teacher Education*, Nol. 9, No. 1, pp. 60-70.

Kolb, D. A. (1984). *Experiential learning: Experience as the source of learning and development* (Vol. 1). Englewood Cliffs, NJ: Prentice-Hall.

Kuh, G. D. (2003). What We're Learning About Student Engagement from NSSE: Benchmarks for Effective Educational Practices. *Change*, Vol. 35, No. 2, pp. 24-32.

Laurillard, D. (2013). *Rethinking university teaching: A conversational framework for the effective use of learning technologies*. Routledge.

Lave, J. & E. Wenger (1991). *Situated learning: Legitimate peripheral participation*. Cambridge University Press.

Leveson, L.; N. McNeil & T. Joiner (2013). Persist or withdraw: the importance of external factors in students' departure intentions. *Higher Education Research & Development*, Vol. 32, No. 6, pp. 932-945.

Margaryan, A.; A. Littlejohn & G. Vojt (2011). Are digital natives a myth or reality? University students' use of digital technologies. *Computers & Education*, Vol. 56, No. 2, pp. 429-440.

Marton, F. & R. Säljö (1976). On qualitative differences in learning, outcome and process I. *British Journal of Educational Psychology* Vol. 46, pp. 4–11.

Marton, F. & R. Säljö (1984). Approaches to learning. *The experience of learning*, Vol. 2, pp. 39-58.

Meyer, J. H. & R. Land (2005). Threshold concepts and troublesome knowledge (2): Epistemological considerations and a conceptual framework for teaching and learning. *Higher education*, Vol. 49, No. 3, pp. 373-388.

Minocha, S. (2009). Role of social software tools in education: a literature review. *Education + Training*, Vol. 51, No. 5/6, pp. 353-369.

Nicol, D. J. & D. Macfarlane-Dick (2006). Formative assessment and self-regulated learning: A model and seven principles of good feedback practice. *Studies in Higher Education*, Vol. 31, No. 2, pp. 199-218.

O'Neill, G. & T. McMahon (2005). Student-centred learning: What does it mean for students and lecturers. In O'Neill, G., Moore, S., & McMullin, B. (Eds.). *Emerging issues in the practice of university learning and teaching.*

Pintrich, P. R. & E. V. De Groot (1990). Motivational and self-regulated learning components of classroom academic performance. *Journal of educational psychology*, Vol. 82, No. 1, pp. 33-40.

Pithers, R. T. & R. Soden (2000). Critical thinking in education: A review. *Educational Research*, Vol. 42, No. 3, pp. 237-249.

Pullan, W.; S. Drew & S. Tucker (2013). *An integrated approach to teaching introductory programming.* Paper presented at the e-Learning and e-Technologies in Education (ICEEE), 2013 Second International Conference on.

Ramsden, P. (1992). *Learning to Teach in Higher Education.* London: Kogan Page.

Rountree, J. & N. Rountree (2009). *Issues regarding threshold concepts in computer science.* In Proceedings of the Eleventh Australasian Conference on Computing Education,Vol. 95, pp. 139-146.

Savery, J. R. (2006). Overview of problem-based learning: Definitions and distinctions. *Interdisciplinary Journal of Problem-based Learning*, Vol. 1, No. 1, pp. 9-20.

Samuelowicz, K. & J. D. Bain (1992). Conceptions of teaching held by academic teachers. *Higher Education*, Vol. 24, No. 1, pp. 93-111.

Schön, D. A. (1987). *Educating the reflective practitioner: Toward a new design for teaching and learning in the professions.* San Francisco.

Shulman, L. S. (1987). Knowledge and teaching: Foundations of the new reform. *Harvard educational review*, Vol. 57, No. 1, pp. 1-23.

Simons, K. D. & J. D. Klein (2007). The impact of scaffolding and student achievement levels in a problem-based learning environment. *Instructional Science*, Vol. 35, No. 1, pp. 41-72.

Sorva, J. (2010). *Reflections on threshold concepts in computer programming and beyond.* In Proceedings of the 10th Koli Calling International Conference on Computing Education Research, ACM, pp. 21-30.

Stroustrup, B. (2008). *Programming: principles and practice using C++:* Addison-Wesley Professional.

Taylor, J. & B. House (2010). An Exploration of Identity, Motivations and Concerns of Non-Traditional Students at Different Stages of Higher Education. *Psychology Teaching Review*, Vol. 16, No. 1, pp. 46-57.

Trigwell, K. & M. Prosser (1991). Improving the quality of student learning: the influence of learning context and student approaches to learning on learning outcomes. *Higher Education*, Vol. 22, No. 3, pp. 251-266.

Trigwell, K.; M. Prosser & F. Waterhouse (1999). Relations between teachers' approaches to teaching and students' approaches to learning. *Higher Education*, Vol. 37, No. 1, pp. 57-70.

van der Bank, C. M. & M. van der Bank (2014). Quality Assurance in Higher Education: A Case Study of the Vaal University of Technology. *Journal of Educational and Social Research*, Vol. 4, No. 1, p. 395.

van der Meer, J.; E. Jansen & M. Torenbeek (2010). 'It's almost a mindset that teachers need to change': first-year students' need to be inducted into time management. *Studies in Higher Education*, Vol. 35, No. 7, pp. 777-791.

Van Rossum, G. & F. L. Drake (2003). *Python language reference manual*: Network Theory.

Wang, F. & M. J. Hannafin (2005). Design-based research and technology-enhanced learning environments. *Educational technology research and development*, Vol. 53, No. 4, pp. 5-23.

Whitchurch, C. (2008). Shifting identities and blurring boundaries: The emergence of third space professionals in UK higher education. *Higher Education Quarterly*, Vol. 62, No. 4, pp. 377-396.

Wirth, N. (1983). On the design of programming languages *Programming Languages*: Springer, pp. 23-30.

Wu, J.-H.; R. D. Tennyson & T.-L. Hsia (2010). A study of student satisfaction in a blended e-learning system environment. *Computers & Education*, Vol. 55, No. 1, pp. 155-164.

Zimmerman, B. & D. Schunk (2008). An essential dimension of self-regulated learning. In B. Zimmerman & D. Schunk (Eds.). *Motivation and self-regulation: Theory, research, and applications*, New York, NY: Tayler & Francis, pp. 1-31.

Chapter Five

Where's the humanity? Challenging the policy discourse of technology-enhanced learning

Sarah Hayes & Paul Bartholomew

Introduction

Technologies for enhancing student learning are now commonplace in higher education. Yet simply introducing new techniques and technologies is not enough. We explore the controversial position that educational technologies are destined for failure as an emancipatory concept unless we radically confront how we discuss technology in policy related to student learning. By challenging policy discourse in a book about technology- enhanced learning, we seek to bring to the attention of readers the concern that if policy and practice become disconnected this has implications for university strategy. The use of a particular type of language which acts as a vehicle for political economic agendas and makes simplified claims in the name of technology may distort the values of human learning communities in higher education. Policy language surrounding technology-enhanced learning embodies a simple economic calculation: *in exchange for the use of technology there will be enhanced forms of learning.* Yet discourse based only on this 'exchange value' (Marx, 1867) inhibits questions being raised about diverse ways students and instructors experience technology.

This chapter makes an important contribution to *Technology-Enhanced Learning in Higher Education* by referring to empirical data to question a particular type of *language* routinely applied to the use of *technology* for *learning*. The empirical approach described in this chapter through critical discourse analysis is just one way to expose policy choices in *language* about *learning* with *technology*.

In United Kingdom (UK) educational technology policy documents (and by extrapolation perhaps more global ones too), 'Technology-Enhanced Learning' (TEL), as a concept label, is often used to articulate a problematic presumption – that learning is (inevitably) enhanced when mediated through the use of technology. We contend that the narrow and largely unconsidered use of this concept label (and related terms) within policy documents has led to a tacit acceptance of a discourse based on the Marxist concept of 'exchange value' (Marx, 1867). Technology, like any commodity, has 'value' which also represents a quantity of human labour. Marx distinguishes between 'use value' and 'exchange value'. 'Use value' relates to human social necessities such as teaching or learning that (in the context of this chapter) a technology might fulfil in conjunction with the labour involved. On the other hand, 'exchange value' is a value that takes the human labour involved for granted to realise a profit in an economic market. This approach seems to be reflected in Technology-Enhanced Learning as a guarantee that the use of technology will enhance learning as exchange value (profit), giving us the notional transactional equation of:

(Learning context) + (introduction of technology) = enhancement of learning

Such 'exchange value'-based policy discourse, constrained to the narrow perception that educational technology provides an economic 'fix' for perceived issues in higher education, conceals a multitude of important assumptions. Discourse predicated on 'exchange value' provides a vehicle for political economic agendas to make simplified claims in the name of technology, which can, according to Greener and Perriton (2005), distort the values of human learning communities. Furthermore, when considered semantically, embedded within the meaning of the three words 'Technology-Enhanced Learning' is a potential foregone conclusion: an assumption that technology has now enhanced learning and will continue to do so (Hayes, 2014). This conceals the need for a debate to remind us that it is humans who design and engage in learning (opportunities), not technology.

We also note that development of educational technology has largely coincided with the development of neo-liberal politics (and the marketisation of higher education) in advanced industrial countries (Jones, 2014). While neo-liberal politics is not the main focus of this chapter, we point out that a history of 'fix-it' policies in education (Selwyn, Gorard, & Williams, 2001) has contributed to a narrow and dominant language about educational technology as always providing an 'exchange value' for learning. Through reading this chapter you will gain the following insights:

1) By sharing some empirical findings from a recent research project that sought to confront a large body of UK policy language, we offer a critique of 'Technology-Enhanced Learning' as a composite term, revealing some surprising results. In a series of examples, we demonstrate through *transitivity analysis* (a form of critical discourse analysis) how a 'process-based' approach in this language isolates humans from their own practices. Potential 'political' and economically-related forms of 'use' become separated from actual, contextual meaning that might be experienced by those learning or teaching in higher education. By 'political', we mean practices that are enacted for the purpose of organising control over a community.

2) We examine some implications from linguistic examples and articulate our critique with diverse critical social theory, drawing on the work of theorists including Marx, Latour, Fairclough, Habermas, and Friere.

3) We suggest that, rather than a simplified focus on 'processes', an alternative way to imagine 'Technology-Enhanced Learning' (TEL) is as a *technology-language-learning* 'nexus' (a composite concept constitutive of the component word-meanings), where claims for enhancement are not just based on the inevitability of 'exchange value' but on an honest and transparent accounting of the human contributions to such endeavours.

What might the term 'technology-enhanced learning' conceal?

The term technology-enhanced learning has become widely adopted in recent years as a way to describe benefits from *"using technology to support learning and related processes"* HEFCE (2009:1). However, TEL, more so than previous terms such as 'e-learning', also *"emphasises how technology adds value"* JISC (2009:8). Some strategy documents even suggest *"a paradigm shift where technology transforms* what *we learn and* how *we learn it"* European Commission (2009:9). If policy documents (and the discourse within) have become a proxy for new power paradigms, then we contend that foundational values once held strong by learning communities may have weakened or be subject to change. Yet in the literature there has been little critique of the fundamental assumptions embedded within the terminology of TEL (Bayne, 2014). Indeed it seems to serve in policy as a form of 'shorthand' for what is, in reality, 'a complex and often problematic constellation of social, technological and educational change' Bayne (2014:1).

While there are many bold positive claims about the *"impact of Technology-Enhanced Learning on roles and practices in higher education"* (Price, 2005:4), research that examines TEL tends to look mostly at impact with a focus on a particular *technology* or the methods of support to help staff implement it. Impact from policy *language* about educational technology, that positions *technology* in a particular worldview for *learning*, tends not to be the main focus. Yet language about technology can reveal things to people as they learn or, alternately, conceal a particularly strong set of economic-based values that underpin the discourse, making the single dominant governing principle of taken-for-granted 'exchange-value' difficult to disrupt.

To support examination of why communities of scholars might want to disrupt this dominant language (that restricts diverse approaches to instructor teaching and student learning) we refer to a recent UK research project. This study was undertaken by one of the authors (Sarah) at Aston University in Birmingham, during 2010 – 2013.

Sarah discusses an episode of critical discourse analysis research

By way of sharing the specific research method that underpins and substantiates the viewpoint we take in this chapter, I offer the following account. I collected and analysed 2.5 million words of UK government policy and university strategy texts written between 1997-2012, in a corpus-based critical discourse analysis (CDA). This approach was aimed at exploring what the language might reveal about how policy is semantically constructed and thus how it might be interpreted by those tasked to enact it.

A corpus is a large collection of real instances of language use. By 'real' I mean that the policy documents which I collected were written by many human beings in different contexts and at different times and thus variety among the documents might be anticipated over the 15-year period scrutinised. In a first step of analysis of my corpus, I applied software called *Wordsmith* to note quantitative patterns emerging through corpus linguistics (Baker, 2006). *Wordsmith* supports corpus linguistic analysis through *keywords* (Scott, 1997) – words that are statistically significant when the language under scrutiny is measured against a comparison corpus, in this case, the British National Corpus. I chose the British National Corpus for comparison purposes because it contains 100 million words of written and spoken English from a wide range of sources. Table 1 below shows some of the keywords that were highlighted and the number of times they appeared in concordance lines within the corpus.

Keyword	Number of instances
Learning	19260
Use	8131
Technology	6079

Table 1: Example keywords and how often they appeared in the corpus.

A concordance illustrates how words and phrases are ordered alongside each other in their actual context of use. Through specific searches in *Wordsmith*, I was able to take a closer look at the words that appeared both before and after the keyword 'use'. In Figure 1, bold text highlights the instances of 'the use of technology'. This phrase is often followed, or preceded, by an expectation <u>to enhance</u> or <u>improve</u> (these instances are underlined) a form of *learning* (denoted in italics).

5659	**the use of technology** <u>can increase</u> *accessibility and flexibility of learning*
5660	**the use of technology** <u>to create</u> *digital archives to improve practice*
5661˙	**the use of technology** <u>to enhance</u> *front line productivity and management*
5665	the agenda <u>to enhance</u> *learning and teaching* through **the use of technology**
5677	produce resources and advice on **the use of technology** <u>to enhance</u> *assessment*
5680	<u>enhancing</u> their skills and confidence in **the use of technology** <u>enhanced</u> *learning*
5681	<u>to enhance</u> **the use of technology** *in learning and teaching* and to facilitate a more
5682	to share information and drive **the use of technology** <u>to enhance</u> *learning*
5683	<u>to improve</u> *the student learning experience* through **the use of technology**
5684	**the use of technology** <u>to achieve</u> *novel and effective learning experiences*
5686	support for **use of technology** <u>to enhance</u> *the learning and teaching experience*

Figure 1: Concordance lines of policy text showing patterns of keywords.

The regularity of the patterns in Figure 1 seem to reinforce the assumption that *in exchange for the use of new technology there will automatically be enhanced forms of student learning.* Having noticed these structures were often repeated within my corpus, we undertook a closer analysis through critical discourse analysis (CDA). CDA provides a more qualitative way to examine not only how language is structured across *concordance* lines of policy text, but also what sorts of values are implicit in these statements and what kind of paradigm might underpin the writing of this policy. We use the word 'paradigm' to draw attention to the particular and distinct concepts or thought patterns that might contribute to a strategy or policy written in a certain style. Yet policy for TEL need not be conceptualised from a paradigm that largely emphasises what 'the use of technology' is doing. There are alternative ways to frame policy and, as discussed by Nygaard when considering the *rudiments of a strategy for technology-enhanced university learning,* "strategy should take its outset in our knowledge of learning" (See Nygaard, this Volume). While we refer to policy to guide different forms of practice in universities, surely it is necessary to also ask *what forms of practice guide policy?*

With these ideas in mind, CDA is *one* way to expose the choices people make (and others may unknowingly replicate) in formulating policy language (Fairclough, 2007). While an analysis of discourse cannot be claimed to prove or alter anything, it offers us a lens through which concrete expressions of expected 'exchange value' from technology might be noticed and discussed. Discourse can 'mould identities' (Massey, 2013) in narrow (often economically-based) terms, which undermines the human interactions (including human labour) implicit within the technology-language-learning nexus. Critically confronting discursive structures in this context is not a negative activity, it simply and usefully empowers conversations about the ways in which *technology*, *language* and *learning* interact. These three constitutive elements, ever-present in learning situations, intersect across what Giroux (1992) refers to as disciplinary borders.

We contend that to be valuable, an exploration of the three constitutive elements should be conducted in a way that is cognisant of the theoretical domains of each, while remaining inquiring of the interfaces and overlaps between them. Therefore, we suggest that together they frame a collated conceptual domain that is more than the sum of the constitutive parts and might rightfully form a legitimate, discrete focus for research into TEL and reflections on associated pedagogic practice. It is hoped that sharing this approach might contribute to visions others may have for a broader theoretical underpinning for educational technology as a developing field of knowledge and research (Conole & Oliver, 2002).

In terms of particular linguistic techniques that might be adopted within a CDA approach, there are many forms of analysis from which a researcher might choose. In my corpus there were 8131 instances of the keyword 'use' which I examined through a method within CDA called *transitivity analysis* (Halliday, 1994). This type of analysis enabled me to label the grammatical patterns of verbs to reveal what *processes* are prioritised and who/what is actually 'doing' these. So taking the components that constitute 'technology-enhanced learning', we might consider: what is the role of *technology*, of *language* and of *learning*? Extending and expanding the term of 'technology-enhanced learning' provides a reminder of the elements (of technology and learning and their semantic relationship as interlinked by language) contained within. This is necessary when this term is frequently condensed into the acronym TEL and its key constituents may be easily forgotten. Whether these key constituents act to undertake tasks, or are acted upon by other constituents, can alter the way in which a reader might experience meaning and perhaps apply this knowledge to practice.

Before discussing some findings from this study, it is worth providing a generic example to demonstrate how *transitivity analysis* works in practice. In Table 2 below, a statement has been made: *"A student is learning at university"*. The components of this statement are broken down and described. 'A student' is labelled as a *noun*, because this is a named participant undertaking a process. The process 'is learning' is labelled as a *verb* and the circumstance 'at university' is acknowledged as an *adverb*. Some things to notice here are that in this sentence the participant, or the actor undertaking the process of learning, is clearly stated. We know *who* is doing the learning and therefore agency is clear.

A student	is learning	at university
Participant (noun)	Process (verb)	Circumstance (an adverb)

Table 2: A generic example of transitivity analysis.

Yet this activity could easily be re-written less transparently, as shown in Table 3, to say: *"Universities are places of learning"*.

Universities	are	places of learning
Participant (noun)	Process (verb)	Participant (noun)

Table 3: One possible way we might rewrite the statement in Table 2.

In Table 3, there are similar components to label but aspects have been missed. For example, to reveal a human subject, more information is required and so I wonder, in relation to *"places of learning"*, *to whose learning do we refer?*

In undertaking a transitivity analysis following the work of Halliday (1994), process types (verbs) are labelled to show what type of actions these are. For example, a *Material* process is a physical act of labour undertaken by an *Actor* (whether human or not) to meet a *Goal*.

In Table 4 below it is clear to see that "Sarah" is the *Actor* undertaking a *Material* process, "is using", and the Goal is "technology".

Sarah	is using	technology
Actor	Material process	Goal

Table 4: How a 'Material' process is labelled in transitivity analysis.

While it may seem a little strange that the *Goal* in this example is "technology", it is worth adding that through the process "is using", "Sarah" is understood to be acting upon "technology". This becomes more significant if we think of transitivity analysis as a way to reveal agency (which refers to the capacity of individuals to act independently and to make their own free choices). In this example "Sarah" is the person with agency, or capacity, to act. If, however, we simply state that "technology" "enhances" "learning", we then attribute agency, or capacity to act, to "technology".

Some further processes that might be noticed through transitivity analysis should help to clarify these points. A process of 'believing' then would be described as a *Mental* process, but *Mental* processes are labelled slightly differently, as shown below in Table 5.

Sarah	believes	innovation is needed
Senser	Mental process	Phenomenon

Table 5: How a 'Mental' process is labelled in transitivity analysis.

In Table 5 "Sarah" is the *Senser* (rather than *Actor*) undertaking a *Mental* process, "believes". "Innovation is needed" is called the Phenomenon (rather than *Goal*). Here again we might consider that "Sarah" has the capacity to undertake this process, but it would change the meaning considerably if in place of "Sarah" we were to insert "This Strategy", which would then attribute agency, or capacity to believe, to a strategy.

A process of 'speaking' would be described as a *Verbal* process in Halliday's method. In Table 6 "Sarah" is now the *Sayer* in a *Verbal* process "criticises", and "quality control procedures" has become the *Target*.

Sarah	criticises	quality control procedures
Sayer	Verbal process	Target

Table 6: How a 'Verbal' process is labelled in transitivity analysis.

Yet if I chose to re-write the statement in Table 6 to replace "Sarah" with "This report" I would no longer be declaring a person or indeed people as responsible for criticising quality control procedures, I would instead be attributing agency to "This report".

Now that you have an idea of how this form of CDA (transitivity analysis) works, I will provide some examples from my corpus to demonstrate its role in this debate. In the concordance lines around 'use' *Material* processes were by far the most common type of process, as shown in Table 7 below.

The figures in Table 7 suggest that many *Material* processes are being discussed in the policy documents in the corpus. As a reminder, *Material* processes are processes of active labour that express the notion that some entity 'does' something which may be done 'to' another entity.

Verbal processes	Mental processes	Material processes
38	49	293

Table 7: Material processes were the dominant process type in the corpus.

A closer analysis of the corpus reveals several interesting observations. First, when examining corpus row 5659, shown in Table 8 below, the *Actor* undertaking the *Material* process, "can increase", is "the use of technology", not a named human being such as an instructor.

The use of technology	can increase	accessibility and flexibility of learning and support resources,
Actor	Process: Material	Goal

address	equality and diversity issues,	and	foster	lifelong learning
Process: Verbal	Target		Process: Material	Goal

Table 8: Row 5659. Transitivity processes = Material, Verbal, Material.

Furthermore, it is "the use of technology" that also undertakes the *Verbal* process to "address" the *Target* of "equality and diversity issues" and the later *Material* process to "foster" the *Goal* of "lifelong learning".

Again, when examining corpus row 5660, a similar pattern can be noticed. In Table 9, the *Actor* undertaking the *Material* process "to create" the *Goal*, "digital archives", is again "the use of technology", not a named human being.

The use of technology	to create	digital archives
Actor	Process: Material	Goal

to improve	documentation of practice	and	to support
Process: Material	Goal		Process: Material

curricular developments as well as more effective use of technology
Goal

Table 9: Row 5660. Transitivity processes = Material, Material, Material.

Indeed, "the use of technology" proceeds to undertake further *Material* processes, "to improve" the *Goal*, "documentation of practice", and "to support" the *Goal*, "curricular developments as well as more effective use of technology". Furthermore, in a curious circular argument, "the use of technology" at the start is expected by the end, to even yield the *Goal*, "more effective use of technology".

In both Tables 8 and 9 the human labour of *using* technology, which could have been expressed in a verb as a *Material* process, becomes expressed as a noun, "The use of technology". This replacement of a verb (*using*) with a noun (*the use of*) is known as *nominalisation*. While nominalisation is a feature of academic writing, when over-used this way it has the effect of turning human labour into a form of commodity discussed more easily in terms of what 'the use of technology' might be profitably exchanged for. Yet in this transformation there is a distinct loss of humanity. The human actions needed "to create" "accessibility and flexibility of learning" (which could be considerable) are no longer accounted for when agency is simply attributed to "the use of technology". To place these observations into context with real experiences, we cite the conclusions of King and Flint, authors in this volume, in relation to "the use of ePortfolios". They concur that *the use of ePortfolios on their own will not enhance student learning*. Introducing and developing student learning through the technology of ePortfolios took King and Flint many hours of academic labour. This included both reflection on experiential learning and efforts to actively embed ePortfolio use within curriculum design (which we believe technology itself is simply not capable of undertaking on behalf of humans). Yet, these human academic interventions are required *to avoid being perceived as merely 'bolted-on'*, so that *'important learning affordances can be achieved'*. (See King & Flint, this Volume).

A further example of this pattern of writing policy that emphasises what 'the use of technology' might be profitably exchanged for, rather than what human teachers and learners (or indeed senior managers) are enabling through *their* use of technology, is provided in corpus line 5661, shown in Table 10 below.

The use of technology	to enhance	front line productivity and management reform	and	sharing	best practice
Actor	Process: Material	Goal		Process: Material	Goal

Table 10: Row 5661. Transitivity processes = Material, Material.

The activities described above cannot be achieved without considerable human effort but here again it is "the use of technology" that is the *Actor* that is 'to enhance' the *Goal* of "front line productivity and management reform" and furthermore undertake the *Material* process of "sharing" "best practice". In Table 11 the nominalisation (replacement of a verb with a noun), is no longer about technology undertaking a *Material* process on the part of humans. This time, human labour (in the form of thinking and mental effort to achieve something) is attributed to a document, idea or an entity.

This strategy for e-learning	strives to	realise the following vision
Senser	Process: Mental	Phenomenon

to use	e-Learning	to enhance	the student learning experience
Process: Material	Goal	Process: Material	Goal

Table 11: Row 5224. Transitivity processes = Mental, Material, Material.

In Table 11, it is "This strategy for e-learning" that undertakes a *Mental* process, as a *Senser*, and "strives to" realise a vision on behalf of humans. Also noticeable is that 'the student learning experience' comes right at the end of a series of processes undertaken, not by humans, but by a "strategy". Students are finally discussed as a static, nominalised singular entity called "the student learning experience" and not as an active, diverse group of people who will experience learning in the plural.

These repeated examples in which a nominalised entity enacts the processes that would normally be attributed to human beings reveal a phenomenon that, without a close linguistic analysis, would be hard to detect. This is the problem – human material practices of learning and doing are persistently de-valued by policy discourse that pre-determines the expected 'return' from technology and labour as commodities. These patterns of words in policy and university strategy statements can alter perceptions of how the labour of learning and teaching with technology is organised. People are removed from statements where they would natu-rally be mentioned as undertaking a task. They are replaced by entities that perform processes for them, like 'the use of technology' 'to enhance' or 'the strategy' that 'strives' on their behalf. Not only do nominalised claims remove any explicit indicator of agency (Simpson and Mayr, 2010: 68) they also remove accountability. This makes it hard to know exactly who makes these choices, whether they are consciously decided or not. Fundamen-tally, transitivity examples reveal how policy discourse can limit people's capacity to manage change. A lack of human representation amounts to a loss of power; if we cannot notice our own performance as co-creators with technology (see Newton, this volume), then we are disconnected from our own practice within the policy for technology-enhanced learning. Policy no longer links with practice, and any aspirations we may have for human practice to inform policy will struggle to succeed.

Implications and insights for further debate

At this time, in UK higher education (and globally) where the reverbera-tions of the global economic crisis are still being felt, policy discourse is being shaped by a neo-liberal agenda, often playing out as a call for greater marketisation of higher education, as is apparent in the UK Government White Paper: *Higher Education: Students at the heart of the system* (BIS, 2011). Universities have responded to this agenda either by accepting the notion of students as customers of the higher education 'offer', or as partners within it. Given the possibility of these two radi-cally different responses, a policy discourse context characterised by a tendency to conceal the need for human agency in the design, delivery and participation in learning opportunities is troublesome to say the least.

In the example texts above, students and lecturers are removed from their connections with the technologies they encounter in real processes of learning and teaching. Their human actions (seen in the analysis as *Material, Verbal* and *Mental* processes) are attributed to technologies and strategies instead. Thus, in this form of language, human social relations, not technology, are discussed as if they were 'things', whereby nominalisa-tions in language result in a form of 'reification' (Lukács, 1971) and human relations become traded as objects. Given that so much human labour now involves digital technologies, this must surely interest educators in terms of what this means for students' learning, and indeed instructors' teaching, in higher education. So, in this second section we consider some implications of these linguistic insights, with reference to critical social theory about *technology, language* and *learning*.

First, in critical theory about *technology*, the broader literature has been strongly criticised in some quarters for omitting discussions about ways that objects and technologies *themselves* might 'act' to transform society, even replace the roles of people (Matthewman, 2011). Technology has been referred to as the 'missing masses' of social theory (Latour, 1992), with the focus on human social interactions alone. According to Olsen

(2003), where theorists avoid discussing technology in literature this is due to a perceived domination of human relationships which can become traded as if they were objects.

However, technology, like language, is part of the social practice of learning in higher education. Students (whether treated as customers or partners in their education) do not simply turn up at university to have technology act on their behalf. Technology is 'constitutive' (MacKenzie & Wajcman, 1999) in people's lives, enabling or constraining what they do inside and outside of university. Students submit ideas through it, they carry it, wear it and search through it constantly as they communicate and learn. While Latour raised the important point about an absence of *technology* in social theory texts, we would argue the *transitivity analysis* above shows an absence of humans in educational technology policy texts. Here, it is *people* that seem to be absent in the language, not *technology*. Technology is discussed not as an intimate personal encounter, but as a 'neutral' external agent, imbued with a calculating political reasoning related to value.

Secondly, in terms of *language*, in the discourse, the natural activities of people learning by using technology seem to become separated from their original constitutive context. Statements like 'the use of technology' then take over to perform the goals of a neo-liberal economic agenda, rather than an emancipatory learning agenda in which people would co-construct their ideas with technology. This then limits what might be envisioned and discussed. Such textual arrangements may not be intentional, yet, collectively and globally, they can build a 'fixed' impression (from one particular paradigm but not necessarily others) of what educational technology means within the university. Thus they form a basis for communicating policy, which we need to question critically.

The role of language in constituting the identities of organisations such as higher education has been explored by linguists as a principal means through which institutions create their own social reality (Mumby & Clair, 1997: 181). Critical discourse analysis is one way to examine what kinds of powerful relationships are negotiated in the discourse (Fairclough & Wodak, 1997: 258) and also to question if it might be otherwise. *Transitivity analysis* is also just one way to examine how language is experienced (Halliday, 1994). However, it enables us to discover who the actors are, who is acted upon, what processes are involved in that action and who or what is missed out. The grammatical choices that are made may not be deliberate but they are still political choices involving power, given these are not the *only* ways to express relationships between students, instructors, technology and learning. These policy statements cannot be verified easily because technology has been separated in the discourse from its social and political contexts, from power and from culture. By this account, educational technologies could be destined for failure as an emancipatory concept if people constantly use language that brackets out (and thus fails to recognise or account for) human endeavour as the only true enabling factor.

Thirdly, in terms of *learning*, critical pedagogy (Freire, 1972; Giroux, 2004) provides a route to informed thought about more inclusive educational relations. Freire famously denounced a *"banking' model of education where knowledge is bestowed on students. To deposit only one version of 'how things are"* negates education and knowledge as processes of inquiry and critique (Freire, 1972:72). If policy routinely treats human and technological relations as if they were simply connections between 'things' to yield an 'exchange value', then this reinforces a banking transactional approach that perhaps calls for a form of resistance. The terrain of the body is an important site of resistance and change in education (Giroux and McLaren, 1989). Our bodies mediate both technology and language in our learning situations and this needs to be acknowledged in our policy language. If people cannot recognise themselves in language about their own learning, they lose perception of their power to change a dominant learning culture. Yet learning involves change as people acquire new knowledge and, in a critical approach towards pedagogy, people need to be empowered not only to interpret the world but also 'to change it' (Marx, 1867).

At the very least, critical pedagogy involves *"critically engaging dominant public transcripts and values within a broader set of historical and institutional contexts"* (Giroux, 2004:34). Once we get past an acceptance of the notional equation highlighted in our introduction, which assumes the inevitability of securing gains from technology deployment within a higher education context, we can engage in action that reclaims people's subjective conceptual space to develop their own critical technological knowledge and contextual digital identities.

TEL as a technology-language-learning nexus

In this last section we suggest that in exploring *technology*, *language* and *learning* critical theory can support alternative and more inclusive understandings of technology-enhanced learning as a *technology-language-learning* nexus in which 'enhancement' is not simply seen in the narrow economic terms of 'exchange value'. Technologies extend our bodies (McLuhan, 2005) and, since the electronic age, our senses too (Matthewman, 2011) but when treated as discrete entities they can hide the political economic context that brought them into being. Therefore, rather than closed statements about universal forms of use, we invite our audience to seek new ways of opening up language about Technology-Enhanced Learning and for humans to reoccupy it.

In earlier analysis, we examined the discourse of TEL to reveal what could be contended as oppressive social practice through the marginalisation of human agency. We argued that in policy language, the crucial linkages and interplay of the constitutive parts of the technology-language-learning nexus can become severed. Re-establishing critical links between human labour and technology, linguistic communication and learning interactions can create new value. Parallel consideration of these three constituents avoids a one-dimensional emphasis on technology in terms of 'exchange value' alone.

We need to reconnect human endeavour with the claimed (economic) gains attributed to technology and strategy and also reconnect people with each other, as policy discourse persistently removes these intimate relationships that are important in praxis. Our use of a 'nexus' to frame discussion reminds us that learning through technology is a complex individualised composition that immerses humans in *technology*, *language* and *learning*. Students and instructors experience these interactions in diverse ways as they endeavour to build knowledge. For constructive debate, these composite human encounters require a language of critique and possibility, not a transactional account aligned to 'exchange value'.

Conclusions

Woven through policy discourse for Technology-Enhanced Learning is a simple economic calculation: *in exchange for the use of technology there will be enhanced forms of learning.* Yet discourse based only on 'exchange value' (Marx, 1867) inhibits raising questions about the diverse ways students experience technology in their learning and throughout life. It also provides a vehicle for political economic agendas to make simplified claims in the name of technology, which can distort the values of human learning communities in higher education.

We argue that in technology-enhanced learning policy literature, rather than being omitted, technologies are very much present. In closed relationships with each other, they are attributed with responsibilities and abilities, to think, speak and act on behalf of people. Humans are not present in this discourse; people are removed from their own teaching, learning and management contexts, from their relationships with technology and with other human beings.

With the focus on technologies not the powerful social and political forces that surround them (including language), important academic questions are not being asked – questions, for example, which address the neo-liberal (and capitalist generally) trend for proliferating technologies to intervene between people or to replace them (Matthewman, 2011). The empirical approach described in this chapter is just one way to expose policy choices in *language* about *learning* with *technology*.

We invite other authors to come forward with further ways to connect critical social theory with the practices of technology-enhanced learning. Solidarity is needed for people actively engaged with *their* technologies in *their* learning situations to re-write themselves into this discourse, and for people using technology to learn what needs to be included in this language, and acquire the power to act. We have suggested a more emancipatory way to reconstruct technology-enhanced learning: envisaging it as a *technology-language-learning* 'nexus' where critical social theory about the composite nexus term, not just the components, might be actively applied to academic practice. This reminds us that there is no automatic 'exchange value' for learning when we interact with technology, no matter how much it is described in this way in policy language. The language promises a lot but on closer scrutiny the choices are made by technologies, not people. This reminds us to question how choices *we* make about technology-enhanced learning can effect change if we are absent from this discourse. If political discourse reduces ways to conceive of our own learning technology practice, then we suggest that, as humans, we have been absent from it for too long. It is now time for us to reoccupy the language...before we are gone from it altogether.

About the authors

Sarah Hayes is a Lecturer in Technology-Enhanced and Flexible Learning in the Centre for Learning Innovation and Professional Practice at Aston University, Birmingham, England. She can be contacted at this email: s.hayes@aston.ac.uk

Paul Bartholomew is Professor of Learning and Teaching and Director of the Centre for Learning Innovation and Professional Practice at Aston University, Birmingham, England. He can be contacted at this email: p.bartholomew@aston.ac.uk

Bibliography

Baker, P. (2006). *Using Corpora in Discourse Analysis*. London: Continuum.

Bayne, S. (2014). *What's wrong with 'technology-enhanced learning'?* In Proceedings of the Networked Learning 2014 Conference, 7-9 April 2014, Edinburgh, UK.

BIS (2011). *Higher education: Students at the heart of the system*. London: TSO, June 2011 Cm 8122.

Conole, G. C. & M. Oliver (2002). Embedding Theory into Learning Technology Practice with Toolkits. *Journal of Interactive Media in Education*, No. 8, pp 1-28.

European Commission (2009). *Educating Europe Exploiting the benefits of ICT*. Online Resource: http://cordis.europa.eu/ictresults/pdf/policyreport/INF%207%200100%20IST-R%20policy%20report-education_final.pdf [Accessed 22 April 2014].

Fairclough, N. and R. Wodak. (1997). Critical Discourse Analysis. In T. A. van Dijk (Ed.). *Discourse as social interaction*. London: Sage Publications, pp. 258-284.

Fairclough, N. (2007). Global Capitalism and Change in Higher Education: Dialectics of Language and Practice, Technology, Ideology. In *BAAL conference: Edinburgh.*

Freire, P. (1972). *Pedagogy of the Oppressed.* Middlesex: Penguin Education.

Giroux, H. A. & P. McLaren (Eds.) (1989). *Critical Pedagogy, the State, and Cultural Struggle.* Suny Press.

Giroux, H. (1992). *Border crossings.* New York. Routledge.

Giroux, H. A. (2004). Critical Pedagogy and the Postmodern/Modern Divide: Towards a Pedagogy of Democratization. *Teacher Education Quarterly,* Vol. 31, No. 1, pp. 31-47.

Greener, I. & L. Perriton (2005). The political economy of networked learning communities in higher education. *Studies in Higher Education,* Vol. 20, No. 1, pp. 67-79.

Habermas, J. (1971). *Theory and Practice.* London: Heinemann.

Halliday. M. A. K. (1994). *An Introduction to Functional Grammar.* 2nd edition, London: Arnold.

Hayes, S. (2014). Learning from a deceptively spacious policy discourse. In *Proceedings of the Networked Learning 2014 Conference,* 7-9 April 2014, Edinburgh, UK.

HEFCE (2009). *Enhancing learning and teaching through use of technology: a revised approach to HEFCE's strategy for e-learning.* Online Resource: http://www.hefce.ac.uk/media/hefce1/pubs/hefce/2009/0912/09_12.pdf [Accessed 21 April 2014].

IIlich, I. (1973). *Tools for Conviviality.* New York: Harper & Row.

Jessop, B (2008). The Knowledge Based Economy. Article Prepared for *Naked Punch.* Online Resource: http://www.nakedpunch.com/ [Accessed 22 April 2014].

Joint Information Systems Committee (2009). *Effective Practice in a Digital Age.* Online Resource: http://www.jisc.ac.uk/publications/ programmerelated/2009/effectivepracticedigitalage.aspx [Accessed 21 April 2014].

Latour, B. (1992). Where Are the Missing Masses? The Sociology of a Few Mundane Artifacts. *Shaping Technology/Building Society: Studies in Sociotechnical Change,* 225-258.

Lukács, G. (1971). *History and Class Consciousness.* London: Merlin.

MacKenzie, D. & J. Wajcman (1999). *The Social Shaping of Technology.* Open University Press.

Marcuse, H. (1991). *One-Dimensional Man: Studies in the Ideology of Advanced Industrial Society.* London: Routledge.

Marx, K. (1867). Capitalism and the modern labour process. Capital, volume 1. In R. C. Scharff & V. Dusek (Eds). (2003). *Philosophy of technology: The technological condition: An anthology.* Oxford, UK: Blackwell.

Marx, L. (1997). 'Technology: The Emergence of a Hazardous Concept', *Social Research*, Vol. 64, No. 3, pp. 965-988.

Massey, D. (2013). Vocabularies of the economy. *Soundings*, No. 54, pp. 9-22.

Matthewman, S. (2011). *Technology and Social Theory*. New York, NY: Palgrave.

McLuhan, M. (2005) *Understanding Media: Lectures and Interviews.* Cambridge, MA: MIT Press.

Morrison, K. (2006). *Marx, Durkheim, Weber: Formations of Modern Social Thought.* Pine Forge Press.

Mumby, D. K. & R. P. Clair (1997). Organizational Discourse. *Discourse as Social Interaction*, 2, pp. 181-205.

Olsen, B. (2003). Material Culture After Text: Re-membering Things. *Norwegian Archeological Review*, Vol. 36, No. 2, pp. 87-104.

Price, S. (2005). *Review of the Impact of Technology-Enhanced Learning on Roles and Practices in Higher Education.* Online Resource: http://hal. archives-ouvertes.fr/docs/00/19/01/47/PDF/Price-Kaleidoscope-2005.pdf [Accessed 23 April 2014].

Scott, M. (1997). PC Analysis of Key Words—and Key Key Words. *System*, Vol. 25, No. 2, pp. 233-245.

Selwyn, N.; S. Gorard & S. Williams (2001). 'The role of the 'technical fix' in UK lifelong education policy' *International Journal of Lifelong Education*, Vol. 20, No. 4, pp. 255-271.

Simpson, P & A. Mayr (2009). *Language and Power.* Abingdon, Oxon: Routledge.

Chapter Six

iBook technology to encourage self-assessment in the classroom

Nicola Bartholomew & Graham Kelly

Introduction

There has been significant interest in the academic community about the pedagogic applications of the *Apple iPad* since its first release in 2010. Yet current literature conveys some mixed messages about the perceived value of this technology in educational contexts. Post-PC mobile tablet computers such as the *iPad* can offer students greater flexibility in how and when they learn (Rankine & Macnamara, 2014). Students have expressed enthusiasm for using *iPads* as learning tools (Davis *et al.*, 2012) and consider them motivating, engaging, interesting and fun. A more cynical viewpoint, also found in literature, has dismissed tablet technologies as novelty items, some contending that any initial enthusiasm for this mobile device, boosted perhaps by glossy advertising, is doomed to fade. Hu (2011) offers polarised opinions which contrast the perceptions of *iPads* as passing novelties with perceptions of *iPads* as 'versatile tools' with a multitude of educational uses; for example, to support self-regulated learning. Subramanian (2012) suggested that the evidence-base was not sufficient to determine whether *iPads* are actually effective learning tools, but adoption of tablet devices for teaching and learning contexts appears to be increasing and, as a consequence, effective models of adoption are being explored (Clark & Luckin, 2013).

The chapter begins by exploring the overarching drivers for

implementing technology-enhanced learning and the potential pitfalls to consider when investing in tablet technologies at an institutional level. It then critiques the application of tablet computers, such as *iPads*, as personal learning tools for study management and considers alternative uses to promote self-assessment, self-regulation and active learning. It continues by examining the multimodal nature of *Apple's iBook* technology as a means to accommodate diverse learning styles within a blended learning context. Finally, it reviews our own practice which explores the use of an interactive formative eBook built using *iBooks Author*, made available on *iPads* within a higher education classroom environment.

The chapter offers an important contribution to this anthology on technology-enhanced learning in higher education because it demonstrates how eBook technology may be embedded within curriculum delivery to support self-assessment. Reading this chapter, you will gain the following insights:

+ how *Apple iBooks* can be deployed as student self-assessment tools in the classroom;
+ how academic staff ownership of learning technology innovations can play a significant role in their adoption by students;
+ how the deployment of a learning technology to change the mode of delivery offers a valuable opportunity to review wider teaching practice.

Drivers for technology-enhanced learning

In England, technology-enhanced learning is promoted by the Higher Education Funding Council for England (HEFCE) as a key part of learning and teaching in higher education. Their revised strategy for e-learning (HEFCE, 2009) highlights the impact technology has made on quality, the enhancement of learning, teaching and assessment while also considering associated advantages, such as improved satisfaction, retention and achievement for students. HEFCE (2009) also identifies quality enhancement and student satisfaction as the key drivers for institutions to invest in new technologies. Furthermore, the significance of assessment is emphasised and HEFCE acknowledges that technology can be deployed effectively to support both summative and formative assessment practice while appealing to a wider diversity of learners. It is reasonable, therefore, that Higher Education Institutions continue to make strategic investments in technology.

HEFCE do raise a cautionary note, emphasising the need for supporting academic staff development and for senior management 'buy-in'. Significant investments could be wasted, as learning technology sits dormant and under-utilised, if academic staff cannot appreciate or realise its potential pedagogic benefits and thus fail to embed it (where appropriate) within curriculum delivery. The impact of any learning technology depends upon how it is used; the technology itself should always play a supporting role to the learning activity (Clark & Luckin, 2013).

While considering investment, it would also be prudent to consider students' expectations of learning technology provision during their university experience. A 2008 survey by Jisc (formally the Joint Information Systems Committee: JISC), conducted via the market research company Ipsos MORI, revealed that students were not looking for technology gimmicks deployed merely for technology's sake; instead, they would only appreciate the use of technology where they could see tangible academic benefits. These students of the digital age also fostered an expectation that academic staff ought to be 'up to speed' with any learning technology that is deployed, although the student respondents were not fully aware of how technology could be used to supplement more traditional methods of teaching. This viewpoint (from 2008) may have already begun to alter as digital technology has claimed an ever-stronger presence within primary and secondary education (Department for Education, 2013). However, it remains incumbent on academic staff to deploy technology where appropriate, to engage learners and to help meet intended learning outcomes efficiently and effectively. We must also be transparent in relation to our pedagogic design choices and take time to explain the benefits of technology to our students while offering a clear rationale for its inclusion within curriculum design. Dobozy *et al.* (in this volume) highlights three types of domain knowledge within the TPACK model presented by Mishra and Koehler (2006) wherein technological knowledge is integrated with content (subject) knowledge and pedagogical knowledge. Congruency between these domains is necessary to ensure effective and contemporary curriculum design and delivery.

At the time of the 2009 HEFCE publication and the Jisc survey,

Apple iPad technology had yet to make its impact, but since then tablet computers have become firmly embedded in our culture. Rainie (2012) reported that a quarter of American adults owned tablet computers and eBook readers, while Statista (2014) predict that almost half of the UK population will be using tablet computers by 2016. An example of an eBook is the *Apple iBook* and this offers not only static digitised text but also multimedia and interactive elements that can afford a "potentially rich educational experience". The challenge for Higher Education today is to know how to respond to these possibilities (Jisc Observatory, 2012).

eBooks as personal learning devices

Tablet computers can be effective when deployed as personal learning devices (Clark & Luckin, 2013; Altena, 2014), providing platforms that can store a multitude of applications and study aids. Nevertheless, universities ought to be cautious if they are considering making an investment in providing tablet computers for students in this capacity. Student use of tablet computers will still be dependent on individual preferences for self-study. In a study to compare student perceptions of laptops and tablet computers, Curtis and Cranmer (2014) reveal that, although tablet computers were considered useful, 68 percent of surveyed students still preferred using a laptop computer for personal learning. This preference was associated with the perceived convenience of word processing; the laptop's large screens; and keyboards and software that make report/ assignment writing easier. This view is supported by the Mavri *et al.* (2014) study that shows student users dislike typing on touch-screen devices due to the amount of screen real estate obscured during typing.

Culén *et al.* (2011) considered the use of the *iPad* for active reading within an academic setting. Their study, which reviewed the use of the *iPad* as an electronic repository for course-reading supplemented by the *iAnnotate* tool for note-taking, revealed that student use of the *iPad* was lower than originally anticipated. A variety of inhibiting factors was identified – for example, students found that taking notes in class was often quicker and easier on paper than with *iAnnotate*. The issue of student ownership was also flagged as significant, as the *iPads* in this context were only available to students on loan and any notes, although stored on the cloud, were wiped at the end of each session. The study suggests that students in this context could not perceive any tangible benefits to using the *iPad* over their own laptop computer or paper for reading or for taking notes. In addition, a study by George *et al.* (2013) indicates that students still prefer paper handouts as study aids.

So, can eBook technology be incorporated more effectively into course delivery to ensure that student engagement warrants investment in tablet technologies? Academic staff 'buy-in' will be a pivotal factor here and there could be latent reservations about learning technologies that would limit effective adoption. Such reservations will be related to variable experience using technology rather than, for example, age-related factors (Eyal, 2014). Garrison and Kanuka (2004) acknowledge that technology supported learning methods although versatile, can potentially yield some *"daunting design challenges"* and Errington (2004:45) suggests that the *"infrastructure for flexible learning innovation exists as much at the level of dispositions as it does on any physically resourced plane"*.

This issue of variable dispositions and willingness to engage with learning technologies reinforces HEFCE's endorsement of faculty development schemes and these will be critical if technology-enhanced learning is to become a key part of our academic practice. In the Culén *et al.* (2011:560) study, it appears that the course instructor did not 'buy in' fully to the technology from the outset, having *"too little time"* to become familiar with the eBook technology and anticipating that *"students would figure out this new technology on their own"*. If technological innovations are to be accepted by students, faith in and adoption of technology-enhanced learning must begin with academic staff so they, as champions, can promote the technology effectively and encourage student engagement. Student achievement has been related to the high levels of enthusiasm and motivation demonstrated by their teachers (Rowan *et al.*, 1997; Covino & Iwanicki, 1996). We might also consider the enthusiasm and drive demonstrated by the 'early adopters' (Moore, 1991) of learning technology within the academic community since these enthusiasts can be the catalysts for innovation and change. Early adopters of innovative practice might become transformational leaders and change agents if they also exhibit the characteristics of champions for change. Howell and Higgins (1990), in their review of literature, identify champion-like qualities such as risk-taking and persistence and these inherent qualities are perhaps necessary to further encourage stakeholder acceptance of any innovation

– including the engagement of students as key stakeholders. Even so, to assure student engagement and achievement, this enthusiasm for using technology-based innovations such as the *iPad* and eBooks must remain underpinned by a transparent, well-planned course design aligned to intended learning outcomes.

Warren (2009), acknowledged that many eBooks can be little more than digitised pictures of a book, offering little added value through multimedia, and highlighted the need for eBooks with greater learning enhancement potential delivered through built-in interactivity. The *iBook Author* application can generate a multimedia environment including interactive elements such as scrolling sidebars, interactive images, galleries and pop-ups, note-taking features and quizzes. In this way, interactive *iBooks* can facilitate active participation in learning as they become cognitive tools to support and develop the cognitive processes of the learner. Nevertheless, Jisc Observatory (2012) warns that students will not necessarily welcome eBook technology unless there are clear advantages to be gained by their use.

iBooks for self-assessment

What about alternative uses for the *iPad* and *iBook?* Eyal (2014) identifies different contexts for students to use *iPads*, including personal and independent learning, but gives equal emphasis to integrating tablet technology into the classroom; here perhaps, is where the real challenge lies. Academic staff must feel confident, both in using learning technology and in the effective course design that integrates technology, to encourage active participation in the classroom. This active approach to learning is encouraged by Biggs and Tang (2011) and is considered particularly important when meeting the learning needs of diverse student populations in higher education today. Although we should encourage note-taking activity as an academic skill, which might empower students to become self-regulated learners (Zimmerman *et al.*, 1996), note-taking can also elicit low levels of engagement and passive learning during traditional lectures (Biggs & Tang, 2011). Self-regulation or self-management of learning describes how learners manage their thoughts, feelings and actions in order to achieve academically (Zimmerman & Schunk, 2001). Self-regulated learners may be distinguished as active learners who control their learning experiences through organisation and rehearsal of information to be learned (Schunk & Zimmerman, 1998). This view also supports a student-centered learning paradigm where students are actively engaged in learning and take responsibility for managing it (Lea et al., 2003). The multimedia nature of iBook technology can offer some key benefits to learners in this context to encourage active learning and self-regulation.

e-Book software may be considered an example of a multimodal information environment. Multimodal (or multimedia) communication is considered essential during the process of designing new technologies (Jewitt, 2006). Multimodal information environments may be defined as learning environments integrating both verbal and non-verbal modes of content presentation (Moreno and Mayer, 2007). The verbal mode of presentation will include elements such as text and audio and the non-verbal mode can include static graphical elements – i.e. illustrations, graphs, maps and dynamic elements such as video or animation. The contiguous integration of words with pictures, described as the spatial-contiguity effect, and the integration of visuals with spoken materials, described as the temporal-contiguity effect, have been associated with the enhancement of learning (Moreno & Mayer, 1999) as audio, digital and visual modes work together to help the learner construct meaning (Frye, 2014; Sorden, 2005). This contiguous presentation of multimedia content can also appeal to different learning styles within a diverse student body (Sankey et al., 2010) and it has been suggested that student performance is improved in learning environments that accommodate individual learning styles (Sankey et al., 2010).

A blended learning approach incorporating technology-based e-learning with traditional instructor-based learning might be seen as a preferred model to accommodate a wider variety of learning styles. Mano-chehr (2006) revealed that students who learn best through lectures, papers and analogies or through laboratories, field work and observations (learning through watching) tend to prefer web-based learning environments. Students who prefer simulations and case studies or brainstorming (learning by doing) prefer in-class instructor-based learning methods.

The iBook/iPad might also appeal to different learning styles as kinaesthetic learners can physically manipulate objects and characters via the touch-screen. 3D interactive images and video files can supplement text for visual learners and audio files support auditory learners. Student-to-student and student-to-academic discussions, emerging around *iBook* activities within a flexible learning classroom environment, can help consolidate these learning styles and reinforce understanding. The light-weight portability of the *iPad* can also encourage collaborative learning since the device can be passed easily between students to encourage multi-user engagement and subsequent discussion (Clark & Luckin, 2013).

Learners have the option to download existing textbooks from *Apple's Bookstore* and academic staff have the option to create their own custom-ised *iBooks* to incorporate course-specific content and self-assessment activities. Existing teaching material and activities from *PowerPoint* pres-entations or *Microsoft Word* documents, for example, can be imported to *iBooks Author* and customized with custom fonts, images, audio or video files by inserting additional 'widgets' such as the Review widget for self-assessment. Self-assessment tests can be embedded within an *iBook* page to supplement the text and review understanding. The widget offers multiple choice options or drag-to-target options. Media files (images, for example) can also be incorporated into such a review test and the more recent *iPads*, with Retina display and 2048 by 1536 resolution at 264 pixels per inch, generate highly detailed images. This can be particularly important if *iPads* are used within a health education context to view medical and anatomical images.

Race *et al.* (2005) signify the importance of student self-assessment and suggest that, as an integral part of learning, it can help students become evaluative, lifelong learners. The deployment of flexible learning materials to include self-assessment exercises can provide essential feed-back to students to guide their cognitive development. Self-assessment in a rudimentary form can be purely diagnostic, focusing the student on areas requiring remedial support while confirming existing competence in other areas (Race *et al.*, 2005). This formative, diagnostic self-assess-ment process can orient students toward their learning goals and provide feedback about how individual performance relates to these goals (Nicol & Macfarlane-Dick, 2005).

In view of the features available through the *iPad*, we wished to explore its application within an educational context. As an example of using *iPad* technology to support self-assessment, below we share a lived experience of our own practice in which *iPads* were deployed in a course review workshop for second year undergraduate radiography students.

We aimed to gather student feedback on the general design of the review workshop and on the perceived value of *iPads* to support self-assessment activities. This feedback was a fundamental element of an ongoing reflective teaching cycle. As members of a course team, we will often review our own teaching practice through mid-term course evaluations or we may gather ad-hoc student feedback during or after individual teaching sessions. This process enables us to gauge the collective knowledge of the student group in relation to the course content, as well as gauging the efficacy of an innovative teaching technique or a change in practice that may influence the learner experience. Effective teachers continually reflect on how they might teach better and are willing to collect student feedback on their teaching (Biggs & Tang, 2011; Dunkin & Precians, 1992).

Course evaluations have a dual purpose for quality assurance and for quality enhancement (Biggs, 2003). Kember and Kelly (1993) suggest that quality assurance mechanisms, such as standardised and regulated end-of-term evaluations, are imposed from above, whereas quality enhancement emerges from a grassroots level (although teaching innovations will typically require central funding). In contrast, mid-course or sessional evaluation can further quality enhancement attributes as the process of gathering intermediate feedback can help underpin the reflective strategy of an academic member of staff aiming to improve his/her practice. Mid-course or sessional evaluations can allow time for the academic to implement an innovation, gather student feedback, and reflect on the innovation while contextualising it within a theory of teaching before implementing the innovation more widely. This way, the informed practice can continue to influence the learning experience of the same cohort. Hansen (1994) acknowledges that end-of-course evaluations often come too late to improve a course or its instructor and mid-point evaluations, which although could be instigated by the course team at any point, rarely are. Perhaps this viewpoint has begun to change in the UK as the Government White Paper: Higher Education – Students at the Heart of the System (2011:6) places greater emphasis on student feedback where '*it will take on a new importance to empower students whilst at university*'.

The student feedback gathered at the conclusion of the review workshop, with examples shared within this chapter, demonstrates the value of actively seeking student perspectives at the point of implementation of a teaching innovation. By offering students regular opportunities to give feedback on their learning experience (and by acting on feedback), we reinforce communication channels and acknowledge students as co-designers of curricula.

Our lived experience

This teaching practice case is located within the context of a course (module) within the second year of an undergraduate radiography programme. The degree programme implements a mixed-mode curriculum whereby students experience traditional didactic lectures supplemented with group discussions, activity-based workshops and online learning activities during scheduled campus delivery time. In addition, fully half of their programme time is spent in a clinical practice environment. The *iBook* self-assessment activity was designed to support a course review session within a broader programme review study day for second year students. This review day was designed to enable students to recap course content during the few weeks leading up to their summative exam week.

Course leaders delivering the second year syllabus collaborated to offer the cohort a series of formative activities over the duration of the study day. As each course within the second year includes an exam-based item of assessment to test (mainly) declarative knowledge, with other coursework having been submitted previously, the course review day enabled participating students (n= 84) to engage with example questions relating to course content. Answers were shared and explained after the formative tests had been completed, either within the review session itself or during the following few days. The course review day afforded students some protected time for self-assessment and it was hoped that, through such participation, they would become familiar with the nature and themes of questions that are typically included in the end of year exams.

The *iBook* was built to be used as an activity within one of the course workshops in the programme study day; a course relating to skeletal radiography and associated image interpretation. The current pedagogic approach for the main delivery of this course uses online audio lectures and activities, handouts and traditional didactic lectures in the classroom.

Students then have the opportunity to review and apply core theory to practice in flexible learning workshops during additional campus-based study time. During these course workshops, the cohort typically receives a short didactic, overview of core concepts. This is supplemented with study activities for students to work through collaboratively in small groups at their own pace. The extant flexible learning activities for such workshops had been generated with *PowerPoint*, largely for the convenience of the course leader, due to familiarity with this software. The *PowerPoint* slides were available to be downloaded from the University's virtual learning environment, *Moodle*, to laptop computers in the workshop. The students accessed workshop content and questions in *PowerPoint*, and these would be ultimately reviewed and answered by the course leader as part of a session plenary. A similar format was used in the course review workshop with the inclusion of the *iBook* resource. The extant method of workshop delivery had proven to be effective, with course pass rates exceeding the minimum benchmark requirements. Furthermore, previous end-of-year evaluations revealed that earlier cohorts valued these interactive workshops. So why interfere with this method of delivery if it appeared to be working? As the Faculty of Health, Education and Life Sciences considers the purchase of hardware to support classroom-based teaching activities and replace existing laptop computers, we felt the course review day would be an opportunity to gauge the effectiveness of *iPads* as learning tools and to gather student feedback on their preferred mode of learning: via *iPad* and *iBook* or via laptop and *PowerPoint*.

One pragmatic reason for change relates to the quality of the current hardware we used to underpin our workshop activities. The forty laptop computers shared by the cohort of approximately one hundred, were bulky, slow to boot up and had fairly short (and getting shorter) battery lives. These computers are stored and charged in large securable mobile cabinets from which they are individually disconnected and distributed across the classroom at the beginning of a workshop session. They are subsequently collected and reconnected to the cabinet for charging at the end of the session. This process of computer disconnection, distribution, boot up, switch off and recharge, impacted significantly on the time available for learning in the workshop. Classroom occupancy is currently at a maximum and another class is always waiting to enter the classroom at the end of any given session. With this in mind, the Faculty of Health, Education and Life Sciences was in a position to review the ageing laptop hardware and consider an alternative and more appropriate replacement solution. The *iPad* was one alternative. Light, slim-line, with sufficient battery lifespan and with instant (always-on) access, it would allow students to get to work on a designated learning activity almost immediately. The changeover time between classes would also be reduced, releasing more time for learning. Although the pragmatics of the *iPad* influenced selection, the primary reason for considering it as an alternative tool for the classroom environment was the ability to generate a formative, interactive self-assessment resource via the *iBook* to encourage self-regulation and that learners would find both relevant and easy to use.

> "I wanted to create a resource that was more interactive for the student; a resource that could help engage the student before, during or after the class to enable the classroom sessions to be liberated for deeper learning. The production of the eBook was undertaken using the iBooks Author application; a tool I had not utilised previously. Through this process I taught myself how to use this application but also how to use Apple technology in general. The process was slow initially, however the process became more intuitive as I persevered. The subsequent eBook consisted of 25 pages of academic content including, images, quizzes or interactive diagrams. The book was created largely from pre-existing content, and took a total of 3 days to build. When comparing the creation of this resource to other teaching resources I would traditionally use, for example PowerPoint slides, it proved to be a much slower process. However, when compared to the construction of other more interactive resources such as online Moodle quizzes, development of the eBook is comparable for time to create the resource".
>
> (Course Leader)

The *iBook* had been designed to share the theory component of the workshop session and to actively trigger self-assessment during study. Students would be able to revisit key concepts before moving on to the self-assessment 'drag-to-target' and multiple-choice test questions that were embedded strategically throughout the *iBook* activity. In this way, students would be self-assessing, monitoring their progress at the point of learning while gaining immediate feedback. They could also gain immediate access to the information they needed to review any incorrect answers, either through the instruction element of the *iBook* activity or, as a wider study strategy, by accessing the Internet. Heick (2012:np) highlights this affordance stating that with the *iPad*, "*learners have the opportunity to 'face' content more immediately*" and there is no delay in waiting for the tutor to actuate learning. Furthermore, the role of the course leader moves from instructor to learning facilitator, better able to facilitate collaboration between him/herself and the students as co-learners (Clark & Luckin, 2014).

During the course workshop, students would undertake a short diagnostic test to gauge their knowledge of course content. Following the test, half the student group was issued laptops to access the *PowerPoint* activity. Students were familiar with this mode of learning as laptops had been used as teaching support tools earlier within the course. The students could work through the activity individually or collaboratively and at their own pace. The second half of the group was issued *iPads* to access the interactive *iBooks* activity. Again, students could work individually or collaboratively. After a period of study time, students were invited to re-take the diagnostic test. In this way, students would see the degree to which their individual test scores had altered after the activity. The course review day was a formative exercise to prepare students for final exams and encourage their self-regulation through the monitoring and evaluation of their own progress. We anticipated test scores would increase overall following a period of self-directed study but, crucially, students were prompted to note for themselves the degree of change between the two results. The highest gain was 51 percent between the pre- and post- test percentage points. In a few cases, a no-change or a decrease in percentage points of up to -5 percent was noted. Where scores had not increased significantly or had decreased, students were prompted to review their own study strategy and to contact personal tutors, course leaders and the Personal Development Department for study skills support. When preparing for exam-based assessments, students are to be encouraged to engage in active study to review course content and test their understanding.

At the conclusion of the course review day, students were invited to offer feedback to indicate whether they felt the day had enhanced their study strategy and to express their views on using either laptops or *iPads* as learning tools. In terms of the overall feedback from the revision day, this proved to be broadly positive. Students valued the opportunity to review course content, practice exam questions and prepare mentally for the pending assessment period.

> "*Thought it was a good idea with the stage 1 & 2 exams with revision in the middle*".

> "*...interesting method to raise awareness of what I actually take in when revising*".

> "*Learnt exam style questions and areas you need to revise more*".

> "*... (gave) me some confidence that I do have a basis of knowledge*".
> (Examples of student feedback following the review workshop)

While reflecting on the course review workshop, we noticed that average scores from post-activity diagnostic tests for the laptop group were comparable to those for the *iPad* user group. If the *iPad* was to be deployed routinely as a learning tool, we did not want it to impose any negative impact on student learning. We must emphasise that our results were gathered to reflect on and inform our own teaching practice and our data were not collected with the intention of making generalised claims for the wider academic community; the practice reported here is context-dependent and we would advocate implementing pilot studies in any new context.

In terms of curriculum development, it was important for us to gather student perceptions of using the different learning technologies in the classroom. In terms of the student feedback we received in relation to the experience of using the *iBook* activity via *iPads* or the *PowerPoint* activity via laptops, similarities were highlighted across both devices. These similarities broadly related to learner control of devices, their ease of use and the opportunity afforded by the workshop to consolidate knowledge.

Learner control

In both instances, students clearly valued being able to control the pace at which they worked through the learning activities:

"gives us the opportunity to go back and forth at our own pace, not so worried about writing everything down and missing important bits which allows you to focus more and retain more information".

(student feedback)

Biggs and Tang (2011) suggest that we should maximise these chances of students *wanting* to achieve intended learning outcomes and a student-centered approach to learning can strengthen student motivations to learn (Cheang, 2009). Our students appreciated the design of the workshop and the learning activities stored on both the laptop and the *iPad* as these shifted the focus of the activity away from the instructor while empowering the students to learn in an active way.

"(I liked being) able to search whatever I felt needed more attention which differed from everyone else".

"I also enjoyed the interactivity; I was able to look up what words meant instantly without having to ask the lecturer and stopping the session".

(student feedback)

Nygaard (in this volume) identifies eight conceptions of learning relating to both individual and a social processes. The classroom as a flexible learning environment enabled students to work individually on the activities at their own pace while offering the opportunity to discuss troublesome knowledge (Meyer & Land, 2003) with their peers or the facilitator. In this way, the classroom became a collegial yet personalised environment.

"(I liked) independent learning in a group – best of both worlds".

(student feedback)

However, for students favouring an intrapersonal learning style, the combination of a social and an individual learning space was not necessarily conducive to their study:

"(I disliked) people working at different paces so 10 different conversations going on at same time".

(student feedback)

Shen *et al.* (2007:271) identify key elements in determining educational activity in a social context as *"compliance with the requirements of others, conformity to the expectations of others, and identifying with the way others work"*. Establishing ground rules at the outset of a social learning activity, while identifying and acknowledging different learner styles, might help ensure learner engagement and satisfaction.

Ease of use

Students generally considered laptop computers and *iPads* easy to interact with. This may be due to student familiarity with both devices, especially when considering the aforementioned increased usage of tablet computers in the UK.

> *"(The laptop) provides the same information as an iPad would. iPads are easier to hand out and return which allows more time for learning"*.

> *"(The laptop) it has a big screen and easy to use"*.

> *(The iPad) "Easy to use, fast, (I liked) the quiz which was useful. The ability to highlight words I didn't understand in order to get a quick translation"*.
>
> (student feedback)

Where some students were less familiar with *iPad* technology, they valued receiving direction and support from their peers.

> *"Me being slightly pc/gadget unfriendly, I was glad to have help from peers. That said, loved it (iPad) and it really got my attention"*.
>
> (student feedback)

Such collaborative opportunities at the point of need may help to promote learner adoption of technology. Shen *et al.* (2007:277) suggest approaches that encourage student collaboration and communication *"may foster peer influence and support for students' adoption of technology"*.

Consolidation of knowledge

Students valued being able to review course content and strengthen their knowledge within a relaxed environment.

> "I felt a bit more relaxed in the session, it kind of felt like using my own laptop at home".
>
> (student feedback)

Zimmerman (2002) suggests that the self-regulated learner will identify their own strengths and limitations towards learning and will take appropriate corrective action when they encounter concepts they fail to understand. Our aim was to encourage this self-regulation process during the course review day and the flexible learning activities with *iPads* and laptops were aimed to encourage dialogue among peers and between tutors and peers. Furthermore, corrective action could be gained through Internet access to wider online resources.

> "Whatever you had just read was consolidated by the little quizzes throughout".

> "You were able to go at your own pace and go back to revisit information. The quizzes also helped to consolidate the knowledge".
>
> (student feedback)

Other considerations

The only consistently negative features identified by students using the Faculty laptop computers as learning tools was their heavy, bulky size and the slow boot-up time. Admittedly, both these factors can be attributed to the age of the computers and both could be resolved to some degree with the purchase of new, ultra portable, slimline laptops (with faster solid state drives) but these can be costly. Tablet computers such as the *iPad* can be a slightly cheaper alternative and the time to get 'up and running' at the beginning of a session with eBooks and other applications is much shorter.

The *iPad* may be seen as both effective and efficient within our context as it generates user feedback immediately at the point of learning. Heick

(2012) also acknowledges that learner familiarity with the *iPad* decreases demand for the user-knowledge required to access information, which in turn allows for greater focus on the information itself and so improves user satisfaction. User satisfaction is a significant consideration as it will influence subsequent engagement with a given learning tool to render it effective.

Our students valued the dynamic and intuitive functionality of the *iBook*, the easy zoom function to view radiological images more clearly and the tactile nature of the tablet device. They also valued the easy-to-access interactive quizzes supplementing the *iBook*. However, it is important to acknowledge that students could access *Moodle* quizzes via any of many web-enabled devices. Furthermore, capturing and logging quiz scores in the web-based VLE *Moodle* would enable the tutor to monitor test scores logged there to subsequently reflect on student progress and to make targeted interventions with individuals, or indeed the whole cohort, as necessary. Our student users also highlighted issues about accessing the learning activity beyond the classroom or on different platforms:

> "Only available on University iPads and not available for use of other tablets".

> "Should be a version where you can access at home without Apple products".
>
> (student feedback)

The *iBook* could have been published to *iBookstore* for student download during independent study but it would only be compatible with Apple devices, limiting the student audience. Institutions also might not want to make course-specific learning activities available globally via *iBookstore*. While learning institutions might have considered the standard purchase of tablet computers for new students, many institutions are now adopting the 'bring your own device' policy to acknowledge student choice of device and individual ownership. Personal devices can then include resources and applications to meet individual user needs. If we were to encourage such a policy, interactive learning applications accessible on a range of web-enabled devices (smartphones, tablets and computers) could be combined with cloud-computing and web-based systems for classroom activities, independent study and tutor monitoring.

The number of formative assessment applications available to educators to enhance the student learning experience is increasing (Dyer, 2014). For example, the *Socrative* application is a student response system compatible with web-enabled devices that enables students to respond to test questions in real time. The academic course team can view reports online with their student groups to encourage reflection and self-regulation while monitoring group progress. Activities within *Moodle* such as 'choice', 'questionnaire' and 'quiz' can be used in similar ways as student interaction and performance can be logged within the *Moodle* system.

As we reflect on our experience using the *iPad* and *iBook*, we are reminded that technology must be given a supporting role for the learning activity that must remain the principal focus. Our aim was to encourage a flexible, student-centered learning environment where students could take the opportunity to formatively review course content and test their knowledge collaboratively or individually. From our perspective, this was achieved, with students accessing activities on either *iPads* or laptops and by paper-based quizzes. Students valued the opportunity to consolidate knowledge and to discuss issues with their peers and tutors. Encouraging and supporting a bring-your-own-device policy to include applications where students can use their personal devices for active engagement within the classroom would afford students an increased sense of empowerment, which in turn could influence student motivations to learn (Nichols, 2006). We could also encourage the development of learning communities wherein students can connect and create and share their outputs for peer review and collaboration.

Academic staff can use the *iBooks Author* application to generate course-specific eBooks, in which learners can access media-rich content at the swipe of a finger, to help meet intended learning outcomes of a given course. Perhaps more crucially, students could be empowered by developing their own content using authoring applications. Tutor-generated eBooks may be deployed effectively to foster the development of declarative knowledge, i.e. knowledge expressed in verbal or other symbolic form. But for a learner to truly understand a concept, the locus of control could be given to them to construct their own eBook resource and their own functional knowledge. This way, the learner actively draws on their pre-existing knowledge and applies it by creating a cohesive learning resource that could be made available for peer-review.

Conclusion

Perhaps the novelty of the *iPad* still appeals to students and this might bias preference of it over laptop computers which could be viewed as equally useful in this context. However, the practical benefits of the *iPad* over a personal computer in terms of storage, battery life and instant access should not be overlooked, and these factors alone could influence purchase decisions within universities. Although the *iPad* was not designed originally for educational purposes, UK school surveys predict a growth in the use of tablet technology with 40 percent of e-learning to be via educational applications by 2020, an increased usage of nearly 12 percent since 2012 (QA Education, 2013). Mobile self-assessment applications could revolutionise teaching in higher education but curriculum designers must embrace this technology fully by linking it to assessment and championing its use to ensure that student acceptance and engagement warrants the initial investment.

We conclude by highlighting that, in addition to learning about the efficacy of the technology within our context, the opportunity of deploying a new technology-based mode of delivery enabled us to reflect, in a very focused way, on what we were expecting from the students. The act of planning and authoring the *iBook* was useful as a way to reflect on what we had taught over the duration of the course. The act of engaging in this rather straightforward evaluation of a device became a 'Trojan horse' for a valuable cycle of practitioner-led quality enhancement, since our reflections of what we have taught and what we expect from our students have prepared us to do a better job next year.

About the authors

Nicola Bartholomew is an Associate Professor (Learning and Teaching) at the Faculty of Health, Education and Life Sciences at Birmingham City University. She can be contacted at this email: Nicola.bartholomew@bcu.ac.uk

Graham Kelly is a Senior Lecturer at the Faculty of Health, Department of Radiography at Birmingham City University. He can be contacted at this email: graham.kelly@bcu.ac.uk

Bibliography

Altena, S. (2014). Implementing iPads as personal learning devices: Making the paperless MBA possible. *The 2014 – 1st International Conference on the use of iPads in Higher Education.*

Baruah, H. (2013). Just in time learning. *IOSR Journal of Humanities and Social Science*, Vol. 12, No. 4, pp. 53-57.

Biggs, J. (2003). *Teaching for quality learning at university. What the student does.* Buckingham, UK: SRHE and Open University Press.

Biggs, J. & C. Tang (2011). *Teaching for quality learning at university.* 4th Ed. Open University Press, pp. 34.

Cheang, K. I. (2009). Effect of learner-centered teaching on motivation and learning strategies in a third year pharmacotherapy course. *American Journal of Pharmaceutical Education.* Vol. 73, No. 3.

Clark, W. & R. Luckin (2013). iPads in the Classroom. What the research says. London Knowledge Lab: Institute of Education, University of London.

Covino, E. A. & E. F. Iwanicki (1996). Experienced teachers: Their constructs of effective teaching. *Journal of Personnel Evaluation in Education*, Vol. 10, pp. 325-363.

Culén, A.; B. K. Engen; A. Gasparini & J. Herstad (2011). *The Use of iPad in Academic Setting: Ownership Issues in Relation to Technology (Non) Adoption. Old Meets New: Media in Education* – Proceedings of the 61st International Council for Educational Media and the XIII International Symposium on Computers in Education Joint Conference. pp. 555 – 563.

Curtis, F. & S. Cranmer (2014). *Laptops are better. Medical students perceptions of laptops versus tablets and smartphones to support their learning.* Ninth International Conference on Networked Learning 2014.

Davis, A. M.; C. Waterbury & R. S. Robinson (2012). Technology enhancement tools in an undergraduate biology course. *Educause Review.*

Dunkin, M. & R. Precians (1992). Award winning university teachers' concepts of teaching, *Higher Education*, Vol. 24, pp. 483-502.

Department for Education (2013). *Digital Technology in Schools.*

Department for Business Innovation & Skills (2011). Higher Education: Students at the Heart of the System. White Paper. The Stationary Office. London.

Dyer, K (2014). 36 digital formative assessment tools for the classroom. *Teach.Learn.Grow. The education blog.* Online Resource: http://www.nwea.

org/blog/2014/update-36-digital-formative-assessment-tools-classroom/ [Accessed on 15 June 2004].

Errington, E. (2004). The impact of teacher beliefs on flexible learning innovation: some practices and possibilities for academic development. *Innovations in Education and Teaching International*, Vol. 41, No.1, pp. 45.

Eyal, L. (2014). Give them a fishing rod... the use of iPads by education students. *The 2014 – 1st International Conference on the use of iPads in Higher Education.*

Frye, S. K. (2014). *The implications of interactive ebooks on comprehension.* Rutgers University Community Repository.

Garrison, D. R. & H. Kanuka (2004). Blended learning: Uncovering its transformative potential in higher education. *The Internet and Higher Education.* Vol. 7, No. 2, pp. 95-105.

George, P.; L. Dumenco; R. Dollase; J. S. Taylor; H. S. Wald & S. P. Reis (2013). *Introducing technology into medical education: Two pilot studies.* Patient Education and Counselling. Vol. 93, No. 3, pp. 522-524.

Hansen, W. L. (1994). Bringing total quality improvement into the college classroom. In G. D. Doherty (Ed.). *Developing quality systems in education.* Routledge, p. 97.

HEFCE (2009). Enhancing learning and teaching through the use of technology 2009/12: a revised approach to HEFCE's strategy for e-learning.

Heick, T. (2012). What the iPad has done to education. *Teach Thought.* Online Resource: http://www.teachthought.com/learning/what-the-ipad-has-done-to-education/ [Accessed 11 January 2015].

Howell, J. M. & C. A. Higgins (1990). Champions of technological innovation. *Administrative Science Quarterly.* Vol. 35, No. 2, pp. 317-341.

Hu, W. (2011). Math that moves: Schools embrace the iPad. *The New York Times.* Online Resource: http://www.nytimes.com/2011/01/05/education/05tablets.html [Accessed 3 June 2014].

Jisc (2012). Preparing for Effective Adoption and use of Ebooks in Education. JISC Observatory TechWatch Series, Report No. 4.

Jewitt, C. (2006). *Technology, literacy, learning: A multimodal approach.* Routledge.

Kember, D. & M. Kelly (1993). Improving teaching through action research. *Green Guide*, No. 14.

Lea, S. J.; D. Stephenson & J. Troy (2003). Higher Education students' attitudes to student-centred learning: beyond 'educational bulimia', *Studies in Higher Education*, Vol. 28, No. 3, pp. 321-334.

Manochehr, N-N. (2006). The Influence of Learning Styles on Learners in E-Learning Environments: An Empirical Study. *Computers in Higher Education Economics Review*, Vol. 18, No. 1, pp. 10-14.

Mavri, A.; F. Loizides & N; Souleles (2014). A case study on using iPads to encourage collaborative learning in an undergraduate web development class. *The 2014 – 1ˢᵗ International Conference on the use of iPads in Higher Education*.

Meyer, J. H. & R. Land (2003). Threshold Concepts and Troublesome Knowledge 1 – Linkages to Ways of Thinking and Practising. In C. Rust (Ed.). *Improving Student Learning – Ten Years On*. OCSLD, Oxford.

Mishra, P. & M. J. Koehler (2006). Technological Pedagogical Content Knowledge: A framework for Teacher Knowledge. *Teachers College Record*, Vol. 108, No. 6, pp. 1017-1054.

Moore, G. (1991). *Crossing the Chasm*. Harper Business: New York.

Moreno, R. & R. Mayer (2007). Interactive Multimodal Learning Environments. *Educational Psychology Review*. Vol. 19, pp. 309-326.

Nicol, D. J. & D. Macfarlane-Dick (2005). Formative assessment and self-regulated learning: A model and seven principles of good feedback practice. *Studies in Higher Education*, Vol. 31, No. 2, pp. 199-218.

Nichols, J. D. (2006). Empowerment and Relationships: A classroom model to enhance student motivation. *Learning Environments Research*. Vol. 9, pp 149-161.

QA Education (2013). Increasing expectation on publishers to develop tablet apps. Online Resource: http://www.qaeducation.co.uk/increasing-expectation-on-publishers-to-develop-tablet-apps/. [Accessed 12 January 2015].

Race, P.; S. Brown & B. Smith (2005). *500 Tips on Assessment*. Routledge.

Rainie, L. (2012). 25% of American adults own tablet computers. *PEW Internet and American Life Project*. Online Resource: http://www.pewinternet.org/2012/10/04/25-of-american-adults-own-tablet-computers/ [Accessed 10 February 2014].

Rankine, L. & D. Macnamara (2014). iPads at the University of Western Sydney (UWS): Initiating institutional transformation. *The 2014 – 1ˢᵗ International Conference on the use of ipads in Higher Education*.

Rowan, B.; F. Chiang & R. J. Miller (1997). Using Research on Employees' Performance to Study the Effects of Teachers on Students' Achievement. *Sociology of Education*, Vol. 70, No. 4, pp. 256–285.

Sankey, M.; D. Birch & M. Gardiner (2010). Engaging students through multimodal learning environments: The journey continues. In C. H. Steel;

M. J. Keppell; P. Gerbic & S. Housego (Eds.). *Curriculum, technology & transformation for an unknown future*. Proceedings ascilite Sydney, pp. 852-863.

Schunk, D. H. & B. J. Zimmerman (Eds.) (1998). *Self-regulated learning: From teaching to self-reflective practice*. New York: The Guilford Press.

Shen, D.; J. Laffey; Y. Lin & X. Huang (2006). Social influence for perceived usefulness and ease of use of course delivery systems. *Journal of Interactive Online Learning*. Vol. 5, No. 3, pp. 270-282.

Sorden, S. (2005). A Cognitive Approach to Instructional Design for Multimedia Learning. *Informing Science Journal*. Vol. 8.

Statista (2014). Tablet user penetration rate in the United Kingdom from 2010 to 2017. Online Resource: http://www.statista.com/ statistics/249124/tablet-penetration-in-the-united-kingdom/. [Accessed 03 June 2014].

Subramanian, C. (2012). New study finds iPads in the classroom boost test scores. *Time Tech*. Online Resource: http://techland.time. com/2012/02/22/new-study-finds-ipads-in-the-classroom-boost-test-scores/ [Accessed 12 January 2014].

Warren, J. (2009). Innovation and the future of e-Books. *The International Journal of the Book*, Vol. 6. No. 1, pp. 83-94.

Zimmerman, B. J. (2002). Becoming a Self- Regulated Learner: An Overview. *Theory into Practice*. Vol. 41, No. 2, pp. 64-70.

Zimmerman, B. J. & M. Martinez-Pons (1996). Development of a structured interview for assessing students' use of self-regulated learning strategies. *American Educational Research Journal*, Vol. 23, No. 4, pp. 614-628.

Zimmerman, B. J. & D. H. Schunk (Eds.) (2001). *Self-regulated learning and academic achievement: Theoretical perspectives*. Routledge.

Chapter Seven

'Reality Bytes': reflections on the lived academic experience of e-portfolio use

Sarah King and Emma Flint

Introduction

Our chapter will examine the potential of e-portfolios to transform the learning experience of students in higher education. Over a number of years, e-portfolios have emerged as technological tools that hold the promise, in an educational context, of supporting and enhancing learning (CRA, 2009). In the first part of our chapter, we will explore the philosophy and theory underpinning their use in the context of developing reflective and experiential learners.

In the second part of our chapter, we share our personal journeys as two academics teaching within the Law School at Birmingham City University (BCU) who have embedded e-portfolios into the structural design of our modules. These contrasting case studies will focus on two quite distinct modules taught within the undergraduate law programme (referred to more commonly in the United Kingdom (UK) as the 'LL.B'). The first case study will examine a skills-based module taught in the first year that was one of the first within BCU to use e-portfolios as a resource for teaching and assessment. With the module now in its fourth year, we will consider how the use of e-portfolios has developed and how the challenges of embedding e-portfolios have been addressed. The second case study will compare the very recent introduction of e-portfolios into a core module in the second year on the LL.B, namely Land Law. As explained below, the e-portfolio approach has been used in this module to develop legal academic skills and enable students to demonstrate the process of their learning, rather than just the product, within a very traditional legal subject. Both case studies will offer an honest appraisal of our aspirations in using e-portfolios, the pressures that come with making significant change to a traditional subject by introducing technology, and the impact of that change on us and our students.

Finally, our chapter will draw together those critical incidents that can impact on the use and value of e-portfolios in higher education and will propose a list of things that make a difference when embedding e-portfolios within curriculum design. We hope that by sharing our lived experiences (which underpins the 'Reality Bytes' notion of our title) we will be able to support others to use e-portfolio technology in their own practice.

The philosophy and theory of e-portfolios

In the UK, the 2005 report *Harnessing Technology: Transforming Learning and Children's Services* (DfES, 2005) prioritised personalised support to learners and envisaged that an individual's progress through the education system would eventually be supported by an e-portfolio, described as a personal online space where learning could take place and achievements would be recorded. This would be available to students throughout their education and beyond, into the workplace and as part of a move towards lifelong learning (explored further in relation to personal development planning later in this section).

As the use of e-portfolios has grown, so has the number of definitions of the term, each perhaps guided by the ultimate end use of the e-portfolio itself. However, there is growing agreement that whatever term is used, any definition must encompass both the product (i.e., the actual digital artefact) and process of learning described by Jisc (a leading agency that champions the use of digital technologies in UK education and research) as *"the rich and complex processes of planning, synthesizing, sharing, discussing, reflecting, giving, receiving and responding to feedback"* (Jisc, 2008:6). For the purposes of our chapter, the definition that most aligns itself with our philosophy of learning and teaching using e-portfolios is that of Sutherland and Powell, 2007 as cited in Jisc (2008:7): *"An e-portfolio is a purposeful aggregation of digital items – ideas, evidence, reflections, feedback etc., which 'presents' a selected audience with evidence of a person's learning and/or ability".*

In our case studies we will discuss how this was translated into our design and allowed our students to share both the products of their learning (a memorandum of legal advice on a problem-based question or a CV for example) and the process that they had undertaken (a research trail or a reflective piece that demonstrates how they sought out and engaged with feedback).

While there is little evidence at present to suggest that e-portfolios have become embedded into the entire UK education system, it is clear that there is an emerging focus on the potential benefits of using them to support learning. In 2007, research commissioned by the British Educational Communications and Technology Agency, ('Becta', a government agency, now closed, that promoted innovative use of technology in learning) examined case studies of e-portfolio use across the whole of the education sector and found they had the potential to have substantial impact on learning outcomes (both pre-declared and emergent) but needed to be part of a *"joined up learning and teaching approach rather than as a discrete entity"* (Hartnell-Young et al., 2007:4). This 'joined up' approach has underpinned our own instructional design and will be discussed further in the next section.

The developments mentioned have a high degree of relevance to the higher education sector. The increasing importance of learner-centred activity (Hager, 2013) and developing employability (Flint, 2014) in our students have contributed towards an interest in developing e-portfolios as a valuable learning and teaching tool. BCU began to consider alternative platforms for e-portfolios in 2007 and subsequently piloted the use of *Mahara* in 2009. *Mahara* is one of a range of open source e-portfolio systems that allows students to create customisable and flexible web pages in which they can upload files, share reflective journals and collaborate with their peers and academic staff. One of its advantages is that it is able to interact with virtual learning environments, such as *Moodle*, (used at BCU). In the School of Law, we developed our *e-Learning Strategy* in 2010 whose goal was to use technology-enhanced learning to develop flexibility in curriculum design and delivery, with a view to enhancing the student experience wherever possible. e-portfolios became a key feature of this strategy and a large scale pilot, discussed in the first case study, was rolled out that year.

e-portfolios and lifelong learning

The development of our *e-Learning Strategy* was also taking place at a time when the need to support students more actively in engaging with personal development planning (PDP) was in sharp focus. A review of the future of higher education in the UK had been conducted in 1997 by the National Committee of Inquiry into Higher Education (NCIHE) and the published Dearing Report recommended that all higher education institutions (HEIs) give their students the opportunity to engage in PDP, defined as: *"A structured and supported process undertaken by an individual to reflect upon their own learning, performance and/or achievement and to plan for their personal, educational and career development"*, NCIHE (1997:372). As a result, the Quality Assurance Agency (QAA), the body responsible for safeguarding the standard of universities in the UK, made it a requirement that all HEIs have PDP mechanisms in place to support students (QAA, 2009).

Inextricably linked to the model of PDP is the concept of reflection. The Dearing Report definition of PDP encapsulates the idea of reflection allowing for lifelong learning by developing a greater sense of consciousness about choices in all personal, academic and professional areas of a student's journey. This is mirrored in the academic theory that underpins the concept of reflective learning (Schön, 1983; Kolb, 1984; Race, 2010). By understanding the context of their actions and making sense of their choices, students are encouraged to take a deeper and more student-centred approach to their learning (see DePew *et al.*, this volume). Reflection allows for a clear recognition of areas for improvement and the ability to action-plan meaningfully for change. Conversely, it allows a student also to recognise what they have done well and ensure that the process underpinning that success can be repeated effectively. It is this process of metacognition at the heart of reflective practice that leads some academics to believe that: *"Perhaps no other concept offers higher education as much as the potential for engendering lasting and effective change in the lives of students as that of reflection."* Rogers (2001:51 as cited in Barnard, 2011).

However, the difficulties in promoting reflective learning in students are well recognised and questions about effectively embedding reflection within curriculum design, along with how to assess reflection, are not new (Bufton & Woolsey, 2010). In terms of the Law School at BCU, we hoped that using e-portfolios within our curriculum design would be an appropriate tool to support the development of reflection in our students and to structure and support PDP. Use of e-portfolios in this way in HEIs is a growing trend (Strivens, 2006). Our first case study outlining our initial use of e-portfolios in a stand-alone 'Skills' undergraduate law module lies within this context.

Case study 1: e-portfolios supporting personal development planning

Skills, Processes and Scholarship (for the purposes of this chapter known as 'Skills') is a first year compulsory module within the LL.B. The module aims to provide students with foundation knowledge of the principal features of the English Legal System and to facilitate the development of many of the practical lawyering, study and employability skills (Flint, 2014) required by students throughout their legal education and into employment (King, 2014).

Prior to the adoption of e-portfolios within the Law School, students were assessed within the Skills module by submitting a paper-based portfolio that demonstrated competence in a number of assessments designed to evaluate the student's ability to conduct legal research, analyse legal texts and communicate orally via a 'moot' (a mock trial). However, the limitations of the logistics of submitting and marking paper-based portfolios in an ever-growing student first year intake meant that the module was ripe for innovation.

In the summer of 2010, colleagues, including the then Skills module leader, were encouraged to get involved in discussions regarding the development of the Law School's *e-Learning Strategy*. As part of this process, a showcase event was held demonstrating to academic staff the opportunities that e-portfolios could offer. Training in using *Mahara* was also organised for all Law School staff during the early curriculum re-design phase. Support and engagement of academic staff is vital to the success of projects utilising new technology: *"Early adopters may run with new ideas, but will struggle to implement them effectively without support from their colleagues and senior staff."* Jisc (2008:16).

As a result of this, the Skills module was re-designed during the summer of 2010 to embed the use of e-portfolios and reflective writing within the module. In the re-designed module, students were solely assessed by an e-portfolio rather than a paper-based portfolio. Students were still expected to demonstrate competency in the same assessments throughout the year, as required by the previous Skills module design. However, the functionality of the e-portfolio also allowed students to reflect on the processes and learning activities in seminars that underpinned those key assessments through the *Mahara* 'journal' function. Students were also expected to demonstrate in their e-portfolio how they had engaged with employability throughout the first year of their studies and had to provide evidence in their e-portfolios of their engagement with PDP. They were also required to include in their e-portfolios copies of their curriculum vitae and copies of their completed PDP activities signed-off by the student's personal tutor.

The choice was made within the Skills module re-design to explicitly assess both the new reflective content and the students' designs of their e-portfolios. This was intended to prompt student engagement with the curriculum design and methods of assessment, a factor that other academics had found difficult when such reflection and use of e-portfolios was viewed as more of a 'bolt-on' to learning (Bufton *et al.*, 2010). However, the assessment weighting for these new elements was relatively small, in terms of the overall weighting of the constituent parts of the e-portfolio (10 percent each for reflective content, engagement with employability and personal tutoring elements and 5 percent for the design of the e-portfolio itself). This minimal weighting was intentional as the previous Skills module leader felt that the reflective process was a personal undertaking for students to navigate and putting too many constraints on the format of reflection would discourage students from engaging with the process.

The initial roll-out of the new Skills module design and use of e-portfolios was ambitious. In September 2010, over 200 first-year law students began the new module and took their first tentative steps into the world of e-portfolio use. From an early stage, it became obvious that the reality of this first implementation roll-out would be a steep learning curve and that, in order to deal with it, members of the Skills teaching team would need to be flexible in adapting to the student response to both the use of e-portfolios and reflective writing. We had assumed that students were 'digital natives' (Prensky, 2001) and it rapidly became obvious that they were not. This finding is echoed by the evidence of other studies exploring the extent to which first year students are 'digital natives' (Kennedy *et al.*, 2005). Students were given initial training in how to use *Mahara* at the outset of the year but it became obvious throughout the year, when they were encouraged to share their e-portfolios with academics for formative feedback, that students were struggling with using *Mahara*. This was not only a student problem – many academic staff in the Law School who were not actively using *Mahara* themselves, also required additional top-up training. However, too often, drop-in *Mahara* support sessions run by IT colleagues were poorly attended and the costs of running such sessions led to perceptions of poor value of this training activity.

Still, modular feedback at the end of the first iteration of the Skills module in April 2011 was generally positive. 117 students out of a cohort of 200 students responded to a questionnaire designed to evaluate e-portfolio use within the Skills module. In response to the question *'How easy or difficult did you find it to create your Mahara e-portfolio?'*, 37 students responded they found *Mahara* easy to use straight away. The remaining 80 students reported that, despite initially struggling with new technology, they found that with perseverance they had mastered *Mahara*:

> "I found the initial understanding on how to create a view a little complicated and I needed a few attempts before I felt confident in completing the task." (Student 1)

Sixty-eight students out of the 117 respondents provided positive feedback to the question *'What did you like about Mahara?'*. Common themes arising from the responses centred on the convenience of the online nature of working with an e-portfolio and the autonomy it can create in learners:

> "It is useful in that work can be submitted from home without the need to be at university." (Student 2)

> "I liked how you had everything in your own hands. I could choose a colour scheme and decide exactly where different things such as my blogs, friends and personal information could go." (Student 3)

"I like the fact that it can be personalised to each individual. This is one feature I found to be quite unique." (Student 4)

Students also seemed to be embracing the positive elements of reflective practice and considering employability from the outset of their academic studies:

"I believe Mahara is useful for selling yourself to potential employers that may want more than just a normal CV as [by sharing your e-portfolio] it gives an insight into someone's personality more." (Student 5)

"You can store important work such as CVs and cover letters in a convenient location where you can access it whenever you want. It is also a good way to reflect on previous years [sic] work and see how you have developed your skills whether it be writing technique or just to add to your CV to make it as complete as possible." (Student 4)

However, the module feedback also revealed a range of student concerns in the 58 responses to the question *'What did you dislike about using Mahara?'*. Analysis of the responses highlighted four key themes: problems with getting a grip on the technology (as explored above); anxiety regarding e-portfolio security; a lack of understanding of the value of reflection; and how to develop reflective writing skills. These themes were not surprising given constraints of curriculum design within the Skills module at that time. Students were not given specific guidance, or teaching sessions/activities within lectures or seminars, on the concept of reflection. This largely reflected the assessment weighting of only 10 percent for this element of the e-portfolio. However, it appeared that this skill was the most alien for the students to grasp and, even though it was only worth a small proportion of the overall assessment marks for the e-portfolio, it seemed to be the most troubling element for the students. In addition, giving students a 'blank page' for reflective content and minimum expectations as to e-portfolio content, caused them anxiety. Rather than embrace the creativity that this could bring, students took a more strategic approach to learning (Ramsden, 1992) and wanted exemplars, plus a more concrete assessment briefing from the outset of the module.

After another positive roll-out of the module in the academic year

2011/12 to a larger student cohort (approx. 240 students) in September 2012, the then Skills module leader retired unexpectedly and left BCU. The Skills module was left without leadership until the new module leader took over in the summer of 2013. This had a considerable impact on the roll-out of the Skills module in 2012/13. While no formal evaluative data was collected from the students, a reflective account from a member of the Skills teaching team during that period gives an overview of the struggles encountered with the module that year:

> "Students and staff really struggled with Skills this year. Without a strong leader guiding both staff in terms of delivery and students in terms of their learning experience the module was very stressful. When [the then Skills module leader] left and there was no time for any handover, we lost a considerable amount of practical knowledge on how to make the module work. Throughout the previous iterations of the module, she had shielded [the previous Skills teaching team] from workload issues regarding marking of the e-portfolios as she first marked the entire cohort herself each year. Students told me they didn't understand how the module worked and what its purpose was. They disliked reflection and did not engage with reflective writing at all. Without a dedicated module leader organising the IT training sessions that helped provide scaffolding and support, students really did not engage in a meaningful way at all with e-portfolios. This year, it felt like the e-portfolios had been relegated to mere repository vehicles for storing information and content."
> (Academic 1)

The appointment of a new Skills module leader brought a fresh impetus to curriculum design within the module. While the e-portfolio remained a key component of assessment (worth 50 percent of the overall mark for the module), the overall design of the e-portfolio and the quality of its reflective content formed the basis of the pre-declared learning outcomes assessed by e-portfolio submission. The new module leader felt that, consistent with the Academic's reflection above, the old design did not really prompt students to become 'intentional learners' (Yancey, 1998 as cited in Bufton et al., 2010: 4); very little of the process underpinning their learning journey in the Skills module was being captured, never mind assessed or evaluated. To counteract this, the pre-declared learning outcomes for the module were redesigned to ensure constructive alignment between learning and teaching activities and e-portfolio assessments (Biggs & Tang, 2011). A clearer set of marking criteria, directly linked to the pre-declared learning outcomes, were drafted and provided to students at the outset of the module in the form of an e-portfolio assessment brief. The diagram below is a visual representation of the pedagogical model that underpinned the curriculum re-design process:

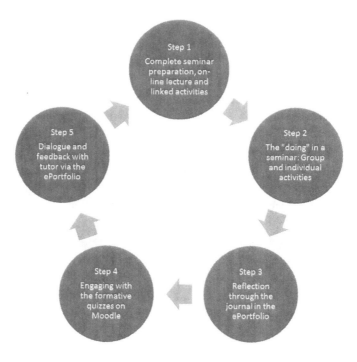

Figure 1: Template layout for Skills e-portfolio design provided to students in 2013/14.

As illustrated in Figure 1 above, Skills students were now expected to reflect after learning and teaching activities within the module, using online lectures and fortnightly two-hour small group seminar sessions which emphasised experiential learning by 'doing' through group and individual activities. To help students structure their reflections and to address concerns about supporting development as reflective practitioners, a whole seminar at the outset of the module was dedicated to reflection. To prepare for this seminar, students were expected to engage with an online lecture that introduced them to the theories underpinning reflection and to some reflective models. Students were then encouraged to use one of these models (Driscoll, 1994) to help structure their reflections by asking themselves three simple questions when completing their e-portfolio journal entries:

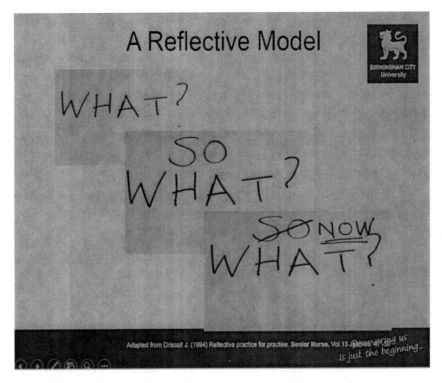

Figure 2: A model of reflective learning (adapted from Driscoll, 1994). Powerpoint replicated with kind permission of Sonia Hendy-Isaac, Senior Lecturer and M.Ed. Programme Director, CELT.

In the accompanying seminar session, students critiqued examples of reflection, using the same marking criteria from the e-portfolio assessment brief that was to be used by the Skills teaching team to assess the students' reflections at the end of the module. In addition, to encourage a more supportive dialogue with students and to prompt student engagement with reflection contemporaneously throughout the module, members of the Skills teaching team for the first time engaged with providing formative feedback on student reflections in the e-portfolio during the course of the academic year.

A different approach was adopted as part of the curriculum redesign process to support students' orientation of *Mahara* as a new technology. Instead of offering voluntary 'drop-in' IT support sessions, IT learner support colleagues were more actively involved and helped the Skills teaching team deliver a Skills seminar early in the year. In that session, students actually created their initial *Mahara* e-portfolio and got specific hands-on training as well as an opportunity to experiment with the different types of content that *Mahara* allows them to add to their e-portfolio, such as videos, pictures and Internet links. We also created an e-portfolio template (an extract from which is shown in figure 3 below). This helped students to understand how to use the different settings in *Mahara* to optimise their e-portfolio. Students are free to ignore the template (and the more creative ones certainly have!) but the template acts as a content aide-memoire and, perhaps more important, allows students, at the outset of the module, to visualise what their e-portfolio could look like (without giving examples of current student work which could prompt issues regarding plagiarism).

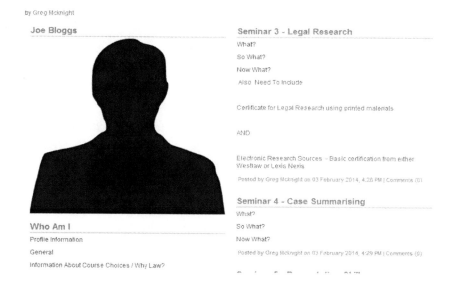

Figure 3: Extract from the template layout for Skills e-portfolio design provided to students in 2013/14.

End-of-module feedback for the academic year 2013/14 has been positive and articulates with the original end-of-module feedback conducted in April 2011. 217 students out of a cohort of 340 responded to a questionnaire designed to evaluate the changes made to the Skills curriculum design, in particular the extra support provided to support e-portfolio use within the module. 196 students out of the 217 respondents found the Skills e-portfolio template 'very useful'. 216 out of the 217 respondents felt that the seminars that contained embedded support for the e-portfolios, such as activities on effective reflective writing and IT support for e-portfolio creation and maintenance, had a positive, direct effect on their eventual summative e-portfolio assessment. Common themes from the positive feedback focused on gaining confidence and showed emerging evidence of respondents taking a more student-centric approach to their studies:

> "I enjoyed writing my diary-esque e-portfolio. I have found that as well as all of the mandatory seminar sessions I had to reflect upon I also ended up reflecting on other sessions (sometimes outside of Skills) that stood out to me as important or unique. Whilst I did my best to follow the marking criteria, my writing did somewhat read as a narrative. This was purposefully done as I did not want to make my e-portfolio a piece of plain coursework following the Driscoll model of reflection to the letter. I wanted to add something of 'me' – some light humour to keep the read interesting. I think I have developed a lot throughout the Skills course. I look back and remember the feeling of worry as I did not know what to do for seminars, I was so worried about getting it wrong. I'm glad to say now that through the process of putting my e-portfolio together, I can see the changes in me and when I now approach seminars, I feel much more confident." (Student 5)

However, academic feedback on the current iteration of the Skills module is mixed. On the one hand, academics report that they have seen a distinct improvement in terms of student work by constructively aligning learning and teaching activities with assessment:

> "In Seminar 3, students complete a legal research exercise, which is assessed by their peers within the seminar session. It is now a far more hands-on session in the library where tutors can take a more hands-on

approach to the experiential learning and feedback process. The e-port-folio assessment brief requires students to then reflect both upon that activity and how they use what they have learnt from the legal research exercise (namely how to conduct effective legal research and how to refer-ence accurately) when completing their summative essay assessment in Contract [Law module]. As a result, I have seen a marked improvement in the standard of engagement with research and referencing plus some really meaningful student reflections from students within their e-portfo-lios on the impact and value of the Seminar 3 activities." (Academic 2)

Other academic feedback, particularly around the increased burden on the teaching team in terms of marking, has not always been positive. As recognised by Strivens (2006), diversity of evidence provided in student e-portfolios can make them harder and far more time consuming to assess. The mechanics of assessment and logistics of the marking process have also proved problematic and time consuming for academics. Solutions had to be found to sharing work between second markers/externals, plus the require-ment to keep assessed student work for a post-marking period, in line with BCU and professional body audit requirements. Also, providing formative feedback via the e-portfolio throughout the year has been challenging:

"I am an active supporter of e-portfolios and the learning affordances they can bring. But there are times this year that I have had to make consider-able sacrifices in terms of my personal life and my ability to research in order to commit to the time required to create the dialogue with students via formative feedback. I am concerned that if student numbers increase again next year, what will be the impact then?" (Academic 1)

This theme of the underappreciated level of human endeavour in creating technology-enhanced learning is echoed in the conclusions of others (see Hayes and Bartholomew, this volume). However, in order to ensure consistency for students, buy-in from the teaching team is vital (see Bartholomew and Kelly, this volume). End-of-module feedback from the current cohort of Skills students highlights the importance of this aspect:

"I have been regularly updating my Skills Mahara e-portfolio throughout the year and it is a bit discouraging when the tutor providing feedback

on my reflections can't even be bothered to update their own Mahara profile with a picture in the same way I am expected to do." (Student 6)

In addition, institutional buy-in is crucial to success. As recognised by Jisc (2008:16):

> "...effective e-portfolio learning is unlikely to occur unless it forms part of a broader commitment to learner-centred, autonomous learning.... despite the drive and energy of individual enthusiasts, large-scale e-portfolio implementation can only be achieved with the support of curriculum managers and practitioners involved in a module."

Since curriculum design should be an iterative and reflective process, solutions to the challenges outlined in this case study, such as use of word counts and using peer feedback, will be explored in the next phase of the module. Despite these challenges, the Skills module leader remains committed to embedding e-portfolios within curriculum design.

By using e-portfolios in the Skills module in the first year of their studies as detailed in Case Study 1 (above), students are supported in the transition to using e-portfolios in a more developed manner in one of the (follow-on) substantive law modules they are required to study in their second year – namely Land Law. This context is shared below as Case Study 2.

Case study 2: e-portfolios in Land Law

Land Law is a compulsory subject on the LL.B, studied at BCU by students within Year Two of the undergraduate programme. It is a challenging subject and one in which students sometimes struggle in the early stages. Some of the concepts that have to be understood are based on ancient law and one of the challenges in delivering the module is finding ways for students to make sense of it and relate it to their everyday lives.

Over the last five years a number of changes have been made to the design of the Land Law curriculum, including assessment. A problem-based approach was adopted in 2011/12, building on successful integration of case-based learning at postgraduate level in the Law School (King, 2014). Class contact time was subsequently restructured to allow for increased small group work and to more effectively embed employability skills alongside the substantive law that was being covered. The learning and teaching activities that were created promoted fuller engagement with learning. The problem was that the assessment method was purely exam-based. While the exam satisfied the requirements for a valid form of assessment that met appropriate academic standards (QAA, 2013) and had been approved by the professional bodies that regulate the law degree, the consequence was that the focus of the assessment was on *product* rather than *process*. The exam-based assessment measured only what the student could write pertaining to what they had learned in relatively artificial conditions (Race, 2010). Student approaches to the assessment suggested that they took a surface approach to their learning during the course of their studies. From a very basic analysis of attendance records, there was a noticeable drop in attendance during the middle part of the programme. The characteristics of surface approaches as set out by Entwistle (1988), Ramsden (1992) and Biggs and Tang (2011) suggest that students taking this line rely on rote learning, receiving information passively and viewing it as simply material that is needed for the purposes of passing an exam. The reality is that a lawyer in practice would rarely be asked to advise a client under timed, supervised conditions without recourse to research materials, so using an exam seemed incongruous with the aim of developing a module that would equip students with skills for practice.

Changing the exam-based assessment to an e-portfolio approach offered the opportunity to rethink the structure and content of the assessment and to refine again the design of the teaching and learning activities within the curriculum to ensure constructive alignment. The early developments that had taken place had been based on the Kolb experiential cycle (Kolb, 1984) enabling students to experience learning through a process of thinking, doing and reflecting on their learning. This iterative process enabling students to develop important academic and practical skills alongside their study of substantive law was one that best replicated professional legal practice. It was important that the e-portfolio was embedded into that curriculum so that it was not perceived by students to be 'bolted-on' and therefore of little value (Hartnell-Young et al., 2007).

The e-portfolio therefore requires students to engage in an ongoing process of learning in which they must plan, research, reflect, and deliver advice on a problem-based question through three pieces of legal writing; a memorandum of advice, an annotated bibliography and a reflective piece. It is intended that students use the *Mahara* 'journal' function for the purposes of reflection, allowing them to share their formative work with academic staff and obtain feedback that will inform and assist their progress. Formative practice and feedback on their progress is also provided through collaborative activity in class with peers and academic staff. Crucially, the final collection of work is produced individually and submitted via the e-portfolio. It is also important that students understand that the e-portfolio is an individual piece of summative assessment and subject to the same assessment regulations as a more typical piece of coursework. The e-portfolio is, therefore, designed to enable students to collect evidence and demonstrate achievement as well as support a *"continuous process of personal development and reflective learning"* (Jisc, 2008:14).

The approach facilitates a model where *"as learners experience critical moments in their learning they can express their responses, collect and organise information and plan their next steps, potentially within one integrated digital environment"* (Jisc, 2008). The result in terms of the Land Law module should be that student learning is shifted from 'product' to a more balanced approach that still values 'product' but also 'process'. The 'product' is focused on the demonstrations of knowledge and understanding through application of law to the problems via the memorandum of advice. The 'process' assessment component provides an opportunity to measure students' ability to research, interpret and evaluate legal concepts, apply them to practical legal problems, propose solutions, continually reflect on their progress, and act on feedback via the annotated bibliography and reflective piece. This creates a more integrated approach (Hager, 2013). Students are now building essential competencies to apply in professional practice in real life situations. This, in turn, more closely aligns with the pre-declared learning outcomes for the module, which now include a demonstration of personal initiative and independent learning and the ability to reflect on learning and act on feedback.

The initial roll-out of the new e-portfolio assessment was not without its challenges. From an institutional point of view, changes of academic staff and issues with timetabling meant that the teaching team as originally envisaged was not eventually involved in the delivery of the module.

New members of academic staff (not previously acquainted with *Mahara*) had a very steep learning curve coming to grips with the technology. For operational reasons it became necessary to reduce the length of the small group seminars, which meant there was less time for academic staff to work on embedding the academic and employability skills into the curriculum.

Early evaluation of students in the first term of their studies on the module revealed that they were engaging to some degree with the assessment process; some had started to reflect on their progress, others had started the research aspect and were beginning to gather resources for their annotated bibliography. Many of those who responded to an evaluation questionnaire in December 2013 requested additional support in terms of structure and content and asked for guiding samples of the artefacts that they had been asked to create. The programme team's response was to provide exemplars (from a different context to the problem question) and opportunities in class to critically reflect on good and less good examples of legal advice. Students were concerned about the technological aspect of using *Mahara* as the vehicle for their assessment. There was a perception that many lacked confidence in developing their e-portfolio, some raised concerns about when and how to share their work online, others preferred to work using their own resources, intending simply to use *Mahara* as a repository for storing the content which they would ultimately submit. The programme team was proactive in their response by offering students a number of opportunities to get technical advice and help on how to create and submit their e-portfolio. However, it remained the case throughout the module that many students seemed to prefer working offline, only engaging with *Mahara* as the due-date for submission approached.

These issues and episodes were all moments when the reality of embedding e-portfolios started to bite. The module had been carefully designed, the declared learning outcomes carefully thought through and the instructional activities mapped to those outcomes and the assessment. There were opportunities for formative practice and feedback through the taught sessions and students were directed in their independent study time towards learning tasks that would support their learning journey. A completely smooth transition to the new form of assessment was not expected but while some of the critical incidents had been anticipated, many others had not, and these had the potential to cause anxiety for academic staff and students. It was vital that we undertook this early evaluation and crucial that there was flexibility in the system to respond to the feedback we were given and support our students as they came to grips with the new assessment.

In April 2014, a month before submission of the e-portfolio was due, a much more detailed evaluation questionnaire was circulated to students. Out of a cohort of 240 students, 100 responded. A range of questions was asked including detailed questions on each of the elements of the portfolio: memorandum, annotated bibliography and reflective piece. Questions were also asked about the use of the e-portfolio as the vehicle for the assessment.

One asked: *"Do you think there are advantages of using an e-portfolio over more traditional forms of assessments, such as essays and exams?"*. 82 students responded 'yes' to this question, 16 replied 'no' and two did not respond. Particularly interesting were the feedback comments, which suggested that those who did not see the advantages tended to dislike using *Mahara* as the e-portfolio platform; one even stating *"I hate Mahara"*. Those who responded 'yes' focused less on the technology itself but more on the opportunities it afforded. They tended to appreciate that the e-portfolio gave students an opportunity to demonstrate a wider breadth of learning and allowed for greater time to be spent reflecting on, reviewing and refining their work prior to submission. A number of students noted that this approach took some of the stress out of assessment and that the technology enabled them to organise their work and spread the workload over the year. One student commented:

> *"The way we are being assessed is different, which is good because I don't believe that exams are always the right way to see how much a person knows."* (Student 7)

Another noted:

> *"By using an e-portfolio it helps us to have an insight into how to operate and be assessed as a professional."* (Student 8)

Interestingly, some students also saw being assessed by this method as putting them ahead of the game in terms of their employability. One commented:

> *"We'll be a step ahead of other universities as the e-portfolio will be used in practice."* (Student 9)

Another commented:

> *"e-portfolios may be used more in legal careers which will give me a head start."* (Student 10)

The embedding of employability skills within the Land Law module and its assessment had been a key aim of the project and it was very pleasing to see that students had acknowledged this. 95 of the 100 students stated that they believed that the skills being developed in Land Law would be of benefit in their future careers.

This feedback was reassuring. It was important to us that students appreciate *why* we introduced the new approaches to assessment, and that they saw the value in what they were being asked to do, even if they found these new methods challenging. The hard work of the teaching team in responding to the early feedback and providing support and scaffolding for the assessment seemed to have paid off with the majority of students responding positively.

It was interesting, however that despite the overwhelmingly positive response to the use of the e-portfolio as a means of assessment, a reasonable number of students did not anticipate continuing to use their e-portfolio as part of their lifelong learning. When asked the question *"Would you continue to use your e-portfolio throughout all of your university modules and into your working life as a means of supporting your continued learning journey?"*, 62 students confirmed that they would, 37 said that they would not and one answered 'maybe'. Those who responded 'no' tended to comment that it would be too time-consuming not necessarily relevant to the job they ended up in, and that they could not see the relevance of it going forward.

This would further suggest that the students' focus is very much on the assessment as the driver rather than the e-portfolio as a lifelong learning tool. It suggests that, given the option to use an e-portfolio to capture learning voluntarily, many would not. It will not become their *"compass through learning"* developed throughout their learning journey (Hager, 2013:157). This is disappointing but not entirely unexpected.

Although we are now developing clear links between the Skills module in the First Year and Land Law in the Second Year, many students will have experienced e-portfolios in the first iteration of the Land Law re-design as an isolated experience, without clear progression from the previous year. We also need to develop opportunities in the Final Year to encourage students to begin to use e-portfolios independently, as part of their learning journey towards achieving their degree.

Finally, a word about early perceptions of marking the Land Law e-portfolios. At this time of writing, hard data about pass rates and progression is not yet available. What does appear clear is that the early approaches of students who worked off-line to produce the work they ultimately submitted did not change throughout the year. Few students chose to use the e-portfolio as a vehicle for reflection, feedback and dialogue as was originally intended. Instead, it became a repository for the artefacts that were produced and simply a vehicle by which their work was submitted. That is not to say that reflective practice, seeking and acting on feedback, and dialogue between students and academic staff and students and their peers was not taking place. It just appears that the environment in which this was happening was not the e-portfolio but rather discussions in taught sessions and other opportunities for face-to-face contact.

This offers an interesting insight into the ways in which students on this module chose to learn. Coming to grips with the complicated concepts in Land Law (described earlier) is perhaps best achieved within a supportive classroom environment and not online. Feedback was perhaps preferred and valued when it was offered face-to-face and not virtually. The affordances of the technology in Land Law were perhaps limited to making a repository for the artefacts that students created rather than providing hard evidence of the learning journey. To the tutor, evidence of a learning process was implicit in the artefacts themselves and did not need to be explicitly present in the e-portfolios submitted.

Conclusions

We agree firmly with the following recommendations that: *"e-portfolio systems and tools must form part of a strategic approach to learning and teaching – it is the pedagogy, not the tool, that comes first"* (Jisc, 2008:17). Our experience and evaluation confirms that the use of e-portfolios on its own will not enhance student learning but, when they are used in conjunction with reflection on experiential learning and actively embedded within the wider curriculum design to avoid being perceived as merely 'bolted-on', important learning affordances emerge.

However, the use of e-portfolios is certainly not as widespread in the UK as it could be, given the pedagogic advantages it can bring (CRA, 2009). As recognised by *Jisc* (2012), there is clear scope for further roll-out of e-portfolios across the wider field of higher education. Coming full circle to the title of our chapter, our reflective case studies tell a cautionary tale of when 'reality bites' in relation to technology-enhanced learning that may help explain this lack of e-portfolio proliferation. As academics with an interest in the learning and teaching aspects of our practice, we did not stumble blindly into the use of e-portfolios. We made informed curriculum design choices that were underpinned by philosophy, theory and, dare we say, professional competence. Yet, in both instances of our e-portfolio use, the learning advantages we hoped to achieve were not fully realised.

We therefore end our chapter with a list of thinking points, based on our own lived experience, that academics may wish to consider in order to make a difference when using e-portfolios. This list is not designed to be exhaustive, and is not a list of 'solutions' *per se* to the challenges we faced, but it may form part of a broader strategy for embedding technology-enhanced learning (see Nygaard, this volume). However, we feel there is value in sharing our perspectives, both good and bad, in an informal yet practical way with the wider higher education community. We hope this may allow other practitioners to develop the flexibility and design resilience required to embrace this technology within their own disciplines.

Thinking points to consider when using e-portfolios

+ Ensure that students understand why e-portfolios are being used. If they understand, they are more likely to engage.
+ Be explicit in the rationale underpinning e-portfolio use and value. Explore with students the impact of e-portfolios as part of a lifelong learning process. This message should be supported by lectures, seminar work and online tutorials.

- Don't assume that students will be masters of the technology and associated terms in the same way that they use and interact with social media. This is particularly relevant to mature and international students.

- Actively involve these who provide IT learner support when designing learning and teaching activities and ensure that training is embedded as much as possible into the curriculum design. Drop-in voluntary training sessions are usually under-utilised by students, which is a waste of IT learner support resource.

- Look at curriculum design across your entire programme when implementing e-portfolios. Try to provide scaffolding and support for students by using e-portfolios across all years of the programme. Use of e-portfolios in isolated unrelated modules is unlikely to add value and will not promote incremental progression of students in e-portfolio use.

- Consider the software tool that your institution uses to support e-portfolios and whether it works in terms of your planned pedagogical model. Can students do what you want them to do? What are the privacy and security controls to assure students of confidentiality in sharing personal reflections?

- From an early stage, consider the quality control processes for your programme within the institution. Think about the submission process, marking and moderation, external examiner input, and audit requirements. These considerations are brought into sharp focus when using electronic instead of paper assessments.

- To facilitate lifelong learning, will your students need to export or transfer e-portfolio content when they graduate? If so, consider when and how to provide training for students on how to complete this task to ensure that the value of the e-portfolio journey is not lost.

- Ensure that students understand that, despite opportunities for feedback (both from peers and academics), e-portfolios are still an individual and personal summative formal assessment. As such, students need to appreciate that e-portfolio assessments are subject to the same regulations (and ultimate sanctions) regarding plagiarism, collusion and collaboration.

- Academic staff engagement with the pedagogy and e-portfolio use is vital. This starts with ensuring academic staff are adequately trained in terms of the technological aspects, which needs to be a continuous process as opposed to an isolated session at the beginning of the academic term.

- Don't assume that the teaching team has the same enthusiasm for e-portfolio use as you do. Student engagement will be adversely affected if they perceive a lack of consistency in academic staff engagement with e-portfolios and the feedback process.

- Manage student expectations with regard to when and how they will receive feedback. Initial feedback is vital to stop early disenfranchisement with reflective learning and e-portfolio use. Lack of academic response to dialogue instigated by the learner can derail the process. Plan clearly how and when feedback will take place within your curriculum design and ensure that this is clearly communicated to your students from the outset.

- Facilitating e-portfolio use will impact academic staff workload, in terms of maintaining ongoing dialogue with students and increasing marking burdens. Can you find solutions at a wider level involving key stakeholders (students, school, faculty, institution) to help mitigate this? Can you use peer feedback among learners to help address this issue?

- Make sure you have some time and space to reflect on your own experiences of using e-portfolios with your students. Remember that programme design is an iterative process. Regular and meaningful evaluation of e-portfolio use and refining your design model are essential. Seek regular feedback from your students to inform your plans going forward.

- Be prepared to be flexible and responsive to the inevitable challenges that will be thrown your way. Don't be afraid to make changes where needed. Try to anticipate as far as possible where those challenges may come from.

The challenges we have faced are not unique to BCU but common to many HEIs. They might be technical challenges (upgrades to the system sometimes throw up unexpected technological problems that cause anxiety for both students and academic staff). They might also be institutional (sudden changes to timetables and resources), related to workload (lack of time allowances for formative feedback and the marking process) or related to academic staff changes.

Finally, the main lesson from our experience is that, as academics, when using technology we need to leave space within our curriculum design to be able to respond when necessary to both expected and (crucially) unexpected challenges. Without this contingency, we run a very high risk of reality 'biting back'.

Acknowledgements

The authors wish to thank their former colleagues Beverley Hopkins and Jonathan Cooper at BCU for their innovation and support in relation to e-portfolio use.

About the authors

Sarah King has recently joined the University of Birmingham as an Academic Practice Advisor and Programme Director for the Postgraduate Certificate in Academic Practice. She can be contacted at this email: s.king.2@bham.ac.uk

Emma Flint is a Solicitor and recently joined the University of Birmingham as a Birmingham Fellow (Teaching). She can be contacted at this email: e.e.flint@bham.ac.uk

Bibliography

Barnard, J. (2011). Reflection on a personal journey: Learning journals in use. *EliSS*, Vol. 3, No. 3.

Biggs, J & C. Tang (2011). *Teaching for Quality Learning at University*. Berkshire: Open University Press.

Bufton, S. & I. Woolsey (2010). 'You just knew what you had to write': reflective learning and e-portfolios in the social sciences. *EliSS*, Vol. 3, No. 1.

CRA (2009). *e-portfolios supporting employer engagement and workforce development. Literature and Practice Review.* Centre for Recording

Achievement. Online Resource: http://www.recordingachievement.org/ employers-cpd/he5p/project/reports.html [Accessed on 3 June 2014]

DfES (2005). *Harnessing Technology: Transforming learning and children's services*. Online Resource: http://www.dfes.gov.uk/publications/e-strategy/ [Accessed on 4 March 2014].

Driscoll, J. (1994). Reflective practice for practise. *Senior Nurse*, Vol. 13, Jan/ Feb, pp. 47-50.

Entwistle, N. (1988). *Styles of Learning and Teaching*. David Fulton.

Flint, E. (2014). Using Case-based learning to enhance undergraduate students' employability. In J. Branch; P. Bartholomew & C. Nygaard (Eds.). *Case-Based Learning in Higher Education*. Oxfordshire: Libri Publishing Ltd., pp. 123-137.

Hager, L. (2013). e-portfolios and the Twenty-first Century: Learning in Higher Education. In C. Nygaard; J. Branch & C. Holthan (Eds.). *Learning in Higher Education – Contemporary Standpoints*. Oxfordshire: Libri Publishing Ltd., pp. 151-166.

Hartnell-Young, E.; C. Harrison; C. Crook; G. Joyes; L. Davies; T. Fisher; R. Pemberton & A. Smallwood (2007). *Impact study of e-portfolios on learning*, Coventry: Becta.

HEFCE (2009). *e-portfolios supporting employer engagement and workforce development. Literature and Practice Review*. Centre for Recording Achievement.

Jisc (2008) *Effective Practice with e-portfolios*. Jisc, UK.

King, S. (2014). Preparing for Practice: Using Case-based Learning to Support Postgraduate Law Students. In J. Branch; P. Bartholomew & C. Nygaard (Eds.). *Case-Based Learning in Higher Education*. Oxfordshire: Libri Publishing Ltd., pp. 105-122.

Kennedy, G.; T. Judd; A. Churchward; K. Gray & K-L. Krause (2008). First year students' experiences with technology: Are they really digital natives? *Australasian Journal of Educational Technology*, Vol. 24, No. 1, pp. 108-122.

Kolb, D. A. (1984). *Experiential Learning: Experience as the source of learning and development*. Englewood Cliffs, New Jersey: Prentice Hall.

NCIHE (1997). *Higher education in the learning society*. (The Dearing Report). London: NCIHE.

Prensky, M. (2001). Digital Natives, Digital Immigrants Part 1. *On the Horizon*, MCB University Press, Vol. 9, pp. 1-6.

Quality Assurance Agency (2009). *Personal development planning evaluation: A guide for institutional policy and practice in higher education*. QAA, UK.

Quality Assurance Agency (2013). *UK Quality Code for Higher Education, Part B, Chapter B6*. QAA, UK.

Race, P. (2010). *Making Learning Happen Making Learning Happen: A Guide for Post-Compulsory Education*. London: Sage Publications.

Ramsden, P. (1992). *Learning to Teach in Higher Education*. London: Routledge.

Rogers, R.R. (2001). Reflection in higher education: A Concept analysis. *Innovative Higher Education*, Vol. 26, No. 1.

Schön, D. (1983). *The reflective practitioner. How professionals think in action*. London: Temple Smith.

Strivens, J. (2006). *Efficient assessment of portfolios*. The Higher Education Academy.

Yancey K.B. (1998). *Reflection in the writing classroom*. Logan, Utah: Utah State University Press.

Chapter Eight

Java Programming Laboratory: a technology-enhanced learning environment for student programmers

Steve Drew & Wayne Pullan

Introduction

This chapter contributes to the anthology on technology-enhanced learning in higher education by describing an innovative, Web-based managed learning system. The system is devised to scaffold novice Java (Gosling, 2000) language computer programmers through self-paced learning activities to provide rapid feedback and access to tutorial assistance whenever and wherever a student is ready to learn. This chapter begins with the underlying learning challenges driving the design of a technology-based system to enhance students' experience of learning to program in Java. It then follows the student-driven, evidence-based development of the system components and presents evidence that the system described is a highly effective technology-enhanced learning environment that positively impacts on student learning experiences and outcomes.

Technology-enhanced learning is about implementing an educational programme that improves learning quality and outcomes in circumstances where technology plays a significant supporting role (Goodyear & Retalis, 2010). Technology-enhanced learning environments are technology-based learning and instruction systems. Interaction with and through such systems allows students to acquire skills and knowledge, usually with the aid of teachers, learning support tools and technological resources (Wang & Hannafin, 2005). The technology-enhanced learning environment described in this chapter can be classified as a managed learning system in which each of the stakeholders in teaching and learning activities can, through technology, actively engage in learning processes. Each student's progress toward learning outcomes can be monitored through the technology and actively guided when necessary – an important feature for maintaining student engagement with learning (Kuh, 2003). Effective engagement and attainment of learning outcomes in such learning environments requires a level of self-regulated learning capability on the part of the student (Delfino & Persico, 2011; see Bartholomew & Kelly, this volume). Self-regulated learning is a characteristic of learners: *"that set better learning goals, implement more effective learning strategies, monitor and assess their goal progress better, establish a more productive environment for learning, seek assistance more often when it is needed, expend effort and persist better, adjust strategies better, and set more effective new goals when present ones are completed"* (Zimmerman & Schunk, 2008:1).

In the context of this study, a technology-enhanced learning environment was designed to allow first-year university students, with a low level of learner maturity and lack of experience in managing their own learning journey, to expand their knowledge and skills and enhance their self-regulated learning ability. Technology was used to structure and manage learning activities to provide regulation of learning and to provide a pattern as a basis for self-regulation. The increasing diversity of Information Technology (IT) degree students creates an environment where there are a high proportion of non-traditional students (Biggs & Tang, 2011; Taylor & House, 2010). A one-size-fits-all approach to curriculum delivery is unlikely to provide optimal student learning experience or learning outcomes. This chapter describes a technology-enhanced learning environment for student programmers that blends face-to-face interaction with computers, mobile communication devices, networks, Internet services, videos, and a range of software. It is an immersive environment that represents both the object of learning (what) and the process of learning (how).

Computer programming languages are designed to provide a human-readable and writeable means of providing instructions for the operation of a computer-based system (Wirth, 1983). All computer software is first written in a programming language that is typed into some form of text editor and saved as a program source file. Using a software tool called a compiler or interpreter, the program source file is then translated into a language computer hardware can read and execute. Traditionally, learning to create software is an evolutionary process of editing, compiling and executing until the desired program properties are accurately implemented. Software systems exist that integrate each of these program development steps and software tools into a single user interface called an Integrated Development Environment (IDE). Novice programmers find themselves learning to set up and operate a complex mix of software including computer operating systems, development environments, and details of the programming language. At the same time, students engage with providing solutions to very abstract problems and data structures, which requires mastery of the programming language, problem solving, and design logic. In the first year of university this creates a very challenging environment in which students must learn in order to succeed. Reducing the complexity of the learning environment, through efficient user interface design and consistent educational design, is a key goal of this technology-enhanced learning environment. It allows students to concentrate on what to learn and reduces emphasis on how to learn.

The technology-enhanced learning environment described in this chapter is the Java Programming Laboratory (JPL) (Pullan *et al.*, 2013) which integrates a number of web communication and application technologies. JPL is designed to complement face-to-face classes and create a managed, active learning (Bonwell & Eison, 1991) experience based on problem-solving and Java (Gosling, 2000) programming language mastery. Essentially, JPL is an evolution of an Integrated Development Environment for programmers into an Integrated Learning Environment for student programmers. The former is a set of tools for programmers to develop computer programs; the latter integrates these tools into a system that supports novice programmers in the development of their knowledge and skills. While this technological solution appears to be highly relevant for helping programming students, it has also been found that the immersive 'shell' and managed learning model is generalisable to a wider range of courses, particularly where student engagement in problem-based learning (Barrows, 1996) is a pedagogic strategy.

The following sections of this chapter describe the learning issues that JPL was designed to address, they then navigate the reader through the approach taken to address these issues. As part of an action learning process (Kember, 2000), the evolution and development of JPL is described, and the impact this technology-assisted learning process has had upon students and tutors is shared. Finally, a conclusion discusses future development and possible research directions.

Contextual learning issues

There are four distinct but related learning issues that JPL was designed to address. First, it is recognised that learning programming is threshold knowledge (Meyer & Land, 2005; Rountree & Rountree, 2009; Sorva, 2010) that is essential to successful progress through Information Technology and Multimedia degrees. Any student learning to program a computer must simultaneously develop proficiency in the programming language and use of the language compiler software, all the while building logical problem solving skills that the language can be used to express. This constitutes an area of troublesome knowledge (Meyer & Land, 2005) that students must master very early in their degree programs and progressively build on throughout their study.

Secondly, modern students have increasingly complex study-life situations and being able to study anywhere at any time is essential (Leveson *et al.*, 2013). A growing trend toward 'blended' and 'online' learning modes may reduce student contact with the learner (and academic) community. This increases their sense of isolation, frustration and confusion, ultimately leading to disengagement (see Cygman, this volume; Wu *et al.*, 2010).

In the early stages of learning to program, it is particularly important to surmount persistent learning challenges and break 'try and fail cycles' before dejection becomes an issue. Small successes build learning momentum and engender enthusiasm in pursuit of solutions to programming problems. For students studying online or undertaking independent, self-regulated learning in the IT disciplines, consistent access to timely expert assistance is paramount (Minocha, 2009).

The third problem relates to the fact that the first programming course is often taught in the very first semester of an IT degree, when students are also dealing with their transition to university and a new learning environment. Programme induction sets the expectation that, for each course, students should spend ten hours per week in related study. Three hours of that are in structured and organised activities in contact with teaching staff . It has been found that, in the remaining seven hours, many students have no idea how to organise their study time and fail to engage in meaningful activities that further their understanding (van der Meer *et al.*, 2010).

Fourthly, student readiness for higher education in the authors' context is diminished. Continuing moves towards 'massification' of higher education (Altbach, 1999) and a local reduction in popularity of many IT-related professions have resulted in lowering entry requirements for IT programmes to maintain budget quotas. This has led to the situation, locally, where a higher percentage of IT students are non-traditional students (Taylor & House, 2010). Non-traditional students are characterised by at least one of the following: low socio-economic status; first-in-family to attend university; lower entry levels with regard to high school qualifications, and full-time students working part-time to fund their studies. Typically, most first-year students can also be characterised by at least one of the following: poor time management skills; a strategic approach to learning (only motivated by assessment items) (Marton & Säljö, 1984); lack of suitable study environments outside of class; and not taking initiative to seek timely help.

In Australian universities, the relative performance of each discipline area, with respect to student retention and student learning experience, determines the proportion of the national Learning and Teaching Performance Allocation received. Similarly, national publication of student retention figures and student experiences of learning by media like the Good Universities Guide influences the popularity of degree programmes and the quality of the student intake. It can be demonstrated that addressing the learning problems positively influences student learning experience and has potential impact on funding, student retention and enhanced attractiveness of IT programmes to potential students.

Developing a solution – The Java Programming Laboratory

In order to address the complex set of learning (and teaching) challenges, an immersive software development environment (Dede, 2009) was designed that provides scaled levels of challenge and self-paced learning to maintain student engagement with learning. The immersive learning experience (Dede *et al.*, 2000) in this case provides access to all of the required learning and communication tools inside a single software environment. JPL provides a learning environment for students to engage with problems and allows teaching staff to focus on 'what the student does' (Biggs, 1999), individually and as a class, to maintain engagement and progression through the learning journey.

Instructional design features of JPL include a component approach (Biggs & Tang, 2011; Pintrich & De Groot, 1990) that is as conceptually 'concrete' as possible: students have to focus only on the topic currently being taught. It presents a problem-based learning approach (Savery, 2006) and provides a large range and number of problems, selected from an even larger range available for each topic. Problems are of scaled difficulty and complexity, designed to scaffold development (Simons & Klein, 2007) for a wide range of student abilities, providing multiple entry points into each topic and additional problems for more advanced students. JPL promotes responsive technology and teacher derived formative feedback (Black & Wiliam, 2009; Nicol & Macfarlane-Dick, 2006) with continuous access to personal and class (group) performance measures and access to just-in-time assistance. It provides a consistent, simple environment for any computing platform with flexible access to the learning environment, available in university computer laboratories or off campus on students' own computers. As a student computer-based application it ensures they can maintain learning momentum and time-on-task even when the Internet may not be accessible. Finally, to maintain originality of learning, JPL does not allow solutions to problems to be passed from year to year. While there are often many possible solutions to a programming problem, the iterative development of a mental model of a solution is essential to the learning process.

JPL's software-based environment allows students to develop their programming skills by starting with simple, targeted, Java code fragments and slowly transitioning to complete Java programs. The fundamental concept underlying JPL is that you can learn basic programming skills by writing many, small, targeted code fragments. With JPL, learning a programming language is devolved into smaller steps of learning and practising computer-based problem solving techniques. Like any language, this simultaneously aids learning of programming language constructs, their syntax and semantics. Problems available in this environment are designed to scaffold student learning through a number of stages, from 'fill in the blanks' exercises to developing Java code fragments and finally full Java programs. All student work in JPL is automatically tested and, as each student performs work on a problem, all activity is logged to a central fileserver. When students are working offline using the JPL application, their progression data is synchronised with the central database once they connect to JPL with the university's intranet. This facility enables the course's convener to monitor class and student performance and investigate any potential issues immediately.

Figure 1 shows the overall system structure of the current version of Java Programming Laboratory. Students interact with the environment collaboratively through lectures and workshops, via the JPL website and an immersive software development environment application called JPLIDE. Accessibility for off-campus students is provided through a Web interface, wJPL, which allows the use of tablets and other mobile computing devices for which JPLIDE, a downloadable application, is not suitable.

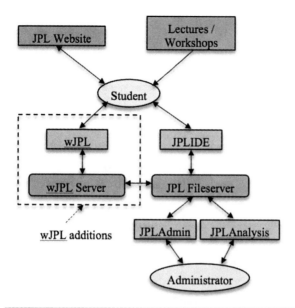

Key	
JPL Website	Online information and resources for students
JPLIDE	Java Programming Laboratory Integrated Development Environment – program development environment
JPL Fileserver	Central database for programming problems, and student progression data
wJPL	Online interface to JPL system emulating JPLIDE
wJPL Server	JPL Web server and interface to central database (JPL Fileserver)
JPL Admin	Administration interface for management of the JPL system
JPL Analysis	Statistical and graphical package for analysis and presentation of student progression data

Figure 1: Java Programming Laboratory (JPL).

All data relating to course administration, the problem bank, and student progress and participation are stored on the JPL Fileserver at the core of the Java Programming Laboratory system. Teaching team members access the system via JPLAdmin in order to administer the system and make changes and updates as needed, and also via JPLAnalysis, through which individual student and class progress can be monitored and learning problems detected and analysed at the earliest possible time.

Technology-enhanced learning activities in JPL

Much of learning to program in Java is supported by classroom learning activities. In this study however, it was found that over 50 percent of student learning activities occurred away from campus. To equitably support student learning at any place or time, a suite of activities including face-to-face and online modes of study was developed. Classroom learning activities involve topic-based discussions and collaborative problem-solving exercises using Java Programming Laboratory. On-campus lab-based workshops provide tutorial assistance while students engage with the current week's exercises accessed through the JPL system. For students engaging with exercises off-campus, a remote assistance feature was also implemented to support learning momentum.

An integral part of Java Programming Laboratory is the use of short (~10 minutes) video tutorials explaining key programming concepts and problem solving techniques. In effect, the student is able to 'look over the shoulder' at the computer screen as an experienced programmer demonstrates both programming language features and computer based problem solving from problem analysis to program implementation. Shorter video tutorials are also used to provide hints for solving problems. These video micro-tutorials that support student learning of individual constructs provide an indexed system of instruction and reviewable examples to support incremental development of problem solving and programming knowledge through guided practice.

Java Programming Laboratory's supporting website contains a number of interactive learning tools, some of which were originally created by Bradley Kjell, Central Connecticut State University (Kjell, 1997). For the first programming course in Java, these include 24 multiple choice quizzes (10 questions) with correct answers supplied on completion, 10 fill-in-the-blank review sessions, and 37 multi-page interactive topic discussions.

JPL's Integrated Development Environment (JPLIDE) was initially developed in Java as an application that could be installed in the range of computing platforms that students might use. Through the application's toolbar, a student can access a range of features including: current course news items; their own performance statistics compared to the rest of the class; access to the current problems; compiling, running and automatic testing of Java programs; problem specific hints; and solutions. Solutions are only released once the relevant topic has been covered in class and also once the student has made a reasonable effort to solve the problem.

Students experiencing difficulties in developing or debugging program code can request tutorial assistance with an automatic email sent to the teacher, who is then able to temporarily take over the student's JPLIDE environment. With sufficient evidence of student attempts to solve the problem themselves, the teacher is able to make code corrections or insert suggestions into the Java code files for students to review or act on.

In order to perform summative assessments of students' knowledge and skills using the JPL environment, JPLIDE also has an 'Assessed' mode. To ensure integrity of assessment in this mode, the computing platform is transformed into a secure environment for assessed workshops; access to other programs such as web browsers and certain editing features is limited to ensure all work is the student's own.

Methodology

In this study, a participatory action research methodology (Kemmis, 2006) involving students, media developers and teaching team, was adopted in order to develop the course using the Java Programming Laboratory learning environment. Starting from the initial model described above, the phases of action research used in the development of the system are described in Table 1. By acting on student and teaching team feedback about experiences and requirements, an evolutionary development and enhancement trajectory was executed.

Phase	Development
2011 Semester 1	Issues affecting student learning in the current course, gathered through student and teaching team evaluations, were noted and an initial JPL system design was created.
2011 Semester 2	First version of JPL system was implemented and 'desktop' tested.
2012 Semester 1	First version of JPL was used with the first programming course cohort at the local campus. Student feedback at mid-semester resulted in changes including student Java files being placed on centralised fileserver and accessed automatically rather than being kept on students' USB drives and having to be accessed manually. JPLIDE was also enhanced to provide solutions to programming problems after a period of time and sufficient engagement. JPL test problem statements were revised to make them easier for students to understand. The JPL Performance Indicator was added so students could compare their progress and achievements with those of all other students in the class. JPLAnalysis was developed to take advantage of centralised log files to provide class level performance analysis.
2012 Semester 2	Implementation of the second programming course version of JPL provided advanced features as needed for more complex software systems. A remote assistance facility was implemented and JPLIDE was enhanced to be integrated into the existing application toolbar menu system rather than using pop-up menus.
2013 Semester 1	Implementation of wJPL was completed to enable JPL use through browsers on tablet computing platforms and to enable two local secondary schools to use JPL without institutional firewall issues accessing JPLIDE. As part of an outreach process, secondary school students successfully completing the programming course are given credit towards their future degrees. wJPL was also trialled as a system for learning other programming languages including Python and C++.
2013 Semester 2	No new features.
2014 Semester 1	NetBeansJPL, an advancement on JPLIDE, was developed to allow students to migrate to an industry standard development environment part-way through Programming 2. The JPL environment was successfully prototyped for a Database Design course so that Java programs can be written to access a remote database essential for Web-based applications and services. wJPL system was extended to programming courses in six local secondary schools.

Table 1: Participatory Action Research phases in the development of JPL.

Alongside the technological developments listed above, a range of face-to-face learning activities was designed to leverage the affordances for learning presented by the Java Programming Laboratory system. Essential educational design was predicated on active learning (Bonwell & Eison, 1991) and problem-based learning (Barrows, 1996) strategies that were both collaborative and interactive. Figure 2 describes the design of the learning activities that students engage with each week and provides an indication of how managed learning is implemented. Figure 3 describes the assessment design for the course that completes the student experience across the semester of study.

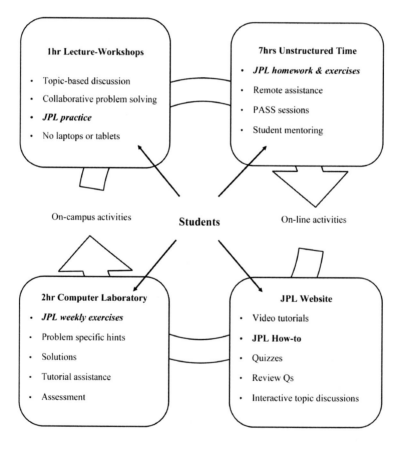

Figure 2: Weekly learning activities.

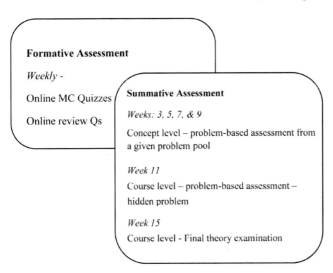

Figure 3: Assessment regime.

Prior to 2013, the lecture-based activities consisted of a presentation of lecture slides with some discussion using a whiteboard. However, in 2013, a revised form of lecture was introduced that incorporated JPL into the large class learning environment. Moving to a workshop format, the first lecture hour is devoted to presenting and discussing content using lecture slides, with the whiteboard for impromptu examples, and the JPL website for online quizzes performed as a group with the class. For the benefit of online and on-campus students, lecture content is also recorded for later review. The second hour is devoted to the class working as a team to solve problems and write Java code. Such sessions always start with a decomposition of the problem into sub-problems, identifying those sub-problems that are mechanical (e.g. getting and storing the data, presenting the output) and those sub-problems that require deeper thought about algorithm (a stepwise solution) design and its translation into Java.

Through individualised learning experiences of tackling problems in their interactions with JPL, students develop a range of different knowledge and skills. As programming knowledge is expanded, so is the quality of the potential solutions to problems and the learning outcomes generated. Collaborative lecture-based activities were devised so that students' experiences and learning could be shared. In order to engender deeper approaches to learning and to develop higher quality learning outcomes (Trigwell & Prosser, 1991) through students' exercise of judgment, the lecturer takes the class down as many wrong paths as possible. This strategy generates discussion about why a particular approach is not a good way to solve the problem or perform the Java implementation. Such exercises are very interactive and normally have enough students with a range of accomplishment levels offering suggestions to collaboratively develop an understanding of how each solution might be derived. This form of lecture has continued into 2014.

In 2013, in response to student perceptions that problems were not appropriately scaled in difficulty, the order of problem set was revised and some new problems added. Data collected by the system on the number of times a program was compiled, and the number of failed test executions in 2012 was used to inform the rank and order of the problems for each topic. In this way the problems with lowest rate of compiles and lowest rate of failed tests were presented to students first. This approach has continued again in 2014.

Learning activities are differentiated so that student-computer interactions are executed during laboratories and unstructured study times. To facilitate concentration, conversation, and collaboration in lectures, students are not allowed to have their laptops open. This removes distractions from the designed learning activity and does not allow students to type discussed solutions into the system as they are presented on the projector during the second hour of the lecture. Experience has shown this can short-circuit the desired learning practice of revisiting and rethinking the solution to the problem later. Instead, students are encouraged to take notes in the lecture and then revisit each problem from the start so the system records the problem as completed by that student based on their own work.

In response to student feedback, the first hour of the first lecture in 2013 (and 2014) was spent demonstrating JPL's Integrated Development Environment using the projector and doing the first few problems. This activity was then repeated in computer labs in Week 1 with the students allowed to run JPLIDE and simply copy the Java code written by the tutor. This gave the students some confidence in starting to use the system and in solving problems.

Five computer lab sessions performed during the semester are executed as summative assessment. Prior to 2013, the assessed problem each student had to solve was hidden in JPL prior to the lab so it was new to the student. In 2013, this was changed so that, a week before the assessed lab, students were given a list of 6 to 8 problems from which one would be chosen at random for them to do in JPL's assessed mode (where they cannot see any prior work and have no other material available). This leveraged students' strategic approach to learning (Entwistle, 1988) and got them to attempt solutions to a range of problems prior to assessment. To test accumulated learning, the last assessed lab session was a hidden problem.

In 2013, a remote assistance facility was introduced where students request assistance by email so that within 24 hours a tutor logs on as the student to fix the issue in the Java code (with appropriate comments) and sends an explanatory email to the student. Also in 2013, Peer Assisted Study Sessions (PASS) were made available for students studying the first programming course. PASS sessions provide a low threat context in which students can ask questions (no academic present) and act as peer mentors to help each other. An investigation of the effectiveness of PASS as an intervention for this course showed that for each PASS session attended by the student, their final grade was raised on average by 1 percent over the cohort average. In 2014, a Student Mentoring scheme was also introduced to provide another avenue of help. Student mentoring provides peer-based assistance for challenged learners but also ensures that knowledge is reinforced and leadership developed for the student mentors.

Discussion

Introduction and development of Java Programming Laboratory has led to an improvement in student experiences of learning, as reflected in automated surveys executed through the system during semester and the formal end of semester student evaluations of course (SEC). Table 2 shows results of automated surveys provided at weeks 5 and 12 with progressive improvements between 1 percent and 8 percent in student appreciation of the JPL system as they became proficient with the learning environment.

Since 2012, end of semester student evaluations have shown a consistently high level of student satisfaction with the first programming course. Table 3 provides a comparison of 2012 and 2013 student experiences with the 2011 course prior to the introduction of JPL as a learning management tool. All tabulated data from this point refers to student and sample populations: 2011 (N=155) with n=55 responses; 2012 (N=155) with n=66 responses; and 2013 (N=130) with n=49 responses.

Question	Week 5	Week 12
The resources provided for this course help me to learn.	3.93	4.29
The problem-based learning activities have provided an effective learning experience.	3.94	4.27
The use of online technologies helped me to learn in this course.	4.05	4.10
This course has engaged me in learning.	3.89	4.11
My skills in analysis and problem solving have increased as a consequence of doing this course.	3.80	4.19
I am satisfied with the teaching facilities available for this course.	3.93	4.31

Table 2: JPL Survey Statistics for the 2012 Introduction to Programming course (mean value of responses, on a scale 1- 5). N=155 students, n=105 responses.

From 2011 to 2012, the impact of introducing Java Programming Laboratory on student perception scores of their engagement with learning Java programming was lifted by 14 percent. Student perceptions of the course organisation were boosted by 11 percent. Corresponding improvements in number of students responding with a Strong Agreement or Agreement were 3 percent for engagement and a massive 40 percent for course organisation.

Student satisfaction with the helpfulness of feedback improved by 18 percent and student perceptions of clarity and fairness of assessment improved by 17 percent. With continued system enhancements, student evaluations have remained relatively high in 2013. There were, however, some notable areas of moderation regarding student engagement with learning to program and the perception of course organisation. Contextual changes including loss of a highly regarded member of teaching staff were most likely factors of influence. Significant continued improvements were noted in student perceptions of provision of helpful feedback on assessment, and in overall satisfaction with the quality of the course.

Student perceptions and satisfaction of their engagement with learning indicates an area of continued enquiry for the development team. Qualitative analysis of student comments on their experience with the JPL-enhanced course reveals some interesting themes. Two open-ended questions were asked of students at the end of each semester: *"What did you find was particularly good about this course?"* and *"How could this course be improved?"* Table 4 shows the most frequent issues and constructs that students have indicated for each year since the introduction of Java Programming Laboratory.

Post Course Survey Question	Mean Score / 5.0			% Satisfaction		
	2011	2012	2013	2011	2012	2013
This course was well organised.	3.8	4.2	4.3	65.0	90.7	83.6
The assessment was clear and fair.	3.6	4.2	4.2	56.7	78.8	75.5
This course engaged me in learning.	3.7	4.2	4.0	76.2	78.8	69.4
The teaching in this course was effective in helping me to learn.	3.7	4.1	4.0	66.6	72.7	75.5
I received helpful feedback on my assessment work.	3.3	3.9	4.1	46.6	62.1	83.7
Overall I am satisfied with the quality of this course.	3.6	4.0	4.2	63.4	78.8	83.7

Table 3: Introduction to Programming post course survey. % Satisfaction is percentage of respondents signalling agreement or strong agreement with the question.

It can be seen that by far the most popular positive comments from students were around the perceived effectiveness of JPL as a learning tool. In 2012, many students indicated that the course was well-structured and organised and the teaching team was helpful, in the level of assistance, both in person and by email. Students also appreciated the problem-based learning approach and remote access to the system. Similar levels of popularity were experienced in 2013 for the effectiveness of JPL as a learning tool, the structure and organisation of the course, and availability of assistance by different modes. Introduction of Peer Assisted Study Sessions (PASS) providing extra student-led workshops shows that students found these as important in effective learning as they do the input of the teaching team.

Student perceptions of required course improvements in tutorial assistance and problem-solving examples have been addressed with new teaching team members and introduction of the PASS program as a student-mentored study assistance. An issue that persists is the perception that there is an assumption of prior knowledge; for some students this leads to knowledge overload in the introduction of concepts around computers and programming. In 2013, the lowest level of student satisfaction was around the perceived affordances of the course to engage them in learning. The relationship between the rapidity of the course introduction, the effective scaffolding of concepts, and student engagement with learning may reveal some important future improvements to the course. A possible approach may be to supplement face-to-face interactions with self-paced tutorials so that each of the early concepts is reinforced and understanding tested with effective formative assessment activities.

Positives (2012)	%	Improvements (2012)	%
JPL – good for learning	48	No ideas	15
Teachers	18	More tutorial help/support	9
Well-structured / organised	9	More scaled JPL problems	8
Helpful assistance in person or by email	9	Slower introduction to concepts	6
		Assumes prior knowledge	5
Problem solving	8	More teacher interaction / explanation	5
Remote access to JPL	8		

Positives (2013)	%	Improvements (2013)	%
JPL – good for learning	41	No ideas	18
Well-structured / organised	10	Slower introduction to concepts	6
Helpful assistance in person or by email	8	More computer theory to link it to	3
Peer Assisted Study Sessions	8		
Problem solving	6		
Teachers	6		

Table 4: Ranking by percentage of sample population of frequent themes revealed in post course surveys.

A representation of student learning outcome changes corresponding to the interventions around JPL are presented in Table 5, where learning outcomes for a cohort are characterised by median mark (%) and distribution of students in each of the grade bands. The table shows that the first offering in 2012 suffered a small reduction in performance over the previous year. There are, however, important variables that affect this apparent change and make learning outcome comparison, particularly from 2011 to 2012, inappropriate. First, the number of concepts taught (breadth of learning) in the course increased and, secondly, the number and type of learning activities significantly changed. Thirdly, the assessment regime has changed to suit the new content and learning system. Such changes, while maintaining professionally accredited assessment standards, amount to a significant intervention.

Year	2011	2012	2013
High Distinctions (%)	16.8	13.5	18.0
Failures (%)	21.3	23.9	20.3
Median mark (%)	59	56	65

Table 5: Cohort learning outcomes statistics.

A more reliable figure is the second evaluation of a new learning system when it has become better understood by the teaching team and 'fine tuning' can be applied to adapt features to the context. The 2013 results show a significant improvement in the learning outcome statistics at that stage. In particular, a significant rise in the median mark, indicating higher grades (better learning outcomes) for more students, and a reduction in the number of fail grades, is a clear indication of improved student engagement with learning (Carini *et al.*, 2006).

Conclusions

This chapter presented Java Programming Laboratory as a novel application of technology-enhanced learning for novice student programmers. Outcomes of using the system as a technology-enhanced learning environment and integrated approach to teaching introductory programming have been shown to be effective. It has been demonstrated that the system impacts positively on student learning experiences and learning outcomes. Recognising the contextual complexity and arcane computer knowledge that must be mastered in order to learn a first programming language, technology is used to manage a student's learning experience effectively toward optimal learning outcomes. Java Programming Laboratory provides an online program development platform and problem-based experiential learning environment that enables academics and students to monitor progression through automatically evaluated learning objectives. In order to provide timely remedial assistance, instructor access to students' achievements on tutorial and assessment tasks allows earliest possible identification of students who are at risk of failing. The system also provides feedback to the academic/teaching team designing problem sets and curricula so they can identify where extra learning assistance or redesign is required. Building on a successful international blended-learning model and open source tools, JPL provides an integrated program development environment that includes automated testing and a comprehensive set of construct-level, video-tutorial resources to aid computer program development and self-paced learning.

Java Programming Laboratory has been used in a number of first programming courses, including at eight Australian secondary schools, an Australian university and a Chinese university, as a generalisable tool for assisting students in different contexts. Further implementations include extension to a second, object- oriented programming-focused course in

Java, courses in C++ (Stroustrup, 2008) and Python (Van Rossum & Drake, 2003), and a database design course involving the Structured Query Language (SQL).

About the authors

Steve Drew is Director of Learning & Teaching in the Griffith Sciences Executive, Griffith University, Australia. He can be contacted at this email: s.drew@griffith.edu.au

Wayne Pullan is Senior Lecturer in the School of Information and Communication Technology, Griffith University, Australia. He can be contacted at this email: w.pullan@griffith.edu.au

Bibliography

Altbach, P. G. (1999). The logic of mass higher education. *Tertiary Education & Management*, Vol. 5, No. 2, pp. 107-124.

Barrows, H. S. (1996). Problem-based learning in medicine and beyond: a brief overview. In L. Wilkerson & W. H. Gijselaers (Eds.). *Bringing Problem-Based Learning to Higher Education: Theory and Practice*, San Francisco, CA: Jossey-Bass. pp. 3–12.

Biggs, J. (1999). What the student does: teaching for enhanced learning. *Higher Education Research & Development*, Vol. 18 No. 1, pp. 57-75.

Biggs, J. & C. Tang (2011). *Teaching for quality learning at university*: McGraw-Hill International.

Black, P. & D. Wiliam (2009). Developing the theory of formative assessment. *Educational Assessment, Evaluation and Accountability (formerly: Journal of Personnel Evaluation in Education)*, Vol. 21, No. 1, pp. 5-31.

Bonwell, C. C. & J. A. Eison (1991). Active Learning: Creating Excitement in the Classroom *ASHEERIC Higher Education Report* (Vol. 1). Washington, DC: George Washington University.

Carini, R.; G. D. Kuh & S. Klein (2006). Student Engagement and Student Learning: Testing the Linkages*. *Research in Higher Education*, Vol. 47, No. 1, pp. 1-32.

Dede, C. (2009). Immersive interfaces for engagement and learning. *Science*, Vol. 323, No. 5910, pp. 66-69.

Dede, C.; M. Salzman; R. B. Loftin & K. Ash (2000). Advanced Designs for Technologies of Learning. In M. J. Jacobson & R. B. Kozma (Eds.). *Innovations in Science and Mathematics Education.* Mahweh, NJ.: Erlbaum. pp. 361–413.

Delfino, M. & D. Persico (2011). Unfolding the Potential of ICT for SRL Development. In R. Carneiro; P. Lefrere; K. Steffens & J. Underwood (Eds.). *Self-Regulated Learning in Technology-Enhanced Learning Environments:* Springer. pp. 53-74.

Entwistle, N. (1988). Motivational factors in students' approaches to learning. In R. Schmeck (Ed.). *Learning strategies and learning styles:* Springer. pp. 21-51.

Goodyear, P. & S. Retalis (2010). *Technology-enhanced learning:* Sense Publishers.

Gosling, J. (2000). *The Java language specification:* Addison-Wesley Professional.

Kember, D. (2000). *Action learning and action research: improving the quality of teaching and learning.* London: Kogan Page.

Kemmis, S. (2006). Participatory action research and the public sphere. *Educational Action Research,* Vol. 14, No. 4, pp. 459-476.

Kjell, B. (1997). Programmed instruction using web pages. *Journal of Computing in Small Colleges,* Vol. 12, No. 5, pp. 113-123.

Kuh, G. D. (2003). What We're Learning About Student Engagement from NSSE: Benchmarks for Effective Educational Practices. *Change,* Vol. 35, No. 2, pp. 24-32.

Leveson, L.; N. McNeil & T. Joiner (2013). Persist or withdraw: the importance of external factors in students' departure intentions. *Higher Education Research & Development,* Vol. 32, No. 6, pp. 932-945.

Marton, F. & R. Säljö (1984). Approaches to learning. *The experience of learning,* Vol. 2, pp. 39-58.

Meyer, J. H. & R. Land (2005). Threshold concepts and troublesome knowledge (2): Epistemological considerations and a conceptual framework for teaching and learning. *Higher education,* Vol. 49, No. 3, pp. 373-388.

Minocha, S. (2009). Role of social software tools in education: a literature review. *Education + Training,* Vol. 51, No. 5/6, pp. 353-369.

Nicol, D. J. & D. Macfarlane-Dick (2006). Formative assessment and self-regulated learning: A model and seven principles of good feedback practice. *Studies in Higher Education,* Vol. 31, No. 2, pp. 199-218.

Pintrich, P. R. & E. V. De Groot (1990). Motivational and self-regulated learning components of classroom academic performance. *Journal of Educational Psychology,* Vol. 82, No.1, pp. 33-40.

Pullan, W.; S. Drew & S. Tucker (2013). *An integrated approach to teaching introductory programming.* Paper presented at the e-Learning and e-Technologies in Education (ICEEE), 2013 Second International Conference.

Rountree, J. & N. Rountree (2009). *Issues regarding threshold concepts in computer science.* In Proceedings of the Eleventh Australasian Conference on Computing Education,Vol. 95, pp. 139-146.

Savery, J. R. (2006). Overview of problem-based learning: Definitions and distinctions. *Interdisciplinary Journal of Problem-based Learning,* Vol. 1, No. 1, pp. 9-20.

Simons, K. D. & J. D. Klein (2007). The impact of scaffolding and student achievement levels in a problem-based learning environment. *Instructional Science,* Vol. 35, No. 1, pp. 41-72.

Sorva, J. (2010). *Reflections on threshold concepts in computer programming and beyond.* In Proceedings of the 10th Koli Calling International Conference on Computing Education Research, ACM, pp. 21-30.

Stroustrup, B. (2008). *Programming: principles and practice using C++:* Addison-Wesley Professional.

Taylor, J. & B. House (2010). An Exploration of Identity, Motivations and Concerns of Non-Traditional Students at Different Stages of Higher Education. *Psychology Teaching Review,* Vol. 16, No. 1, pp. 46-57.

Trigwell, K. & M. Prosser (1991). Improving the quality of student learning: the influence of learning context and student approaches to learning on learning outcomes. *Higher Education,* Vol. 22, No. 3, pp. 251-266.

van der Meer, J.; E. Jansen & M. Torenbeek (2010). 'It's almost a mindset that teachers need to change': first-year students' need to be inducted into time management. *Studies in Higher Education,* Vol. 35, No. 7, pp. 777-791.

Van Rossum, G. & F. L. Drake (2003). *Python language reference manual:* Network Theory.

Wang, F. & M. J. Hannafin (2005). Design-based research and technology-enhanced learning environments. *Educational technology research and development,* Vol. 53, No. 4, pp. 5-23.

Wirth, N. (1983). On the design of programming languages. *Programming Languages:* Springer, pp. 23-30.

Wu, J.-H.; R. D. Tennyson & T.–L. Hsia (2010). A study of student satisfaction in a blended e-learning system environment. *Computers & Education,* Vol. 55, No. 1, pp. 155-164.

Zimmerman, B. & D. Schunk (2008). An essential dimension of self-regulated learning. In B. Zimmerman & D. Schunk (Eds.). *Motivation and self-regulation: Theory, research, and applications,* pp. 1-31.

Chapter 9

Enhancing student learning in online nursing education using ApprenNet technology

Diane D. DePew, Frances H. Cornelius and Carol Patton

Introduction

Contemporary healthcare delivery environments demand practitioners to be critical thinkers and to respond appropriately to unfolding situations. Healthcare environments are often described as chaotic, frenetic, and complex. It is essential, therefore, that faculty members prepare nursing students to apply critical thinking skills to guide appropriate responses in their practice.

A number of technology-focused teaching methods address critical thinking, but there is a lack of tools for assessing appropriate responses to situations. Online education of healthcare professionals typically occurs through synchronous or asynchronous discussions and written assignments. These methods can lead to compartmentalising rather than integrating learning domains.

The challenge is to construct learning activities which develop high-level critical thinking skills and which engage students in learning activities which facilitate idea exchange in the online classroom. Not only do students need to be prepared to think critically, but they must also be able to articulate relevant knowledge and communicate effectively and persuasively with the interdisciplinary team. Faculty members, in turn, must be able to conduct authentic assessment of students' mastery.

The purpose of this chapter is to examine ApprenNet as an effective method for assessing students' critical thinking and appropriate response to specific situations. ApprenNet is an innovative Web-based teaching approach reflecting online simulation to enhance student learning. ApprenNet links learning experiences from real situations to the online classroom. It provides a rich opportunity to engage learners in critical thinking learning activities requiring appropriate responses. It is also a means of exchanging ideas with peers and faculty members. ApprenNet is a methodology rooted in learning theories and an e-learning framework.

This chapter begins with an introduction of the ApprenNet technology and follows with an examination of the theoretical foundations of cognitive apprenticeship and experiential learning. It continues with an overview of the ApprenNet technological process to support learning in a nursing program. Finally, we offer a discussion of the outcomes of the technology to support learning. The key lesson from this chapter is that technology can be used to link classroom and practice via structured learning activities which permit faculty members to assess student performance.

The chapter contributes to this anthology on technology-enhanced learning by introducing a technology that offers authentic assessment of students in the online environment. It also discusses the impact of the technology on learning in higher education.

Historical perspectives on ApprenNet technology

In 2011, ApprenNet, conceived by Karl Okamoto, received a National Science Foundation (NSF) Small Business Innovation Research (SBIR) Phase I grant to build a web platform for teaching entrepreneurial law practice. Law students were given a legal challenge from real life, such as acquisition, and were required to provide a response to a client. The experiment was a success. In 2012, the NSF awarded ApprenNet a Phase II SBIR grant to continue to build its online learning platform and share it with other disciplines. Since its Phase II grant, ApprenNet has been used in the health professions, education, and business schools. Corporate America has also begun to use ApprenNet to develop workforce readiness skills in employees. In December 2013, the NSF granted ApprenNet a second Phase I grant to test its platform with science, technology, engineering, and mathematics (STEM) educators in an effort to improve K-12 student achievement in STEM.

Currently, 25% of U.S. law schools use ApprenNet technology on some level for developing transactional law practice skills. Business schools at Colorado State University, Temple University and Drexel University use it for case analysis, presentation and communication skills. Classroom management and communication skills (how to explain concepts to students clearly and how to have difficult conversations with parents or other teachers, for example) are being taught with ApprenNet in undergraduate and graduate programmes.

At this time, both graduate and undergraduate nursing programmes at Drexel University, in hybrid and fully online courses, use ApprenNet technology. Courses using the technology are leadership, ethics, and education. Because of ApprenNet technology, Drexel nursing students receive a 'value-added' student learning experience and course evaluations indicate a high degree of student satisfaction with ApprenNet technology in the online classroom.

ApprenNet technology

Tsai *et al.* (2011) report self-efficacy is challenged, and can be strengthened, through intervention and training. ApprenNet's Web-based technology consists of a three-phase process allowing educators to create and assign a structured learning exercise. The design of the exercise provides a controlled and orchestrated learning experience for the student with the goal of eliciting the desired performance/response which permits the faculty member to assess student mastery. There are steps through which the student must progress in each phase to achieve the desired activity goal (Figure 1).

In Phase 1, the learning exercise requires students to watch a recorded video. The recorded video presents a challenging scenario depicting a situation likely to be encountered in practice. The scenario requires students to respond to the situation through role-play while using critical thinking skills and applying knowledge, skills and/or attitudes. The second step provides the opportunity to practise the skill by responding to the challenging scenario via video. In the third step, students are able to review their performance, reflect critically on it and make adjustments if necessary. This first phase provides the opportunity to 'learn by doing'.

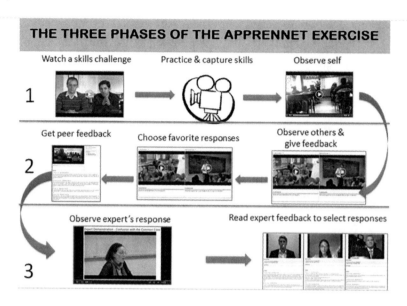

Figure 1: The Three Phases of ApprenNet Structured Learning Activity.

In Phase 2, students can learn from their peers through a three-step process. First, by viewing peer responses, students are able to compare their responses to those of their peers. Next, students give constructive and collegial feedback to their peers using, as a guide, a rubric provided by the faculty member. Peer review consists of reviewing a designated number of video responses by peers in their online classroom. Once the student reviews the designated number of these, the student formulates collegial and constructive peer feedback that all students in the online classroom can view. This step solidifies for students the link between the performance and the assessment criteria. Finally, students receive peer feedback which can be utilised to improve understanding and improve future performance.

Barbera and Linder-VanBerschot (2011) indicate a need to focus on both process and results in online learning. Feedback is the key mechanism in the development and enhancement of learning and is a foundational underpinning of ApprenNet technology in the online class-room (Brown, 2005; Chickering & Gamson, 1987; Mutch 2003; Orrell, 2000). Feedback fosters higher-level thinking (Lasso, 2006) leading to individual improvement (Hubba & Freed, 2000).

In Phase 3, students view an expert's video response to the challenge and the expert's feedback to select students. The final step in Appren-Net's pedagogically-grounded theory is expert response to the challenge scenario, in which the expert answers the same questions as the students. This consists of a video recording by an expert in the specific content area which students and their peers have presented on and discussed. The expert response provides an opportunity for students to reflect and benchmark with the expert response their critical thinking, knowledge, skills, and attitudes. At all levels within this activity, students are able reflect on their own responses, those of their peers, and that of the expert.

ApprenNet technology's design captures simulated realistic practice which approximates the real world environment to specific course content. For example, the nursing student is presented with a challenge which involves application of knowledge or skills guided by evidence-based research and best practice. The simulation activity has goals at each phase of the process that stimulate students to think critically and reflectively on their learning (Table 1).

Activity	Activity Goal
Phase 1	
The student 1. Watches a skills challenge 2. Records him/herself practicing the skill via video 3. Critically observes his/her skills	The student learns *by doing*
Phase 2	
The student 1. Observes other student responses 2. Gives feedback to other students 3. Receives peer feedback on his/her response	The student learns *from peers*
Phase 3	
The student 1. Views an expert's video response to the challenge 2. Reads expert feedback to select students	The student learns *from experts*

Table 1: Activity and Desired Activity Goal within the Three Phase Process of an ApprenNet Exercise.

Reflection allows an individual to recognise performance strengths and weaknesses (Chickering & Gamson, 1987). Then, an individual can specifically direct his/her efforts towards improvement by remediating his/her identified deficiencies and adjusting his/her approach to future learning tasks (Lasso, 2010). Ultimately, the individual's reflection allows him/her to transfer lessons learned to new and different situations (Goode, 2000). Feedback from the ApprenNet learning exercises first interrupts the student's linear learning progression (Goode, 2000) and identifies an individual's strengths and weaknesses (Chickering & Gamson, 1987). This type of interruption leads to reflection and higher-level learning, a process which aligns with Nygaard's (this volume) statement that "*learning involves acquiring new personal knowledge, skills, and competencies which can be used to resolve forthcoming challenges in life*". There is a clear and compelling need to educate students in a manner consistent with the world of work and what professionals do in real life (Hirumi, 2013).

Theoretical underpinnings

This section provides an overview of the learning and technology theories that provide the foundation for ApprenNet. We start with cognitive apprenticeship and experiential learning, both constructivist learning theories. We end the section with Hirumi's (2013) three levels for planning e-learning interaction model.

Cognitive apprenticeship

Cognitive apprenticeship rethinks the traditional apprenticeship of task formation to cognitive use in a variety of contexts. Conceptual and factual knowledge is encouraged to develop a deeper meaning. The goal is to decontextualise knowledge so it can be used in other areas and in problem solving. Cognitive skill requires "*externalisation of processes that are usually carried out internally*" (Collins *et al.*, 1987:4), and learning through guided experience encourages the development of self-correction and self-monitoring. These are crucial metacognitive skills.

Collins (1989) describes six characteristics of cognitive apprenticeship:

+ situated learning;
+ modelling and explaining;
+ coaching;
+ reflection on performance;
+ articulation;
+ exploration.

Technology affords the environment – the context – in which to create real world situations which cannot be realised in a classroom. 'Modelling' shows how a process works, and 'explaining' gives reasons why the process happened that way. 'Coaching' allows for individual feedback on specific performance and offers a different perspective on the process. 'Reflection on performance' gives students the ability to replay their performance against peer and expert performance. 'Articulation' forces students to think about and explain their thought process. 'Exploration' guides students to find new solutions to problems (Collins, 1989).

Technology provides an environment with resources for cognitive apprenticeship. Putting students in virtual situations to articulate a problem solution with feedback, modelling and coaching, and then providing peer and expert coaching upon which to reflect, is the basis of the ApprenNet methodology.

Experiential learning theory

The groundwork for experiential learning theory was laid by Dewey, Piaget, Lewin, Rogers, and others. In 1984, Kolb refined the concepts into two learning aspects: processing and perceiving. Processing is how we do things and perceiving is how we think about things. Both are integral components of experiential learning. The processing continuum includes active experimentation (doing) and reflective observation (watching). The perceiving continuum includes concrete experience (feeling) and abstract conceptualisation (thinking). Figure 2 shows how these continua interact. The four quadrants are the learning styles based on the intersection of the student's perceiving and processing continuums.

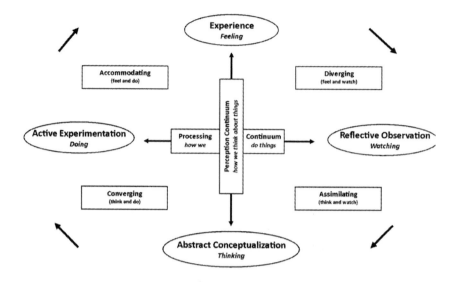

Figure 2: Kolb's Experiential Learning Theory.

Kolb's (1984) model emphasises the need for discovery and self-reflection. Learning occurs in a cycle; a person experiences something then reflects on it. This reflection leads to the incorporation and refinement of concepts which then lead to implications for action. ApprenNet affords the experience and reflection throughout the learning exercise.

Three Levels for planning e-learning interactions

Instructional technology offers methods for learners to be immersed in the learning aspect of education. There are unlimited ways to integrate technology for learning consisting of human and nonhuman interactions. However, technology use does not inherently mean an increase in the quality of education. *"Frameworks are necessary to help organize and apply our knowledge of research and theory, and properly integrate the use of emerging technologies to facilitate elearning"* (Hirumi, 2013:2). Hirumi (2013) describes three levels for planning e-learning interactions. The levels guide the *"alignment between learning theories, instructional strategies, and planned interactions"* (Hirumi, 2013:3).

Level I is learner-self interaction. This consists of the mental and metacognitive processes which students use for learning. Learning theory describes these internal processes. The instructional strategies (Level III interaction) are selected based on the designer's values and beliefs of how and why people learn (Level I interaction). That is, the learning theory which the designer subscribes to directs the selected technology strategies. The selected strategies then guide the design and sequencing of the user interface (Level II interactions). The sequencing of these strategies provides the instructional events of human and nonhuman interactions for learning (Figure 3). The user interface of ApprenNet provides interactions between learner-learner, learner-instructor, learner-other (expert), learner-content, and learner-tool. These interactions are the experiences upon which the learner reflects.

Application of ApprenNet technology in the online classroom

This section of the chapter will present a complete structured learning exercise. We will provide a step-by-step example of how this tool is utilised within our courses. Each structured learning exercise is designed to elicit demonstration of critical thinking to address a specific, reality-based situation.

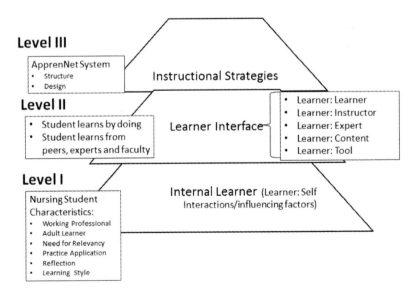

Figure 3: Three Levels of Planned eLearning Interactions as Applied to ApprenNet.

Learning exercise

Challenge ▸ Peer Review ▸ Expert Response ▸ Analysis

Instructions

Challenge: Watch the video below. You are a colleague of Terri Burns. She is troubled about the situation and reaches out to you for advice. What would you say to her? What evidence would you consider?

As you prepare your response, be sure to review the following articles located in Module 4. You may also consult the literature and the recommended readings as you prepare your response.

1. MedlinePlus: Advanced Directives (www.nlm.nih.gov/medlineplus/advancedirec-tives.html)
2. End-of-Life Ethical Issues (Chapter 15)
3. The Right to Die (Chapter 16)

Submit a video response between May 19 and May 25 at 11:50pm EST. Your response should not be longer than 3 minutes. If you need assistance, select 'Help & Support' (located on the right side of the screen).

You must submit your response by the due date to receive any credit for this activity.

Peer Review: You will be expected to review 6 peer responses any time between May 26 and June 1 at 11:50pm EST. You will be required to review and rate 3 pairs of peer submissions (for a total of six) using the provided rubric. Remember, you are expected to provide constructive and collegial feedback using this rubric.

Reviewing 3 pairs of responses unlocks access to an Expert Response and the top peer-rated submissions.

If you have any questions about this assignment, please post your question in the Q&A Discussion Forum in Blackboard. If you are having technical difficulty, please use the 'Help & Support' button on the right side of your screen.

Figure 4: ApprenNet Challenge Ms. D & the Interdisciplinary Team: Patient Self-Determination.

Students receive a brief introduction to the learning exercise and are instructed to view a video challenge (Figure 4). This scenario involves Terri Burns, a staff nurse working on the oncology unit at a busy inner city hospital. She has a troubling experience at work and reaches out to her colleague (the student) for guidance. For the purposes of this chapter, a transcript of the video is provided (Table 2).

After watching the skills challenge, the student records him/herself practising the skill via video and during this process, critically observing his/her skills: 'learning by doing'. Frequently, students will re-record their response after they have critically reviewed their performance.

Terry Burns: I have a problem that I hope you can help me with.

Colleague: What's the problem?

Terry Burns: As you know, I work on an Oncology unit at the City Medical Center. The other day, during rounds with the Gynecology Oncology team, I met Ms. D, a 33 year old female with stage IIIC ovarian cancer. Her situation is not good. The cancer has spread throughout her abdomen and inguinal nodes. She has malignant ascites and a bowel obstruction. Her condition has worsened so she has to have daily paracentesis. The Team has told her that they will have to operate to partially alleviate the obstruction. Ms. D told the team she has schizophrenia and has not been taking her psychotropic medication for quite some time because they are 'poison'. Ms. D told me "I may be crazy, but I'm not stupid. The treatment is going to kill me. I don't want it."

The Oncology Team told her that the treatment is the only chance to cure her cancer and they will contact the family against her wishes to make sure she gets the proper treatment.

I am troubled by this situation. Do you think that Ms. D is capable of making her own decision? Or do you think the team should intervene? What do you think I should do?

Table 2: Scenario Script.

Next, the student observes other student responses, gives feedback to other students and receives peer feedback on his/her response: 'learning from peers' (Figure 5). Students are instructed to view and provide constructive, collegial feedback to peers' responses to the scenario using a Likert-scale grading rubric.

Figure 5: Phase Two: Viewing Peer Responses and Giving Feedback.

In the final phase, the student views an expert's video response to the challenge and reads expert feedback to select students: 'learning from the expert'. In this step, the students view the response from Dr. Amy Jones, a nurse ethicist who has served as chair of the hospital's ethics board. Viewing the expert's response stimulates the student to reflect on his/her own performance and reinforces higher-level learning (Figure 6).

Measuring ApprenNet success on student learning through outcome data

This section includes the outcome data we have collected thus far in our use of the ApprenNet technology. It begins with quantitative and qualitative data and concludes with the impact this technology-enhanced learning has had on teaching and learning.

Figure 6: Phase Three: Viewing Expert Response.

Quantitative data

As with any new teaching technology, it is essential to assess and measure outcome data and metrics to evaluate the impact and effectiveness of changes to the learning environment. Evaluation should be both formative and summative, with reports of learner assessment experience in online environments (Mao & Peck, 2013). Our evaluation includes qualitative and quantitative outcome data regarding the ApprenNet technology application in the online classroom.

ApprenNet has been implemented in online courses for nursing undergraduate and graduate levels. The undergraduate programme is for those with a Registered Nurse license seeking their Baccalaureate degree. The graduate course, Ethics, is one of the core courses required of all students seeking Master's degrees. The other graduate course where ApprenNet is used is in a nurse educator specialty course on teaching strategies. Immediately after the end of a term, students are asked to complete an anonymous online questionnaire. Data were gathered on the students' perception of how easy ApprenNet activities were to use, added to learning, and increased their ability to provide constructive feedback. The undergraduates were also asked how ApprenNet activities increased enhanced engagement in learning. Table 3 shows the results based on a 5-point Likert scale from 118 undergraduate and 85 graduate students.

	Undergraduate	Graduate
Measure	Mean	Mean
Ease of Use	4.46	4.23
Add to Learning	3.45	4.38
Add to Engagement	3.95	
Constructive Feedback	2.70	4.59

Table 3: Evaluation of ApprenNet from Undergraduate and Graduate Nursing Students.

The post-licensure nursing students reported a high degree of satisfaction with ApprenNet technology's ease of use. Graduate nursing students reported high degrees of satisfaction with ApprenNet technology's ease of use, enhancement of learning, and skill in providing constructive peer feedback. The type of student in each group could explain these differences. The RN-BSN student is typically in the programme to obtain a nursing position in acute care (most acute care hospitals in urban areas require the Baccalaureate for employment) or to keep their position as required by their employer. The graduate student is seeking to advance their practice.

Qualitative data

We obtained qualitative data from the undergraduate and graduate students with an open-ended question: *"Describe your experience using this learning methodology"*, as part of the online anonymous survey, noted above. Four major themes emerged: (1) different learning domains, (2) technology interaction, (3) reflection, and (4) thought provoking.

It was clear from the analysis of the research data that ApprenNet utilises the cognitive domain and the affective domain. As one student stated:

> "I thought it was a great benefit in that you were able to hear and visu-
> alise the speaker's tone – sometimes content and/or meaning is lost or
> misunderstood when simply reading the written word. By being able to
> hear the tone in the speaker's commentary as well as visualise the body
> language you are able to get a clearer understanding of the speaker's
> meaning".

There was also added value to using the technology. For example, one student stated:

> "Overall I thought the use of ApprenNet was useful in my learning expe-
> rience for the material in this course. I also appreciate that it helped my
> timidness related to public speaking. The feedback and constructive criti-
> cism was [sic] very helpful".

The technology interaction, or as Hirumi (2013) would state, 'learner-tool' interaction, proved to be a hurdle for some. As one student shared:

> "The thing that took me longest was figuring out how to use the camera
> and upload the video on my computer. I had never used my computer
> camera before so I felt like it was a lot of wasted time that I could have
> spent on something else. The website was user friendly, however, so once
> I was able to record my video it was easy to upload".

This was a consistent theme:

> "This was the first time using this, it was a little confusing at first. After
> using it I was able to navigate the system".

There were also those who embraced the interactions. For example:

> "I enjoyed using the ApprenNet system. I thought it was a smart way to
> interact with the students in class and hear other opinions" and "It was
> my first time having "meets", I found it informative and motivating to
> improve my public speaking skills!"

For some, the 'learner-tool' was not conducive to learning. For example, students said:

> *"Overall I am just not an online-type of student therefore this learning methodology wasn't particularly engaging".*

And:

> *"It was weird. Not my style of learning".*

Of course, there was the dissenting comment:

> *"I did not like the Apprenet [sic] application. It's nice to know that there is something else out there other then [sic] Discussion Boards for online learning. But I am not a visual learner. Using Apprenet [sic] it seems as if you are taking speech class and expected to be proficient in talking (not looking at your notes) while answering questions. I am very nervous in front of the camera and hated this experience".*

The use of a video response did increase student anxiety for some. However, providing the 'why' of the activity – articulating a viewpoint is critical in the profession – and indicating that the grade was not photogenically-based reduced anxiety. Once the students were given this information, the comments about being videotaped and anxiety decreased.

It was evident that when using the ApprenNet technology, the students engaged in reflection on their learning. As noted by students:

> *"The ability to record a presentation in private and to refine it prior to posting the presentation relieved alot [sic] of stress and self-judgment".*

And:

> *"It was something different then [sic] other classes. It helped with my confidence. I actually noticed things about me that I did not realise I do, so after watching myself I am more conscious about how I talk".*

The reflection went beyond self to a comparison of their performance to others. For example:

> *"The ability to review others opinions regarding the subject matter provided different insights into the material".*

And:

> "I was very nervous at first. I learned a lot by watching the other students and trying to incorporate those things into my next meet".

Perspectives on the technology changed as well:

> "i [sic] did not think I would enjoy this, but I really did. It was engaging and was nice to see how other classmates interpreted the information given".

This suggests that the use of ApprenNet does enhance learning through reflection, an aspect of both cognitive apprenticeship and experiential learning theory.

Finally, the data showed that including ApprenNet technology was thought-provoking. As one student stated:

> "It is always a good thing to learn how to use new formats. Just having to organise your thoughts and present your information in an unfamiliar format forces you to look at your conclusions in a novel way. I was a little uncomfortable at first but I find it interesting and thought provoking to see my peers present their conclusions".

The application of the time constraint prompted a different way of thinking:

> "I felt ApperNet [sic] was an innovative way for students to observe, evaluate, address, and communicate. It was difficult composing a 3 minute response. This process helped me to identify the specifics of a given situation and formulate a thoughtful and concise response. The subjects evoked strong emotions, which made responding in 3 minutes difficult. I suppose this helps to take the emotion out of the conversation allowing for critical thinking. a [sic] great experience in learning".

This suggests that ApprenNet enhances learning through the content and the technology.

Impact on teaching

Through this activity, faculty members were able to determine the students' mastery of the content and ability to effectively articulate a persuasive response to the challenge. Incorporating literature to support their responses demonstrated scholarly learning. Typed discussion boards and papers take time for teachers to give feedback and grade. With ApprenNet, faculty members can streamline their workflow. The engagement of the students in the learning process has an overall positive effect through reflection and critical thinking.

Using the Technological Pedagogical Content Knowledge (TPACK) model (see Dobozy *et al.*, this volume), the ApprenNet platform offers an 'off the shelf' solution to the required technological knowledge. The content and pedagogical knowledge still resides with the expertise of the faculty member and the input of the expert response into the exercise enhances the content knowledge.

Impact on learning

Based on the data and observations of the video responses, it is clear that students were able to measure their own performance against their peers and the expert response. Students develop self-confidence in their ability to communicate effectively and persuasively by supporting their position with evidence and develop skills in application of evidence-based practice. Using peer reviews, integrating external expert responses and including written feedback to use the highest rated responses, learning occurs on the cognitive and affective levels.

Conclusion

ApprenNet is a pedagogically-grounded, theoretically-based online technology that adds value and enhances student learning as evidenced in online nursing education. ApprenNet technology consists of three steps and engages nursing student learning through learning experiences from the real world into the online classroom. These real world learning experiences prepare nursing students with enhanced capacity to care for

patients in diverse healthcare environments and enhance nurse retention as a result of critical thinking through ApprenNet application of
course-related knowledge, skills, and attitudes. Evaluation and outcome
data indicate high levels of nursing student satisfaction with ApprenNet
technology. Students report learning through engaging learning activities with rich feedback and the opportunity to practise answering tough
questions from real world experiences.

Nurse educators are challenged to prepare a nursing workforce
grounded in knowledge, skills, and attitudes, ready for a challenging,
demanding and vital career in diverse healthcare delivery environments.
ApprenNet technology helps prepare students across levels of nursing
education for the realities of healthcare by fostering and promoting critical
thinking that enhances patient care quality, safety and nurse satisfaction.
ApprenNet technology has potential for broader application in a wide
variety of educational disciplines other than law and nursing and can be
used in fully online courses and in traditional settings.

About the authors

Diane D. DePew is an Assistant Clinical Professor at the College of
Nursing & Health Professions at Drexel University. She can be contacted
at this email: d.depew@drexel.edu

Frances H. Cornelius is a Clinical Professor and Director of the MSN
Advanced Role Program at the College of Nursing & Health Professions
at Drexel University. She can be contacted at this email: fc28@drexel.edu

Carol Patton is an Associate Clinical Professor at the College of Nursing
& Health Professions at Drexel University. She can be contacted at this
email: cmp358@drexel.edu

Bibliography

Barbera, E. & J. A. Linder-VanBerschot (2011). Systemic Multicultural Model for Online Education: Tracing Connections Among Learner Inputs, Instructional Processes, and Outcomes. *The Quarterly Review of Distance Education*. Vol. 12, No. 3, pp. 167-180.

Brown, S. (2004). Assessment for Learning. *Learning and Teaching in Higher Education*, Issue 1, pp. 81-89.

Chickering, A. W. & Z. F. Gamson (1987). Seven Principles for Good Practice in Undergraduate Education. *American Association for Higher Education and Accreditation Bulletin*, Vol. 39, No. 7, pp. 3-7.

Collins, A. (1989). *Cognitive Apprenticeship and Instructional Technology*. Cambridge, MA: Illinois University (Urbana: Center for the Study of Reading. Bolt, Beranek and Newman, Inc).

Collins, A.; J. S. Brown & S. E. Newman. (1987). *Cognitive Apprenticeship: Teaching the Craft of Reading, Writing, and Mathematics*. Cambridge, MA: Illinois University (Urbana: Center for the Study of Reading. Bolt, Beranek and Newman, Inc).

Goode, V. M. (2000). There is a Methodology to this Madness: A Review and Analysis of Feedback in the Clinical Process. *Oklahoma Law Review*, pp. 223- 228.

Hirumi, A. (2013). Three Levels of Planned ELearning Interactions: A Framework for Grounding Research and the Design of ELearning Programs. *The Quarterly Review of Distance Education*, Vol. 14, No. 1, pp. 1-16.

Huba, M. & J. E. Freed. (2000). *Learner-Centered Assessment on College Campuses: Shifting the Focus from Teaching to Learning*. Boston: Allyn and Bacon.

Kolb, D. A. (1984). *Experiential Learning: Experience as the Source of Learning and Development*. Englewood Cliffs, NJ: Prentice-Hall.

Lasso, R. A. (2010). Is Our Students Learning? Using Assessments to Measure and Improve Law School Learning and Performance, 15 Barry L. Rev. 73, *John Marshall Institutional Repository*, pp. 75-106.

Mao, J. & K. Peck (2013). Assessment Strategies, Self-Regulated Learning Skills, and Perceptions of Assessment in Online Learning. *The Quarterly Review of Distance Education*, Vol. 14, No. 2, pp. 75-95.

Mutch, A. (2003). Exploring the Practice of Feedback to Students. *Active Learning in Higher Education*, Vol. 4, No. 1, pp. 24-38.

Orrell, J. (2006). Feedback on Learning Achievement: Rhetoric and Reality. *Teaching in Higher Education*, Vol. 11, No. 4, pp. 441-456.

Tsai, C. C.; S. C. Chuang; J. C. Liang & M. J. Tsai (2011). Self-Efficacy in Internet-Based Learning Environments: A Literature Review. *Educational Technology & Society*, Vol. 14, No. 4, pp. 222-240.

Chapter 10

Using mobile technology to enhance field education: a blended learning model

Leon Cygman

Introduction

This chapter is an important contribution to the anthology on technology-enhanced learning in higher education because it demonstrates that using mobile technology will increase the pedagogical value in courses that require some of the objectives to be studied in an unsupervised, out-of-the-classroom environment. Learning in this type of environment will be referred to as field education.

This chapter will give you the following three insights:

1) how field education can be enhanced with mobile and Internet technologies;

2) how distance education theory can be used to support a technology-enhanced learning environment in higher education;

3) how mobile technologies can provide a resource for self-reflection and data analysis in education.

Aviation has taken its place in the realm of higher education. Those wishing to become pilots can earn their wings and an aviation-related degree at one of a multitude of post-secondary institutions. Currently, there are over 300 (AvScholars, 2007) universities and colleges in North America offering degrees in aviation. With the looming pilot shortage, academically trained pilots are actively sought by major airlines around the world (Clark, 2013).

When I was learning to become a pilot, I was asked to perform manoeuvres, such as stalls and spins, which were very frightening. After the instructor ensured I was able to perform these exercises safely, he sent me out on my own to practise. I was aware I had to demonstrate proficiencies to a flight examiner to acquire a pilot's license but I did not think it was worth risking my life to practise these exercises without my instructor in the cockpit. When I returned from these supposed practise sessions, I was debriefed by my instructor. I told him that I had not only practised these manoeuvres but I was also getting comfortable with them. I finally chose to master these skills only when accompanied by an instructor, which slowed my progress to attain a pilot's license. Meaningful dialogue was not possible in this independent learning environment because the instructor could never be sure which skills I had practised or what my level of proficiency was.

I am now Chair of the Mount Royal University Aviation programme in Calgary, Alberta, Canada. I am always looking for innovative ways to increase the educational value of flight education and to ensure students are, in fact, practising manoeuvres as briefed by their instructors. In this chapter, I will discuss how adding technology to flight education can significantly improve learning outcomes and create better dialogue between student and instructor.

The purpose of this chapter is to provide a solution for instructors who want to increase meaningful dialogue with students engaged in field education. It begins by describing the problems faced by instructors unable to provide meaningful feedback to students as a result of the limited interaction inherent in field education. It then proposes a technology solution and provides an example of how the technique was implemented in flight education. The chapter continues by discussing how the implementation of a communications medium can support meaningful dialogue, strengthen the learning outcomes, and enhance student engagement. Finally, it provides a recommendation for a technology-enhanced solution to strengthen the link between the instructor and the student and it will inspire a strategic approach to using technology-enhanced learning solutions in higher education, also discussed by Nygaard (this volume). Although the case discussed in this chapter is related to flight education, the concepts can be applied to any post-secondary environments where field education is necessary.

Federal regulators mandate the regiment of flight education standards, which consists of dual flight training, an instructor accompanying the student in the cockpit, and solo training, in which the student takes the aircraft on their own in order to practise what they have been taught in dual flights and learned from classroom theory. This creates an interesting dilemma for both the student pilot and the instructor. If the student is doing his/her learning at a distance without an instructor present, how can the student be evaluated on his/her performance or be given feedback for improvement? In this chapter, I examine how the use of mobile technology can solve this problem and create a blended learning environment that can enhance courses involving field education.

Background

Until the recent proliferation of mobile devices, students performing field work were away from Internet stations and were known to reference online resources. With the proliferation of tablets and smart phones, students increasingly have access to a wealth of information away from the classroom. There is now a bring-your-own-device (Khaddage et al., 2013) movement in education where students are encouraged to use their own mobile devices as learning tools rather than relying on computer-based web browser technologies. These mobile devices contain basic tools, such as web browsers, which have taken distance education into a new learning technology paradigm. Although these devices can be brought into the field, they have not been powerful enough to support the demands of learning management systems (Wang & Higgins, 2005). This issue has been further compounded by the expensive data plans required to access web servers.

Incorporating mobile technology into field work can enhance student learning. In the case where students must leave the classroom in order to have a complete educational experience, mobile technology can be used to bring new and exciting possibilities to higher education. For example, a geology student can take a picture of a rock formation and geo-tag it to document its exact location.

Problem

The requirements of students performing field education emerges from the demands of the course as determined by the instructors and, in the case of aviation education, government regulators. In North America, flight education is governed by national standards set out by the Federal Aviation Administration in the USA and Transport Canada in Canada. These agencies dictate the types of fieldwork required in order for the student to be granted a rating or license. For example, of the 65 flight hours required by Transport Canada for a commercial pilot license (CPL), 30 hours must be solo practice. The regulations are also very prescriptive on the types of solo practice required. For example, one of the requirements for the CPL is that the student must undertake a solo flight of at least 300 nautical miles (nm) from point of departure, including at least three landings at places other than the departure point, and the flight must be conducted within flight parameter limits prescribed by Transport Canada (Transport Canada, 2009, 2013).

In field education, students must have a clear understanding of the objectives before they venture out on their own. Before a solo training flight, a student is briefed by the instructor on the objectives to be accomplished. On return from a solo flight, it is vital that the instructor debrief the student on all aspects of the learning experience in order for this flight to have a successful learning outcome. According to Transport Canada (2004), the instructor must provide the student with an assessment of the student's performance based on flight test standards (Transport Canada, 2009). This assessment must include both the strong and weak points and advice on how to correct any errors. The ensuing dialogue cannot be meaningful because the only information available is limited to the student account of the exercise.

As with all education modalities, the instructor must be fully cognisant of the student's level of progress in order to plan subsequent lessons. Solo flights are an integral part of flight training but the student must fully and honestly report his/her progress. The problem with this method of instruction is that the instructor can never be sure that the student report was an accurate reflection of the solo flight. Perhaps the student's practice was not as successful as indicated or the student did not practise the briefed exercises. The instructor might be under the false impression that the student is further along in the flight curriculum, causing confusion, delays in progress and a possible deterioration of trust between student and instructor (Bogo *et al.*, 2007).

Theoretical background

Field education can be equated to distance education because there is an attempt to impart knowledge to students when they are at a distance from each other (Wedemeyer, 1981); thus, exploring a distance education theory to support a solution is appropriate.

Transactional distance theory

One of the core distance education theories, transactional distance, was developed by Moore (2000). This theory is *"invaluable in guiding the complex practice of a rational process such as teaching and learning at a distance"* (Garrison, 2000:3). It suggests that if learning outcomes in any distance education course are to be maximised, transactional distance needs to be minimised.

Moore's (2000) theory postulates three interactive components:

1) structure – the way a course is delivered by the communication medium;
2) dialogue – dialogue between the student and the teacher;
3) student autonomy – individual student's sense of personal responsibility and the degree of self-directedness.

As shown in Figure 1, transactional distance is lessened in courses with high levels of dialogue and little predetermined structure. Transactional distance is also determined by student autonomy exhibited in the control the student has in the process of learning (Moore & Kearsley, 1996; Moore, 2000; Saba & Shearer, 1994). Teaching situations involving different transactional distances require unique or specialised instructional techniques (Transactional Distance Theory, 2002).

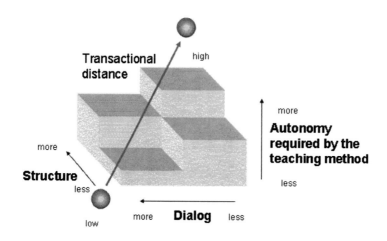

Figure 1. 3D model of transactional distance (Stover, 2004).

Moore (2000:24) describes structure, as "*the ways in which the teaching programme is structured so that it can be delivered through the various communications media*". Without a communications medium, students participating in aviation studies may also lose connection with other facets of the educational structure, which is important in minimising transactional distance. According to Chen (2001), the instructor's recognition that students need technical interaction might contribute to enhancing the teaching-learning experience in the distance learning environment. Therefore, the addition of a communication medium, such as discussion boards or live chat tools, is pivotal for minimising transactional distance.

Dialogue, as explained by Moore (2000:23) is a "*series of interactions having positive qualities*". Dialogue must be purposeful, constructive and valued by each party (Moore, 2000); without any tangible evidence of the fieldwork performed, meaningful interaction would be difficult to establish. Although the instructor might debrief the student's experience in the field, positive interaction can be aided by the use of a communication medium and "*has a direct impact on the extent and quality of dialogue between instructors and students*" (Moore, 2000:23).

Student autonomy in field education is quite prevalent and is described by Moore (2000:26) as "*the extent to which, in the teaching/learning relationship, it is the student rather than the teacher who determines the goals, the learning experiences, and the evaluation decisions of the learning programme*".

When transactional distance is high, students share a greater responsibility for their learning and must use their personal judgment about what, when and where to study. Students must be highly autonomous in order to be successful in distance education systems where transactional distance is great (Kearsley, 2000). Those students with a high level of autonomy are emotionally independent of an instructor and are self-directed, resulting in high transactional distance. Students with low levels of autonomy tend to depend on the instructor for guidance through the course structure and have a tendency to display more dependency throughout the learning process (Mueller, 2003). This careful balance must be negotiated by the student and may be difficult to achieve, especially by those students who are not prepared for this type of educational environment (Furman *et al.*, 2008), thus hindering the field experience. Moore (2000) argues that increased avenues of communications may permit students to exercise and develop the appropriate amount of autonomy to be successful in a distance education course.

Blended learning theory

Garrison and Kanuka (2004) define blending learning as the integration of face-to-face and distance learning, to help enhance the classroom experience and the extension of learning, through the innovative use of information and communication technology. The part of blended learning missing from typical field education is the innovative use of information and communications technology. Adding a communication medium to field education would not only help shorten the transactional distance but would also align field education to a blended learning modality, thus gaining all its advantages.

As field education is performed outside the confines of a classroom, the communication medium must consist of a technology that can be taken with the student. Mobile technologies have made this possible with tablets and smart phones equipped with the necessary capabilities of connectivity and educational functionality. These mobile technologies have been added to the list of the communications media necessary for blended learning, which is successful when technology and teaching inform each other (TeachThought, 2013) and create an independent learning experience. As reported by Lonsdale *et al.* (2004:7), *"the personal nature of these technologies means that they are well suited to engaging students in individualised learning experiences, and to giving them increased owner-ship (and hence responsibility) over their own work".*

A pedagogical framework for mobile learning

Empowering students at the centre of a technology-enriched educational experience will impact on the role of the educator but theory and prac-tice must be aligned to create a cohesive and effective model of education (de Freitas & Mays, 2013). Another theory applicable to this study was postulated by Yeonjeong (2011), who introduced a theoretical mobile learning framework by using transactional distance theory. The theory is augmented with a new dimension to reflect the characteristics of mobile technologies that support both individual and social aspects of learning. The framework, as shown in Figure 2, consists of the four types of mobile learning (m-learning) generated in the context of distance education:

1) high transactional distance socialised m-learning (Type 1);
2) high transactional distance individualised m-learning (Type 2);
3) low transactional distance socialised m-learning (Type 3);
4) low transactional distance individualised m-learning (Type 4).

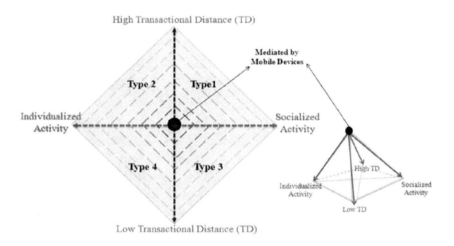

Figure 2. Four types of mobile learning: A pedagogical framework (Yeonjeong, 2011).

Application

Although most small training aircraft are equipped with global positioning system (GPS) technology for navigation purposes, the recording functions are limited and do not provide a format that can be easily reviewed. In order to increase benefit from a solo flight experience, the student pilot can carry a GPS-enabled mobile device onboard the aircraft and capture flight parameters of the aircraft (position, speed, and altitude). On return to the classroom, the data can be downloaded and superimposed on a topological map. The GPS data capture is made in real time and the playback can be viewed in a similar way. The instructor and student can review the outcomes of the flight, highlight the important data points and discuss key educational issues revealed by the data capture.

There are many mobile applications, or apps, in both iOS™ and Android™ that can accomplish the data capture using global positioning systems (GPS) technology. This study used the Android™-based app called GPS Logger™. Figure 3 shows the GPS Logger™ screen.

Figure 3. GPS Logger™ screen.

This app can capture flight parameters and record the data in both GPS Exchange (GPX) format and Keynote Markup Language (KML) file formats. The Extensible Markup Language (XML)-based file, which is stored on Google Drive™, can be easily interpreted by Google Earth™ to create a marked path of the flight along with the flight parameters.

In one case, a student pilot planned and departed on the required solo navigation flight with a GPS-enabled device onboard. According to Transport Canada's limits (Transport Canada 2013), the flight was to be carried out within an altitude of +/- 100 feet of determined altitude. On the student's return, the instructor downloaded the GPX file, superimposed it on Google Earth™ and analysed the data. The instructor was able to determine whether the flight was carried out within limits. As seen in Figure 4, a portion of the flight exceeded the assigned altitude of 6,500 feet by over 200 feet.

Without the GPS-enabled device on the flight, the instructor would have no evidence that the student strayed from the assigned objectives. The student might not have been aware that parts of the flight were beyond the acceptable limits. With the GPS data examined, a meaningful face-to-face discussion can take place between instructor and student to accurately debrief and coach the exercise. The dialogue, based on actual flight parameters, would accurately depict errors and successes, allowing for the opportunity to explore causes and discuss possible solutions. The GPS-enabled device was able to bridge the gap between the student pilot and the instructor, elevating the educational experience for both parties.

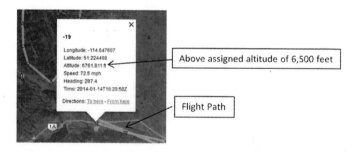

Figure 4. Google Earth™ interpretation- altitude higher than assigned.

Discussion

In the many trials conducted to test the above application, both the student and the instructor witnessed extremely valuable additional benefits. The student pilot's fieldwork was understood better, enabling meaningful dialogue and feedback. The instructor was in a better position to guide the student through the solo flight experience and accurately recommend next steps in the student's flight education syllabus. The application's value is also supported by distance education theories and mandated flight education methodologies (Moore, 2000; Transport Canada, 2009).

Transactional distance

The addition of mobile technology to field-based studies has a distance education impact of shortening transactional distance and impacting the three components of Moore's (2000) theory.

GPS tracking can act as the communications medium, providing data for interaction between the student's work in the field and the instructor's feedback. It can also provide the minimum structure necessary to accommodate and be responsive to the students' needs and create a better learning environment, as well as creating opportunities for honest reflection and action planning. GPS tracking would act as the link to the instructor. The student performs the fieldwork independently but still receives the educational pillars of practise, feedback and testing.

The data provided by the GPS tracking tool during a solo flight provides a method by which a flight can be thoroughly monitored. It creates a record of the experience, which allows for a meaningful dialogue and interactions between student and instructor. As in most cases of field education, the student will bring back some evidence of the study performed, but the analysis of data from a communications medium provides additional understanding between student and instructor.

Field education is performed away from the classroom and instructor and the student is given specific objectives to carry out while continuing to receive ongoing guidance. The addition of the GPS tracking tool promotes the generation of knowledge by the student. It allows the student freedom to explore objectives while still being able to share the experience with the instructor. Calvin *et al.* (2005:116) reported that *"students can identify their learning needs and work with the instructor to develop criteria for successful achievement and lessen the transactional distance".*

Blended learning

Another significant benefit of adding GPS tracking technology to a solo flight is that it adds an information and communications technology component to the field education part of the course and, as defined by Garrison and Kanuka (2004), results in a blended learning modality. There is much literature to support blended learning as a very effective modality (Attardo *et al.*, 2013; Fleck, 2012; Fox *et al.* 2013). The solo flight component augmented with GPS mobile technology would gain pedagogical advantages from both the student's and instructor's perspective.

In flight education, the level of success of the 300 nm solo flight is dependent on careful flight planning and skilled execution. The instructor can verify the student's plan and, with the addition of GPS mobile technology, examine the execution. In most cases, the student pilot is aware of any deviation that occurred during the flight, but the opportunity to verify both successful and unsuccessful portions of the exercise are of great benefit to the student and the instructor. According to Glazer (2011:3): *"students in a blended learning course make more and richer connections between what they are learning and what they already know".*

Giving the instructor the ability to debrief the student on the execution of a solo flight fosters a better understanding of the student's abilities and allows the instructor to guide better the student's progress. This, in turn, provides meaningful learning outcomes for the student, thereby promoting deeper engagement with the learning experience (Merriam *et al.*, 2006). It can also create a stronger bond and lessen the transactional distance between the student pilot and the instructor. This bond is very important (Brookfield, 1985) in flight education as most of the training is done in a one-on-one setting. This sentiment is found in blended learning environments as Vaughan (2007:86) reported: *"faculty almost universally reported feeling more connected with their students and knowing them better".*

One of the criticisms of blended learning is that its focus is on the teacher to create knowledge as opposed to the student taking responsibility

(Carbonaro *et al.*, 2008). Adding mobile technology to field education would support the theory of constructivism that suggests students construct new knowledge based on their experiences (Chen & Liu, 2010). Student pilots on GPS-enhanced solo flights would be able to replay their own experiences and be more active in constructing knowledge based on their interpretations of the exercises (Al-Huneidi & Schreurs, 2013).

Yeonjeong's mobile learning framework

GPS technology helps create a low transactional distance in solo flight education. As the student is alone during the training flight and the dialogue is solely between the student and the instructor, the experience would fall into the Type 4 category of Yeonjeong's (2011) mobile learning framework. In this case, *"the instructor leads and controls the learning in an effort to meet individual students' needs while maintaining their independence"* (Yeonjeong, 2011:94).

When using GPS technology, the Type 4 category of mobile learning implies low transactional distance because learning processes are better matched with the student's progress. Additionally, the flexibility and portability made possible by the GPS technology supports individualised learning. One of the advantages of the Type 4 category is that students are typically learning in self-directed or independent modalities. The mobile device supports this type of learning by tailoring to the needs of the students in order to help them achieve their learning goals (Sawyer, 2006; Yeonjeong, 2011).

In preparing for the Type 4 category of learning, flight curriculum designers and instructors should understand the complete learning environment, both in the classroom and in the fieldwork. Yeonjeong (2011) also recommends that they provide appropriate guidance in order to lead students through the completion of tasks and assignments.

Flight education perspective

According to Transport Canada (2004) and the Federal Aviation Administration (2008), flight instructors must use the demonstration-performance method for flight training. This method consists of five steps:

1) explanation;
2) demonstration;
3) student performance;
4) supervision;
5) evaluation.

The first two steps can be done either in the air or on the ground depending on the objective. The last three steps would only be possible during and after a dual flight. In the case of a solo flight, these three steps can be facilitated by the use of GPS mobile technology.

As shown in Figure 5, the GPS technology ties together the last three steps of the demonstration-performance method, with the components of Moore's (2000) transactional distance theory acting in the intersections.

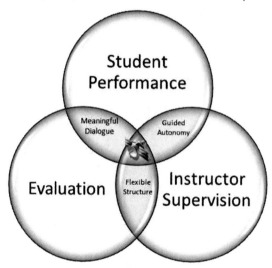

Figure 5. Transaction distance and demonstration-performance method.

The supervision and evaluation of the solo flight adds a flexible structure to the flight education course. Student performance and evaluation can now be accomplished through dialogue. Student performance and supervision provide a basis for interaction as the student experiences guided learning, developing the appropriate level of autonomy. The intersecting factors of meaningful dialogue and flexible structure lessen the transactional distance, providing ongoing guidance to support the demonstration-performance method, thus maximising the educational experience of the solo flight.

Recommendations

Recording the GPS data becomes a valuable educational resource for both the student and instructor. It be used not only to evaluate the exercise and determine the next steps in the learning, but also to provide a record that may be used as part of a student portfolio. Therefore, I recommend the following:

1) incorporate GPS mobile technology within field education;

2) use the resulting GPS data to debrief the field activity and facilitate meaningful dialogue;

3) minimise the course structure, allowing students the flexibility to adjust course materials in order to suit their needs, based on analysis of field work outcomes;

4) provide ongoing guidance to field work students through the use of communications technology.

Implementing similar mobile technology in any required off-campus activity would be beneficial in many ways. The educational value of adding mobile technology to field education is that it provides an avenue for follow-up and discussion. It tracks the activity using multiple parameters that then can be discussed with the instructor, providing an avenue for self-reflection based on data gathered. It will also support a blended learning environment that, as suggested by Long et al. (2013:1726), creates *"a potentially more robust educational experience than either traditional or fully online learning"*. GPS data provides a documented record of the activity for archival and research purposes and, in the case of flight education, a lightweight flight data recorder improves information gathering as recommended by the Transportation Safety Board of Canada (2013). Using technology for self-reflection and assessment has additional benefits as discussed by Bartholomew and Kelly (this volume).

An additional career-oriented educational benefit would be realised from implementing GPS technology. A report by Davies et al. (2011) claims that one of the drivers of change that will shape future work skills will be graduates' ability to interact with data and understand how to use the data to design desired outcomes. Another driver of change will be the required ability to understand and work with new media. Adding mobile technologies to field education would also better prepare the graduate for the technology-based work place of tomorrow.

Conclusion

Taking learning outside the classroom is not a novel concept. The development of mobile devices that can accompany students has greatly increased the learning potential. Part of realising learning outcomes is documenting the student's world as they move through it (Woodill, 2012). It is also important to note that the majority of students and instructors favour the utilisation of mobile technology in an educational environment (Abachi & Muhammad, 2014; Chen *et al.*, 2012).

Jong *et al.* (2012) developed a GPS-system to monitor students on field exercises. These researchers reported that students rated their field experiences more desirable than past experiences without the monitoring system. Instructors valued the ability to engage and motivate the students during the field exercise and were able to make the experience more student-centred.

Abrami *et al.* (2012) defines the next generation of interactive distance education (IDE2) as purposeful, interactive distance education. IDE2 should be designed to facilitate more meaningful interactions that are targeted, intentional, and engaging. To better engage students in learning, strategies and techniques for knowledge acquisition must be considered. *"It is time to create a new set of principles that better reflect the ideals of a contemporary higher education experience, principles which recognize and utilize the capabilities of new and emerging information and communications technologies"* (Cleveland-Innes & Garrison, 2012:225).

GPS technology is one of many mobile learning tools that can be used in higher education. Adding mobile technology to field education can be implemented in many disciplines and has been proved very beneficial. Alexander (2004:35) stated that *"the physical vs. the digital, the sedentary vs. the nomadic—the wireless, mobile, student-owned learning impulse cuts across our institutional sectors, silos, and expertise-propagation structures"*. It is important to note that technology itself does not increase learning, but its intelligent and imaginative implementation can shift the outlook of the teacher-learner relationship, creating mutual responsibility and empowerment of learning for students (see Newton, this volume). Students in higher education will form their own awareness of the world around them if they are involved in gathering data from a variety of sources made possible through the use of technology. Speaking for educators, Moller et al. (2012:18) stated, "*we owe it to ourselves and our future to harness the synergy of emerging technology and instructional design to usher in the next generation of unconstrained learning*".

About the author

Leon Cygman is the Chair of Aviation, General Management and Human Resources programs at Mount Royal University in Calgary, Alberta, Canada. He can be contacted at this email: lcygman@mtroyal.ca

Bibliography

Abachi, H. R. & G. Muhammad (2014). The Impact of m-Learning Technology on Students and Educators. *Computers in Human Behavior*, Vol. 30, pp. 491-496.

Abrami,P. C.; R. M. Bernard; E. M. Bures; E. Borokhovski & R. M. Tamim (2012). Interaction in Distance Education and Online Learning: Using Evidence and Theory to Improve Practice. In L. Moller & J. B. Huett (Eds.). *The next generation of distance education: Unconstrained learning.* New York: Springer, pp. 49-69.

Alexander, B. (2004). Going Nomadic: Mobile Learning in Higher Education. *EDUCAUSE Review*, Vol. 39, No. 5, pp. 28–35.

Al-Huneidi, A. M. & J. Schreurs (2012). Constructivism Based Blended Learning in Higher Education. *International Journal of Emerging Technologies in Learning*, Vol. 7, No. 1, pp. 4-9.

Attardo, D.; T. Doan & C. Levesque-Bristol (2013). *Fostering Blended Learning: Successful Partnerships and Faculty Development for Institutional Change.* Online Resource: http://docs.lib.purdue.edu/impactpres/1. [Accessed on 20 June 2014].

AvScholars (2007). Online Resource: http://www.avscholars.com/Aviation_Colleges/Aviation-Colleges-Schools.htm [Accessed on 20 June 2014].

Bogo, M.; R. Power; C. Regehr & G. Regehr (2007). When Values Collide: Field Instructors' Experiences of Providing Feedback and Evaluating Competence. *The Clinic Supervisor*, Vol. 26, No. 1-2, pp. 99-117.

Brookfield, S. D. (1985). Self-directed Learning: A Critical Review of Research. *New Directions for Adult and Continuing Education*, No. 25, pp. 5-16.

Baumgartner, L. M.; R. S. Caffarella & S. B. Merriam (2006). *Learning in adulthood: A comprehensive guide*. San Francisco, CA: Jossey-Bass.

Carbonaro, M.; J. Drummond; S. King; E. Taylor; F. Satzinger & E. Snart (2008). Integration of e-learning Technologies in an Interprofessional Health Science Course. *Medical Teacher*, Vol. 30, No. 1, pp. 25-33.

Calvin, J.; C. Overtoom; D. S. Stein; C. E. Wanstreet & . E. Wheaton (2005). Bridging the Transactional Distance Gap in Online Learning Environments. *American Journal of Distance Education*, Vol. 19, No. 2, pp. 105-118.

Chen, C. Y.; S. H. Huang; H. Y. Kao; C. H. Lin; W. H. Wu & Y. C. J. Wu (2012). Review of Trends from Mobile Learning Studies: A Meta-analysis. *Computers and Education*, Vol. 59, No. 2, pp. 817–82.

Chen, I. J. & C. C. Liu (2006). Evolution of Constructivism. *Contemporary Issues in Education Research*, Vol. 3, No. 4, pp. 63-66.

Chen, Y. (2001). Dimensions of transactional distance in the World Wide Web learning environment: A factor analysis. *British Journal of Educational Technology*, Vol. 32, No. 4, pp. 459-470.

Clark, M. (2013). Closing the Gap on the US Airlines' Pilot Shortage. *Defense Transportation Journal*, Vol. 69, No. 4, pp. 12-16.

Cleveland-Innes, M. & R. Garrison (2012). Higher Education and Postindustrial Society: New Ideas About Teaching, Learning, and Technology. In L. Moller & J. B. Huett (Eds.) *The next generation of distance education: Unconstrained learning*. New York: Springer, pp. 221-233.

Davies, A.; D. Fidler & M. Gorbis (2011). *Future Work Skills 2020*. Online Resource: http://www.iftf.org/uploads/media/SR-1382A_UPRI_future_work_skills_sm.pdf. [Accessed on 04 January 2014].

deFreitas, S. & T. Mayes (2013). Technology-Enhanced Learning: The Role of Theory (Second Edition). In H. Beetham & R. Sharpe (Eds.). *Rethinking Pedagogy for a Digital Age*. New York: Routledge.

Distance-Educator.com (2014). *Introduction to distance education: theorists and theories — Charles Wedemeyer*. Online Resource: http://distance-educator.com/introduction-to-distance-education-theorists-and-theories-charles-wedemeyer [Accessed on 20 June 2014].

Federal Aviation Administration (2008). Aviation Instructor's Handbook. Online Resource: http://www.faa.gov/regulations_policies/ handbooks_manuals/aviation/aviation_instructors_handbook/media/ FAA-H-8083-9A.pdf [Accessed on 19 February 2014].

Fleck, J. (2012). Blended Learning and Learning Communities: Opportunities and Challenges. *The Journal of Management Development*, Vol. 31, No. 4, pp. 398-411.

Fox, J.; E. Fynan & K. Lothridge (2013). Blended learning: Efficient, Timely and Cost Effective. *Australian Journal of Forensic Sciences*, Vol. 45, No. 4, pp. 407-416.

Furman, N.; J. Gookin; K. Paisley & J. Sibthorp (2008). The Pedagogic Value of Student Autonomy in Adventure Education. *Journal of Experiential Education*, Vol. 31, No. 2, pp. 136-151.

Garrison, D. & H. Kanuka (2004). Blended Learning: Uncovering Its Transformative Potential in Higher Education. *Internet and Higher Education*, Vol. 7, No. 2, pp. 95-105.

Garrison, R. (2000). Theoretical Challenges for Distance Education in the 21st Century: A Shift from Structural to Transactional Issues. *International Review of Research in Open and Distance Learning*, Vol. 1, No. 1, pp. 1-17.

Glazer, F. S. (2011). *Blended Learning: Across the Disciplines, Across the Academy. New Pedagogies and Practices for Teaching in Higher Education*. Herndon: Stylus Publishing.

Kearsley, G. (2000). *Online education, learning and teaching in cyberspace*. Belmont, CA: Wadsworth.

Khaddage F.; G. Knezek & K.-W .Lai (2013). Blending Student Technology Experiences in Formal and Informal Learning. *Journal of Computer Assisted Learning*, Vol. 29, No. 5, pp. 414-425.

Jong, M. S. Y.; E. T. H. Luk & J. H. M. Lee (2012). An Integrated GPS-supported Outdoor Exploratory Educational System—EagleEye. *Proceedings of the 20th International Conference on Computers in Education*. Singapore: Asia-Pacific Society for Computers in Education.

Long, T.; G. T. Lotrecchiano; L. Lyons; P. L. McDonald & M. Zajicek-Farber (2013). Blended Learning: Strengths, Challenges, and Lessons Learned in an Interprofessional Training Program. *Maternal & Child Health Journal*, Vol. 17, No. 9, pp. 1725-1734.

Lonsdale, P.; L. Naismith; M. Sharples & G. Vavoula (2004). *Literature Review in Mobile Technologies and Learning*. Bristol, United Kingdom: Futurelab.

Merriam, S. B.; R. S. Caffarella & L. M. Baumgartner (2006). *Learning in Adulthood: A Comprehensive Guide*. San Francisco, CA: Jossey-Bass.

Moller, L.; D. Robison & J. B. Huett (2012). Unconstrained Learning: Principles for the Next Generation of Distance Education. In L. Moller & J. B. Huett (Eds.) *The next generation of distance education: Unconstrained learning*. New York: Springer, pp. 1-19.

Moore, M. G. (2000). Theory of Transactional Distance. In D. Keegan (Ed.). *Theoretical Principles of Distance Education*. New York: Routledge, pp. 22-38.

Moore, M. G. & G. Kearsley. (1996). *Distance Education: A Systems View*. Belmont, CA: Wadsworth.

Mueller, C. (2003). *Transactional Distance*. Online Resource: http://tecfaetu.unige.ch/staf/staf9698/mullerc/3/transact.html [Accessed 20 June 2014].

Saba, F. & R. Shearer, R. (1994). Verifying Key Theoretical Concepts in a Dynamic Model of Distance Education. *The American Journal of Distance Education*, Vol. 8, No. 1, pp. 36-59.

Sawyer, R. K. (2006). *The Cambridge Handbook of the Learning Sciences*. New York: Cambridge University Press.

Stover, A. B. (2004). *Learning Architecture Online: New directions for distance education and the design studio*. Online Resource: http://home.comcast.net/~abstover/learning_arch/learning_arch_05.html [Accessed 22 February 2014].

TeachThought (2013). Online Resource: http://www.teachthought.com/blended-learning-2/the-definition-of-blended-learning [Accessed 20 June 2014].

Transactional Distance Theory (2002). Online Resource: http://cde.athabascau.ca/cmc/transactional.html [Accessed 20 June 2014].

Transport Canada (2004). *Flight Instructor Guide: Aeroplane*. Ottawa: Transport Canada.

Transport Canada (2009). *Flight Test Guide: Commercial Pilot Licence: Aeroplane*. Ottawa: Transport Canada.

Transport Canada (2013). Online Resource: http://www.tc.gc.ca/eng/civilaviation/regserv/cars/part4-standards-421-1086.htm [Accessed 20 June 2014].

Transportation Safety Board of Canada (2013). Online Resource: http://www.tsb.gc.ca/eng/recommandations-recommendations/aviation/2013/rec-a1301.asp [Accessed 20 June 2014].

Vaughan, N. (2007). Perspectives on blended learning in higher education. *International Journal on eLearning*, Vol. 6, No. 1, pp. 81-94.

Wang S. & M. Higgins (2005). *Limitations of mobile phone learning.* Wireless and Mobile Technologies in Education, IEEE International Workshop. Tokushima, Japan. 28-30 November 2005.

Wedemeyer, C. A. (1981). *Learning at the back door: Reflections on Non-Traditional Learning in the Lifespan.* Madison: The University of Wisconsin Press.

Woodill, G. (2012). Moving from e-Learning to m-Learning. *The Canadian Learning Journal,* Vol. 16, No. 2, p. 34.

Yeonjeong, P. (2011). A Pedagogical Framework for Mobile Learning: Categorizing Educational Applications of Mobile Technologies into Four Types. *International Review Of Research In Open & Distance Learning,* Vol. 12, No. 2, pp. 78-102.